DR. BARNARDO

920

From a photograph taken shortly before his death

DOCTOR BARNARDO

PHYSICIAN, PIONEER, PROPHET

CHILD LIFE

YESTERDAY AND TO-DAY

by

J. WESLEY BREADY

Ph.D. (London)   B.D. (Toronto)
M.A. (Columbia) B.D. (Union N.Y.)

LONDON
GEORGE ALLEN & UNWIN LTD
MUSEUM STREET

FIRST PUBLISHED IN DECEMBER 1930

W2377

PREFACE

As the sub-title suggests, the task which I have set myself is larger than simply writing the life of Dr. Barnardo. He and the Homes he founded are my central theme; but his achievement I have striven to co-relate with those of his spiritual forbears throughout an unparalleled era of social reform, in which the child came finally to loom large as a social asset of incalculable worth. Barnardo's work, therefore, is treated not as an isolated phenomenon, but as a vital tributary to a mighty river of social endeavour, which carried hope, power, spiritual renewal and practical achievement wherever it flowed. Hence Chapter I, designed to suggest this historical background, is, of necessity, painted on a large canvas.

For the past nine years it has been my privilege to devote practically all my time to social and historical research, beginning with the early eighteenth century and continuing through to a consideration of problems vexing the present day. This work is a part of that study.

The investigations behind my book, *Lord Shaftesbury and Social-Industrial Progress*, caused me forcibly to realize, first, the close relationship between the endeavours of Shaftesbury and Barnardo, and, secondly, the profound significance of Barnardo's work as a pioneer movement in child-welfare advance. Barnardo's lifelong campaign on behalf of the "urchin" and "sprat" of city streets, with its watchword "Save the Child", followed in the immediate succession of Shaftesbury's Ragged Schools. As a teacher in one of these schools he had revealed to him the poignant challenge of the outcast child. Nor is it without significance that this medical missionary student began his lifelong crusade with Shaftesbury's blessing.

No other characters in British history have proven themselves such effective friends of unfortunate children as these two. But not only do their labours reveal much that is common: more vital, their achievements sprang from the same spiritual source. Indeed, historically, we may go farther back; for, on the oft-repeated confession of the leaders concerned, the origin and succession of Britain's richest reform inheritance are clear. Briefly, they may be stated thus. As the Evangelical Revival was the fount from which Wilberforce and his associates derived inspiration to champion the cause of the slave, so Wesley, the great prophet of that revival, and Wilberforce, were Shaftesbury's spiritual forerunners in his epic struggle, as champion of the industrial worker; while these noble souls, in turn, were Barnardo's inspiring precursors in his crusade as champion of the outcast child.

But these men were not only champions; they were emancipators. Wesley, in an age of frigid rationalism, emancipated the heart and conscience of Britain; Wilberforce emancipated the slave; Shaftesbury emancipated the industrial worker; Barnardo emancipated the destitute child. Yet all maintained stoutly that they themselves were first emancipated by Christ: and each looked to the Christ-Spirit as his guiding star.

*   *   *   *   *

My thanks are specially due to Dr. Barnardo's widow; to the late William McCall, for many years Chairman of the Barnardo Council; and to Mr. Harry Elmslie, Barnardo's brother-in-law, for placing large packets of invaluable letters and other private papers in my hands. I desire also to express my indebtedness to the Homes' "Director of Migration" for his unwearying patience in facilitating arrangements whereby my wife and I were enabled to visit the many centres of Barnardo's work; while again, my gratitude is due to the Council of the Homes, who, as a body, have proffered much assistance; to the Governors, Superintendents, Matrons, and other officials of different Branches, whose kindness I can never forget; and, not least, to the hundreds of "old boys and girls", who through letters, interviews, etc., have thrown a revealing light on Barnardo's character, and on different aspects of the Homes' work.

It is a pleasure to record again my indebtedness to the never-failing courtesy of the officials and attendants in the different departments of the British Museum Library, at whose hands I have been the recipient of much help.

J. WESLEY BREADY

81, St. Mary's Grove
   Chiswick, W.4
      London, December 1930

CONTENTS

ILLUSTRATIONS

DOCTOR BARNARDO
PHYSICIAN, PIONEER, PROPHET

CHAPTER I

A GREAT AWAKENING

"THE earlier half of the eighteenth century in England", says the *Cambridge Modern History*, "was an age of materialism, a period of dim ideals and expiring hopes; before the middle of the century its character was transformed; there appeared a movement headed by a mighty leader, who brought forth water from the rocks to make a barren land live again." [1]

This is the judgment of an English historian. What is the verdict of great scholars abroad? Professor Élie Halévy, of the Sorbonne, Paris, has given us perhaps the most penetrating study of English Modern History yet made. In the course of his titanic labours he has dissected both the political and economic institutions of Britain: in neither can he discover the secret of her social development. He is forced back upon the Evangelical Revival as the chief inspiration of all that is most heroic in modern Britain. Maintaining that it brought under its influence first the Dissenting Churches, then the Establishment, and finally secular opinion, he proceeds: "We shall explain by this movement the extraordinary stability which English society was destined to enjoy throughout a period of revolution and crises; what we may truly term the miracle of modern England, anarchist but orderly, practical and business-like, but religious and even pietist." [2]

Again, Dr. Parkes Cadman, one of the most remarkable of our American contemporaries, proclaims his continent's

[1] Vol. vi, p. 76, written by H. W. V. Temperley.
[2] *History of the English People*, p. 339 (vol. i. of translation from the French).

debt to Britain for this Revival. In his brilliant book, *Three Religious Leaders of Oxford*, referring to its guiding prophet, he says: "Happy is the nation which gave him to the highest possible service. Incalculable are the obligations which North America and the world at large owe her for such a gift. Blessed are the people in whose midst he moved, vigorous without vehemence, neither loud nor laboured, but like a fixed star of truth and goodness, a pattern of private excellence and public virtue." [1]

Not everyone would agree with these high tributes. But whoever might dissent, Dr. Barnardo, the central character of the present study, to all of them would have said "Amen!" The inspiration of his life-work is directly traceable to this religious renewal.

Moreover, even among those who would contest the above judgments, it would be admitted, that to the latter half of the eighteenth century is traceable a *Great Awakening of Conscience*, which acted as the nursing-mother of social reform. From this awakening sprang a new valuation of human life, a new passion for justice and equity, a new vision of society as a unified whole, a new hatred of bestiality, a new impulse to subjugate cruelty and oppression. This humanitarian awakening, too, gave birth to the famous philanthropic movement which, maturing in the nineteenth century, expressed itself through a thousand organizations designed not only to provide self-help and moral dynamic, but also to brighten and sweeten human relationships.

The reality, then, of a great eighteenth-century awakening of conscience is admitted on all sides. The only debatable point is its *immediate cause*. And when all evidence is sifted, two inspiring forces stand out in clear relief: one, the Evangelical Movement in Britain; the other, the Radical Movement on the Continent, often loosely styled the Humanitarian Movement. Now Dr. Barnardo, as later will appear, came under the power of both spheres of influence.

The book deals with Wycliffe, Wesley and Newman (New York, 1916).

It therefore behoves us briefly to survey the tenor and trend of these movements.

Thoroughgoing secularists will hear of only one inspiration to the humanitarian awakening. To them its richest fruits are traceable to the "philosophers" of the French Revolution. Rousseau and Voltaire are their supreme gods; while around these "all-highest", on thrones of less resplendent glory, are grouped a galaxy of minor "divinities", including Montesquieu and Diderot, Mirabeau and Turgot, Quesney and Mably. Such names, though suggestive of widely different systems of thought, are to the uncompromising rationalist synonymous with the highest good; while the French Revolution, for which they paved the way, is regarded as the foundation of modern liberty and progress.

Now, that the French Revolution accomplished much, no one will deny. Yet, when all credits are recorded, there remains a huge debit sheet. For decades, even to those at first sympathetic, the Revolution suggested little but chaos. It is easy to say that Britain greeted the dawn of the Revolution and became affrighted by its shadows. In the perspective of distance there is much to be said for and against this catastrophic eruption. But it is suggestive that thousands of liberal, high-minded Englishmen, like Wordsworth and Fox, greeted the advent of the Revolution with joy, yet, seeing its first fruits, came to loathe it. It must be remembered too that the "philosophers" of the French Revolution drew the substance of their teaching from the English Deists. Yet, under the domination of Deism in England, social conditions sank to an appallingly low ebb; and until the great Religious Revival began to kindle the imagination and touch the emotion of the populace, they rapidly were becoming worse.

Again, it is notable that in France the chaos of an uncontrolled Radicalism gave place to the iron discipline of a military despot; for only under the tyranny of Napoleon's legions was order re-established. And though in this re-establishment some Radicalism was preserved, its chief ingredient was reaction. France, indeed, came to learn that Revolution is, at best, but an indifferent road to progress, and that it runs great danger of inflicting as many evils as it cures; for with the gradual return of sanity, as France began to build afresh upon the ruins of the past, it became increasingly obvious that radicalism, divorced from moral and religious values, is an empty husk.

But whatever be the source of social reform on the Continent—whether secular Rationalism here contributed little or much—in England the problem is less complex and less confused. Here the transition from the old social order to the new was accomplished without bloodshed. Hence, no war-hysteria perverting judgment, we are able to trace in truer perspective the source of reform.

To maintain that the social progress of modern Britain is all traceable to one fountain-head would be folly. But to say that it is chiefly traceable to one source, is an assertion backed four-square by stubborn historical facts. England, prior to France in the eighteenth century, experienced a Great Awakening of Conscience, initiating an irresistible impetus toward reform. That awakening was the outcome of a vehement reassertion of vital religion, known as the Evangelical Revival, which, proclaiming the Fatherhood of God and Brotherhood of Man, emphasized "the infinite value of even the downmost soul".

Before the advent of this Revival, English history, for half a century, affords a sorry spectacle. Deism and Rationalism —the one scarcely distinguishable from the other—dominated every aspect of ruling-class life. With the utmost correctness, God was bowed off the stage of Time. Revelation became a word wholly taboo in "thinking" circles, while "Nature", whatever exactly it meant, was a word of magic power. All the smart set spoke of Natural Law, Natural Rights and Natural Religion: all chattered about being natural, following Nature and communing with Nature.

But meanwhile every noble emotion, aspiration and sentiment was suppressed as vulgar. Religion, even Sir Leslie
Stephen reminds us, was forced into a strait-waistcoat;
and only for police duty was it given free scope.[1]

This period called itself the Age of Reason; but under
its Arctic skies the springs of human compassion were
frozen up. England rapidly was degenerating into a nation
of castes: and a large proportion of her population were
outcasts. Social conditions were ghastly. The slave-trade
flourished, and from year to year increased. It represented
more capital and returned larger profits than any other
branch of high-sea trade. Every year, to supply its demands,
scores of African villages were razed to the ground, and
thousands of natives—men, women and children—were
transported into "living death". Intoxication, tribe warfare,
arson, rapine and plunder were its means of procuring
victims.[2] During the march of the eighteenth century,
millions of Africans were sold, while still more were mur-
dered, committed suicide or died in "middle-passage".[3]

Up to the middle of the eighteenth century, public-houses
in hundreds were swinging signs: "Drunk for One Penny.
Dead Drunk for Two Pence." Some added, "Free Straw."
The phrase "drunk as a lord" had then a literal significance,
many "great lords" priding themselves on being "four",
"five" and "six-bottle" men. In some eighteenth-century
mansions are to be seen "peeping galleries", designed that
the ladies after dinner might "peep down" on the gentlemen and offer wagers whose husband or lover would longest
retain his chair. Drunkenness, in fact, was accepted as a
mark of "manly manners"; though when a lord-bishop

---

[1] See Sir Leslie Stephen's *English Thought in the Eighteenth Century*, 2 vols., 1881.
Though a rationalist, Sir Leslie freely admits the stilted artificiality of the
period.
[2] See Wilberforce's numerous addresses and pamphlets on this subject.
[3] Cf. Newton (Rev. John), *Thoughts on the African Slave-Trade*, 1788; also
Africanus : "Remarks on the Slave-Trade and the Slavery of Negroes in a
Series of Letters," 1788 (dedicated to Granville Sharp). See, too, the diagram
of a slave-ship in Thomas Clarkson's *History of the Abolition of the Slave-Trade*.

became intoxicated he explained that it was "as a lord, not as a bishop", that he indulged so freely. Hogarth's famous paintings, "Beer Street" and "Gin Lane", are faithful presentations; while his less famous picture, "An Election Entertainment", depicts, all too accurately, the contaminating influence of alcohol upon political life.[1]

Yet slavery and drunkenness were not isolated phenomena. Chief among sports was prize-fighting: never more popular than when a woman was pitted against a man. Cruelty to animals, also, contributed largely to sport, for cock-fighting, dog-fighting and bear-baiting were familiar to every village green. Betting and games of chance, again, were universal pastimes among high and low: one bishop owed his mitre to the fact that he had wagered a highly placed lady £5,000 he would *not* be made a bishop.

The penal code was then ferocious. Free Britons could be hanged for one hundred and sixty offences: for shooting a rabbit on a gentleman's estate, for picking a pocket to the extent of eighteen-pence; even for appearing on the king's high-road with blackened face. Women, too, could still be burned alive for witchcraft, arson or forgery: a barbarism not prohibited till 1794. Nor was the *administration* of justice much superior to the penal code. During a large part of the eighteenth century, judges counted on receiving from £2,000 to £3,000 each as New Year presents from the Bar practising under them. Press-gangs, crimps and trading justices were part of the accepted order, while pillory, stocks and whipping-posts were official instruments of correction. The hanging of petty criminals, too, was made a "public show", defended even by Dr. Johnson:[2] and the prisons into which even debtors and their families were thrown, were torture-chambers so foul as to revolt the imagination of our age. Men, women and children were

[1] See George, D.M.: *London Life in the Eighteenth Century*, 1925; Sydney, W. C.: *England and the English in the Eighteenth Century*, 2 vols., 1892; Lecky, W. E. H.: *History of England in the Eighteenth Century*, new ed., 1892.
[2] See Romilly, Sir Samuel: *Observations on the Criminal Code*, 1810.

huddled together in indiscriminate fashion; chains, strait-
jackets and the like were constantly in use; while Prison
Governors were encouraged to extort bribes.[1]

Indeed, the social life of Britain, far into the eighteenth
century, exhibits in full measure the debauchery sown
by the Restoration régime. The Established Church was
utilized as a Government machine. A degrading system
of pluralities and sinecures was everywhere in vogue.
Thousands of poor curates, who did the hack-work for their
"superiors", were "passing rich", not, like Goldsmith's father,
with £40 a year, but with £20; while their ecclesiastical
"betters", heaping plurality on plurality, were sometimes
not content with £20,000. Nowhere was class snobbery
more pronounced than in the Establishment, where "big
plums" went to scions of the aristocracy. Though all the
national education of the "common people" was entrusted
to the Charity Schools of the Established Church, one
eighteenth-century archbishop and his sons were annually
receiving more national income than the entire revenue
of these schools. Is it surprising, then, that hundreds of
Charity School teachers were illiterate, or that their average
pay was less than that of a labourer? Is it surprising that
"*the* Church", hating "enthusiasm", taught the "sinfulness"
of "being righteous overmuch".[2]

Ignorance and total illiteracy were, among the working
classes, almost universal. Contemporary tables in a Medical
Research Committee Report show that early in the eighteenth century, 74·5 per cent. of all London children died
before their fifth birthday. Brothels were attached to nearly
all gin-shops, and not infrequently to theatres. The children
of besotted parents were commonly sold into handcraft
"apprenticeships", which forced upon them economic conditions little short of slavery: often, in cellars, attics and

[1] Howard, John: *State of Prisons in England and Wales*, 3rd ed., 1874.
[2] See *Martyrdom Sermons*, 1757–1770. Bishop Newton's Sermon before the
House of Lords, p. 9.

sheds, mere infants laboured twelve to fourteen hours a day. But why multiply instances? The pressure of cold facts substantiates to the hilt the verdict of the *Cambridge Modern History*: the age was "one of materialism"—"a period of dim ideals and expiring hopes". Though nominally it worshipped Reason, its God was Mammon; it took for granted the superiority of property over the personality of the poor.[1]

*　　*　　*　　*　　*

In the revolt against these conditions, and in the crusade to humanize them, certain schools of rationalism, beyond doubt, played a valiant rôle. Who will deny that radicals, like Owen and Place, were true friends to the industrial worker? Who will minimize the influence of Utilitarians, like Bentham and the Mills, on the political and philosophical outlook? Who will make bold to say that their slogan, "The greatest happiness to the greatest number", did nothing to lay low the usurpations of the few, or that it resulted in no benefit to the masses? Can it be contended that even arch-egoists, such as Paine and Cobbett, or premature political agitators, like Lovett and O'Connor, have contributed nothing to social emancipation? Or again, will anyone deny to Secularists, turned in the mould of Holyoake and Bradlaugh, a certain influence in sharpening the wits and cultivating the intellects of their compatriots? Beyond doubt, these and other rationalists contributed to the common weal.

One point, however, must be emphasized: all the rationalists cited above belong to the second or third—not the first—generation of their order. All succeeded the Great Awakening of Conscience, and therefore stood under moral obligation to a movement whose spiritual tenets they ridiculed.

---

[1] For a list of books and documents dealing with this period, see Bibliography in the author's *Lord Shaftesbury and Social-Industrial Progress* (section on "Shaftesbury's Predecessors", pp. 417–424).

Hence, admitting that the broad stream of social reform within the English-speaking world has been fed by many and different tributaries, we are none the less forced, by overwhelming evidence, to the conclusion that its primary source is the series of mountain-springs thrown up by the Evangelical Revival. As Green has pointed out, one of the noblest results of that Revival was "the steady attempt which has never ceased from that day to this, to remedy the guilt, the ignorance, the physical suffering, the social degradation of the profligate and the poor". Then, significantly, he adds: "It was not till the Wesleyan impulse had done its work that the philanthropic impulse began." [1] In another connection Green says of this revival: "It changed, after a time, the whole tone of English society. The Church was restored to life and activity. Religion carried to the hearts of the people a fresh spirit of moral zeal, while it purified our literature and our morals. A new philanthropy reformed our prisons, infused clemency and wisdom into our penal code, abolished the slave-trade, and gave the first impulse to popular education." [2]

Professor Thorold Rogers, in his exhaustive study *Six Centuries of Work and Wages*, declares that he does "not believe the mass of the peasants could have been moved at all, had it not been for the spiritual and educational stimulus they received from Methodist [3] organizations".

As for the inspiring genius of the Evangelical Revival, few men of any age or country have touched the social problem at so many angles; and no man who ever spoke the English tongue has left behind him a nobler memorial, by way of influence over his fellows. In 1774, thirteen years before the Abolition Committee was formed, Wesley published his treatise, *Thoughts Upon Slavery*, and never was there a more searching exposure of that monstrosity. His attacks on the

[1] Green, J. R.: *History of the English People*, vol. iv, p. 1618.
[2] See *A Short History of the English People*, p. 736.
[3] The word "Methodist" was often used instead of the much more comprehensive word "Evangelical", which has *no denominational limitation*.

liquor traffic, with its ravages on hearth and home, are not less prophetic. Nowhere are the moral implications of this traffic more trenchantly set forth. Wesley made the British public realize that drunkenness is a disgrace; he shamed the "peeping galleries" out of use; he silenced the stupid boasts of "five" and "six-bottle" men; he started the first militant temperance movement the English-speaking world has known.

War he repudiated as the antithesis of every Christian virtue—"a horrid reproach to the Christian name, yea to the name of man, to all reason and humanity".[1] Economic tyranny and political corruption he never wearied of condemning; rotten boroughs and feudal land laws he held up to public scorn; the bloodthirsty penal code and the legal chicanery by which it was interpreted and executed he exposed to the withering blast of his moral indignation. Taxes on workmen's food and turnpikes on the highroads he denounced as wicked machinations saddling the common people with burdens too grievous to be borne. Intimate contact with Ireland caused him to discover in England's treatment of that unhappy land the sure seeds of revolt; while her persistence in forcing upon the Irish, ecclesiastical institutions alien to their sympathy made his blood boil. As for pluralities and sinecures, which had so corrupted the National Church, he lost no opportunity of exposing them; whereas the prevailing prison system he described as "a nursery for all manner of wickedness", and never did he cease to work for "humane treatment".

In spite of organized opposition and mob violence, Wesley visited every town, village and hamlet throughout the kingdom; and as the *Cambridge Modern History* says: "Wherever he passed he left memorials in the shape of schools,

[1] See "Address to the more serious part of the Inhabitants of Great Britain respecting the Unhappy Contest between us and our American Brethren" (1776).

mission-rooms, meeting-houses and unions for prayer, for charity and for self-help." [1] At a time when British society was ripe for chaos or anarchy, Wesley, labouring fourteen to sixteen hours a day, made the mute, illiterate population vocal: he gave them their first lessons in democratic organization, in sobriety, self-discipline and self-help. Sir Josiah Stamp scarcely overstates the case when he asserts that "Wesley and Shaftesbury together . . . by evolution of opinion and sympathy", saved Britain from "bloody revolution".

Fifty years before the outbreak of the French Revolution this rugged prophet had taught to his outcast countrymen three mighty principles: Liberty, Equality, Fraternity. But these principles he taught not with the cynical superiority of Voltaire, nor the demagogical arrogance of Rousseau. In their gods he had little faith. Had he not been raised in an atmosphere of rationalism and materialism, and rebelled against it? He came, therefore, preaching not his own wisdom, but the wisdom of God through Christ. Hence his emphasis was spiritual to the core; and when he spoke of Liberty, Equality, Fraternity, he spoke not in terms of class hatred or revolution, but in terms of the Kingdom of God upon earth.

To appraise the *social fruits* of the Revival which started with Wesley would require volumes. That the abolition of the slave-trade, and finally the emancipation of all slaves within the Empire, was an immediate result, no historian will deny. Even Jeremy Bentham admitted this: "If to be an anti-slavist is to be 'a saint'," he declared, "sainthood for me. I am a 'saint'." [2] True, a few other Rationalists cast in their lot with "the saints"; but the whole campaign, waged in the teeth of furious opposition, was organized and led by zealous converts of this revival. Granville Sharpe, William Wilberforce, Thomas Clarkson, Zachary Macaulay, Sir James Stephen, William Cowper and John Newton were

[1] Vol. vi, p. 84.　　　　　　　　　[2] Halévy, op. cit., p. 510.

all products of the Evangelical Movement; and so also were the noble band of Nonconformists, particularly Quakers, who rendered them valiant support. The crusade, too, was conducted in the language neither of economics nor politics, but of religion. Again, in tracing the pioneer movements for popular education, the same influence is patent. Green says, the Sunday-school marked "the beginning of popular education".[1] But whence came the inspiration of that world-stirring institution? The impulse behind Wesley, Hannah More and Robert Raikes, its chief founders, is too well known to need comment; while as for its army of teachers, they all had drunk at the same fountain-head. Then, too, the British and Foreign School Society and the National School Society, representing Nonconformity and Church of England, and founded respectively by Joseph Lancaster and Dr. Bell, were avowed by-products of the same spiritual succession; while, again, the most romantic, courageous and heroic of all forerunners of national education sprang from the same parent stem; for the Ragged School Union, which inspired hundreds of paid and thousands of voluntary teachers, Bible in hand, to work daily among the outcasts and criminals of our great cities, owed everything to the religious spirit. Lord Shaftesbury and all his Ragged School colleagues, including such noble characters as Quintin Hogg, Lord Aberdeen, Dr. Guthrie, Professor Leoni Levi, George Holland, the Baroness Burdett-Coutts and Dr. Barnardo were Evangelical zealots to the bone.

The hard-fought campaigns to humanize the prison system and the penal code are equally suggestive. John Howard and Elizabeth Fry were zealous Nonconformists; the former was a devoted friend of Wesley, and both were thoroughgoing "Enthusiasts". A study of John Howard's book, *The State of the Prisons in England and Wales* (1774), and of Mrs. Fry's *Life* by her daughters, will remove any doubt as to the inspiration of prison reform. In the case

[1] *History of the English People.* vol. iv, p. 1619.

of the parliamentary leader of the fight to humanize the penal code, facts are different. Here, a rationalist taking the lead, religious organizations fell into line; but Sir Robert Romilly was on terms of thorough understanding with "the saints". Raised under Evangelical influence, he was a warm admirer of Wilberforce; and in the campaign against the slave-trade he, like Bentham, cast in his lot with "the saints".

The origin of the Protestant World Missionary Movement is now universally known; comment would be superfluous. All the great Protestant Missionary Societies of the English-speaking world grew up in the wake of this Revival: and who can estimate their contribution toward the advent of world-brotherhood and world-peace?

Coming nearer home, if we examine the facts of the long-fought campaign to humanize the factory system, we find that nine-tenths of the leaders were the avowed progeny of Protestant Evangelical religion. Admittedly Robert Owen took up his position with rationalists of the left wing; but, by marriage, he had entered into the heritage of a Christian "enthusiast"—his father-in-law, David Dale. Indeed, when he was still a stripling, the New Lanark reforms were well under way; and when, in 1800, he took over the management of Dale's factories, he simply carried forward, with his father-in-law's money, the humanitarian policy the latter had inaugurated; while Dale retired *to labour as an Independent Preacher and general philanthropist*.

As for the other leaders in this campaign, whose avowed purpose it was to suppress every vestige of "industrial slavery", they were religious zealots almost to a man. Lord Shaftesbury, their parliamentary chief, continually described himself "an Evangelical of Evangelicals"; repeatedly he asserted that were it not for his Faith he neither would have entered nor continued in the fray. Among his lieu-tenants the same inspiration is equally apparent. Richard Oastler was a local preacher and the son of a local preacher;

R. J. Stephens was a Methodist parson; John Wood, the great cotton manufacturer, who largely financed the crusade, was a fervent Bible Christian, as was also Philip Grant. Michael Sadler exhibited his "enthusiasm" in religious verse; G. S. Bull was an Evangelical clergyman of the Church of England; while as for John Fielden, though in mature years he was a Unitarian, as a young man he had been a Sunday-school teacher, and it was then that his lifelong enthusiasm was kindled.[1] Again, the work-men's official organizations were permeated by the same zeal. In May, 1847, just after the Ten Hours Bill had passed its final reading in the House of Commons, a National Convention of Workmen's Delegates was assembled in London, which, expressing *"deep gratitude to Almighty God"* for the great success attained, pledged itself "to promote by every means in its power the RELIGIOUS AND SOCIAL BLESS-INGS which it was *the object* of the Bill to extend to the factory workers".[2]

Finally, approaching the great Philanthropic Movement of the nineteenth century, to which Dr. Barnardo made so large a contribution, here again direct relationship to this religious succession is everywhere apparent. The move-ment which gave to Britain free hospitals, insane asylums, recreation fields, public parks, gymnasiums, workmen's institutes, the Y.M.C.A. mission-halls, crèche systems and child-welfare centres—it, too, sprang up on soil fertilized by the Great Awakening of Conscience; it, too, had as its noblest prophets "twice-born" men.

In a word, the Eighteenth-Century Revival of Religion changed gradually for good the whole tone and trend of British life. It set up higher moral standards, purged our literature, cleansed our Court life, revitalized the National Church, and remoulded the character of the British people.

[1] For the detailed history of this industrial crusade, see *Lord Shaftesbury and Social-Industrial Progress*, chaps. xiii–xix.
[2] See *Halifax Guardian*, May 22nd, 1847.

Coming as a second, but more spiritual and more universal, form of Puritanism, it baptized the English-speaking world with purging and illuminating fire from off the Altars of God.

*   *   *   *   *

Strange, therefore, that despite this incomparable succession of social reform there remained, in the heart of Christendom, a wild tribe of homeless and destitute children, of whose existence the general public never dreamed, and before whom even the Ragged Schools acknowledged defeat. Yet such was the case.

In the big cities there existed a clan of street urchins, living nowhere and sleeping anywhere; here to-day and gone to-morrow: a closed fraternity of the underworld who knew no grammar and spoke largely by signs; whose only school was the school of debauchery and crime; who were ignorant of the meaning of morality, and never heard even the primary tenets of Christianity; who had no means of livelihood, and "picked up" their living where best they could; who hated policemen and loathed the name of Law; who felt, by an animal instinct, that society was at war against them, and knew well that they were at war against society. A veritable fraternity of the underworld was this tribe of street-arabs; furtive, feverish, vermin-ridden: members of the human race, but living a life akin to that of scavenger animals; emerging into vision here and dissolving into thin air there; dodging in and out of lanes, alleys and markets by day—by night they prowled forth into wider areas to seek their meat: and now, having satisfied their appetite and deposited in their pockets, perchance, a store for the morrow, slinking off to rest, they sheltered themselves in stables or barges, under tarpaulins, boxes or barrows—anywhere offering shelter from the cold, so long as they were beyond reach of the police and hidden from the sight of man.

Here, then, was Barnardo's problem, and, like his predecessors in a glorious succession of reforms, he faced it unabashed. He was a product of the Evangelical Revival, and into its humanitarian heritage he entered heart and soul. In fact, without the Great Awakening of Conscience, inspired by a mighty outpouring of spiritual power, Dr. Barnardo's Homes, the greatest child-rescue system yet known, could scarcely have been born; for through the previous succession of reforms flowed the human sympathy essential to ransom the outcast child.

CHAPTER II

THE CHILD'S CHAMPION

IT is a truism that a man's life is best interpreted through his work. In Dr. Barnardo's case "the work was the man!" The Homes, which his faith inspired and his initiative built, reflect more than anything else the spirit and genius of their founder. Hence, before relating the dramatic challenge that moulded his destiny or the romance of his career, let us pause for a glimpse at the proportions of his work.

In 1866 Thomas John Barnardo, a medical student in the London Hospital, saw a sight which, piercing to his heart, uprooted his life-plans and caused him to dedicate his career to the succour and guardianship of the outcast child. Less than forty years later he died in harness, a happy martyr to "The Children's Cause". To-day his Homes can survey sixty-four years of unbroken service, during which 110,000 children have been redeemed from a condition of destitution, pauperism, or crime; while nearly half a million other unfortunates, mostly kiddies and youths, have been helped by free gifts of clothing, meals and temporary lodging. To-day Barnardo's Homes can point with pride to the opposite ends of the earth, in Canada and Australia, where "old boys" have become Cabinet Ministers of State, ministers of religion, missionaries, doctors, barristers, solicitors, head masters of schools, college lecturers, dentists, Church organists, directors of business houses, manufacturers, contractors, etc. With equal pride can they point to "old girls" who are professional singers, expert musicians, missionaries, nurses, school teachers, lecturers, music mistresses and heads of business houses; more important, they can point to Barnardo girls who are the beloved helpmates of men pursuing every skilled trade and in all the learned professions. Several "old girls" have creditably taken their places beside their husbands as mayoresses of Colonial towns.

It speaks well for the loyalty Barnardo's Homes inspire in their protégés that some 11,000 "old boys" *voluntarily* responded to the Call of Empire during the Great War, casting their lives into the jaws of death, in defence of hearth and home.[1] It is suggestive, too, that over half of them enlisted, not on English, but on Canadian soil, thus proving their title as real "ambassadors of the Commonwealth of Free Nations"; and so valiant was their endeavour that among them were men cited for every distinction, from the Victoria Cross down.

Equally creditable is the record of Barnardo's boys upon the Seven Seas. Both the Royal Navy and the Mercantile Marine boast large numbers of "old boys", not a few of them officers, some even commanders. But whether officers or plain "Jack Tars", their Barnardo training has helped them to present their worthy quota towards Britain's high reputation for chivalry at sea.

Not least important in Dr. Barnardo's scheme was the manner in which he, like his Master, dignified the humbler crafts. To-day his Homes can point to all the skilled trades, and there too, as a result of training in the Homes, are a regiment of Barnardo boys, masters of their craft, happy in their work, vigorous, respected citizens.

Nothing, however, speaks more eloquently of the spirit of this work than the support of "old boys and girls". Yearly, from Canada alone, to say nothing of Great Britain and other quarters of the Empire, former wards pour into the Barnardo treasury thousands of dollars;[2] and whether the gift be $1 from a girl who has just received her "first pay", or $100 as a Christmas remembrance from a "boy" ten years married, who writes to tell of the purchase of his "own farm", and send photographs of his wife and children, almost always there is expressed the desire that the enclosed

[1] This number is quite *exclusive* of the "Marchmont" boys, though the Marchmont Homes are now incorporated in Dr. Barnardo's Homes.

[2] Last year's contributions from old boys and girls in Canada alone was nearly $4,000.

THE BOYS' GARDEN CITY

1. A gift from England's Schools
3. A corner of the "City"

2. "Dinner is over"
4. Some boys in tableau

THE WILLIAM BAKER TECHNICAL SCHOOL

1. In the power house   2. A tinsmith shop
3. The main building   4. Young shoemakers

remittance "may help a bit toward doing for some destitute child what the Homes did for me". Hundreds of letters to Headquarters contain even more touching references: often it is stated that "twice every day" the correspondent lifts up his voice in thankfulness to God for the Homes "and the chance they gave me".

So much by way of a racing glance at the Homes' record. But where, and under what conditions, has this work been wrought? To-day Dr. Barnardo's Homes include nearly one hundred distinct organizations, each with clearly defined responsibilities; and these organizations operate in some two hundred separate buildings, each designed for a specific need, and all vibrant with life. The Administrative Headquarters are in Stepney Causeway, the heart of East London; but the nucleus of the Homes is the open country of the South of England, where, in different quarters, amidst the beauty of woods, hills, flowers and streams, the kiddies learn the charm of rural life. From here, however, Branches and Ever Open Doors extend throughout the Kingdom; while distributing quarters in Canada and Australia mark the outposts.

Now, to describe in detail the hundred centres wherein the Barnardo process of life-equipment is carried on would fill volumes. A bird's-eye view of five or six will reflect something of their founder's aim.

The Girls' Village Home, where 1,400 girls are housed in more than eighty separate cottages, has been styled "the loveliest village in the world". Often has it been acclaimed by artists, architects and landscape gardeners "*England's* most charming village". And whether the prospect be that of May or December, the stately church, presented by an anonymous donor, the ivy-mantled hospital, the gift of Australian and New Zealand admirers, the superb Barnardo Memorial, and the Cairns Memorial House, seem perfectly situated as sentinels, guarding the serenity of an ever-green and ever-enchanted girls' world. During no season of the

c

year, in any part of these grounds, will you find a sign: "Keep off the Grass." Every village girl plays gaily on the green; but all have learned to reverence the beauty of flower, shrub and tree.

Not less captivating than the village green is the orderly life of the cottages. Each cottage is a separate home, and each home has its own "mother", generally a young, vigorous widow of refinement, who directs, or rather leads, the affairs of the household. In most cottages dwell sixteen to twenty girls: a few, house twenty-five. But in every case the family spirit prevails. Scarcely a cottage is without its toddling baby, and none is without its big sister, of fifteen or sixteen. The older girls love to look after "baby" and their "little sisters"; and every lassie, from nine or ten up, helps "mother" with the daily round. Hence, although all the girls from four to fourteen go to school, and although all have plenty of time for play, the elder schoolgirls—along with one or two above school age—perform nearly all the household duties, so that the real task of the "mother" is that of supervision. The little maidens dust and scrub, make beds, sweep, cook, wash dishes, peel potatoes, run errands and attend to a thousand duties, thus making all run like clockwork. Often have I felt as I moved among smiling faces, visiting at random different cottages and inspecting every quarter from pantry to wardrobe, that cleaner cottages could nowhere be found.

The unit of the village, then, is the cottage, wherein are all the essentials of a happy home, not excluding a fine assortment of dolls, teddy-bears, rocking-horses, etc., presented by admirers. And although it often happens that a tricycle or dollies' pram is given to some fancied child, the gift always is shared, in the best of grace, with this lassie's sisters; for life in each cottage is co-operative. Yet the *community* life of the whole village is not less attractive than that of the individual cottage. To see the fourteen hundred girls assembled in their beautiful church with their mothers

and teachers, singing some familiar hymn, is a sight to
rejoice angels' hearts. The school, too, is large, light and
airy; and whether engaged in reading, history, geography
or physical drill, the girls look almost as happy as when
romping on the green, or gathered in their own cottages
for tea. But "fullness of life" is interpreted through other
vehicles than sport, church, school and home. That great
artist, the late Sir George Frampton, after coming into
intimate contact with Barnardo's work, made its support
one of the master enthusiasms of his life. Not only did he
give the Homes some of his own rarest paintings, but he
persuaded other first-rank artists to do likewise. So the
village boasts a splendid art collection of appropriate
pictures, which always are suggesting to the girls' minds
the sense of colour, beauty and charm.

Other aspects of this community's life are equally arresting. In the excellently equipped laundry, girls beyond
school age, who soon are to earn their living as "maids"
in England, or as household helpers Overseas, do all the
washing and ironing not only for the village, but also for
all Barnardo institutions within a reasonable radius of the
village. This means that every week the laundry girls wash
and iron many thousands of articles; and let the sceptic
visit the laundry, which, like all Barnardo departments, is
open to inspection, and he can judge for himself how well
the work is done!

But the charter of all Barnardo's Homes is: "*No Destitute
Child Ever Refused Admission.*" Accordingly there are, among
these fourteen hundred girls, cripples and specially delicate
children; while, naturally, the village is not wholly free
from outbreaks of disease. But for both the crippled and
the sick special preparation is made. The Australasian
Hospital, a magnificent building, is as cheery a children's
hospital as one could find; and its seventy beds, some of
them endowed, are always ready to minister to the health,
not only of village children, but also of boarded-out girls,

and even of "old girls" in special need of treatment. As for the cripples, they are members of "families" along with their healthy "sisters"; but, as many are too deformed ever to fend for themselves, and as they have no friends anywhere on earth save Barnardo's, the village opened up a large Embroidery Department, where under skilled tuition, by warped bodies but radiant spirits, is produced the most exquisite needlecraft. Some of the cripples are over thirty years old and have been with Barnardo's since babyhood. Barnardo's was their first home, and will remain their last on earth. Yet, deformed as they are, they could teach millions of healthy-bodied people the secret of cheerfulness.

Ten minutes drive takes you from the Girls' Village Home, Barkingside, to the Boys' Garden City, Woodford Bridge. In this "City", peopled by more than seven hundred Barnardo boys, you find a totally different environment. The scene is bolder, more virile than that of the Village Home. Fewer flowers and shrubs, fewer lawns and dove-cots meet the eye: far less of quiet, serene beauty makes itself felt. Here, unmistakably, is a *boys'* world.

Well over fifty acres comprise the "City" estate, and if the houses are larger and less surrounded by flowers, shrubs and lawns than is the case at the Village Home, the spacious playing-fields are more provocative of robust endeavour. Football, cricket and other field sports are always in prominence; while even the trees of this boys' paradise are sturdy veterans which, having defied a thousand storms, rear out their giant boughs on high, challenging the lads to climb aloft and learn the secret of their strength.

In the Boys' Garden City, as in the Girls' Village Home, the cottage is the unit; and here, too, each cottage has its "mother", while the "sons" and "brothers" of each family perform the household duties. And well they do them, too. For although here each "family" consists of some thirty sons, the rooms are as spotlessly clean as though all the sons were daughters. Indeed, when paying an unexpected visit you drop into cottage after cottage and inspect the rooms, you get the impression that you could eat from the floor of any cottage in the "City" and not imbibe a speck of dirt. At dusting and sweeping, scrubbing and polishing, bed-making and dish-washing, the boys are as dexterous as the girls. But what a task for the House Mother to keep this large family in order! True, it is a mighty challenge, but every mother is there because she feels it to be her vocation—not her job. Nearly all the "mothers" are smiling cheerfully at their task, and if you ask them about the boys, you are sure to get the reply: "They are just wonderful! We would far rather have boys than girls. They are heaps more fun!"

But how can a matron in the Garden City mother thirty boys, while in the Village Home the average family is not above twenty? Are boys so simple a problem in comparison with girls? Certainly not! The reason for the larger family in the "City" is the different organization of life. The boys here do not eat in their cottages as do the girls at Barkingside: instead, they assemble for meals in Canada Hall, a fine building presented by Canadian admirers, which, with its clock-tower, rises to prominence in the centre of the "City".

But this hall is more than a dining-room. Save on Sunday mornings, when the "City" *en masse* turns out for worship at local churches, it serves as convocation centre for all purposes whatsoever.[1] Every week, during autumn and winter, it is the scene of educational films, lantern talks, community singing, special lectures, etc.; while every Sunday evening, all the year round, it witnesses a Mission Service, at which the Governor of the "City", or some equally qualified person, gives a twenty-minutes' talk on a Bible topic: and to feel the pulse of this meeting, particularly when the boys break into song, is a tonic to one's spiritual health.

---

[1] Owing to the generosity of friends, a Chapel is now being erected in the Garden City grounds.

The swimming-pool is another centre of interest; for a magnificent pool it is, and the boys love it. But we dare not stop to elaborate its charm. Go, visit it yourself, and you will find the scene presented by these erstwhile destitute lads, now manœuvring on the diving-boards, now sporting in the water, conjures up a picture not less captivating than that confronting you at Golden Gate Harbour, where, around towering, sun-kissed rocks, are myriads of glossy seals: some basking in the brilliant light; some gliding from the burning rocks into the deeps beneath; some exhibiting their "stunts".

But hold! Enthusiasm for this "City of Boys" already has carried us too far; and no more space is left to tell of its educational schemes, its hospital, club rooms, library or scout corps. Nor can we pause to tell of its bakery, where every day some two thousand large loaves are made— enough not only to feed these ravenous lads, but to supply *all* the Homes within reach of its van. Here, as in the case of the Girls' Village Home, a hundred aspects of the corporate life cannot even be suggested. Only a series of visits can reveal the "City's" wonder. One thing, however, must be mentioned—the spirit of the place. A prominent Poor Law administrator, after visiting this Home, said he would give ten years of his life if he and his colleagues, who represent the Government's Poor Law Schools, could develop such fellowship as he had there witnessed.

To see the fraternity between "big boys", about to migrate or start life in the trades and little chaps recently transplanted into the "City" from one of the Homes for smaller lads, leaves a memory not easily erased; but to observe the devotion of the "City" to its governor and his wife, or to see a "family" huddled around its "mother" as she reads a good story, would make glad the heart of every lover of boys.

"Goldings", two miles from Hertford, commanding an eminence in the midst of a superb district, is the seat of the William Baker Technical School. This industrial training centre was originally a country mansion surrounded by a large estate. But the day came when its owner no longer felt justified in maintaining it; so, desiring to see it utilized for some "good work", he offered it to Barnardo's at a fraction of its value. The offer was thankfully accepted, and after extensive alterations Barnardo's craft schools were transferred from Stepney Causeway to this spacious, wind-swept abode.

After internal alterations, this mansion provided seven excellent dormitories, sufficient for 300 boys, while its ground-floor apartments made ideal classrooms. To feed these 300 growing lads a dining-hall had, of course, to be erected,[1] but the fine set of stables and out-houses were, as by magic, transformed into workshops, where more than a dozen skilled trades are mastered. And as you watch these once-destitute lads, whistling at bench, last, anvil or lino-type; as you observe the close relation between their fingers and minds, as you examine the beautiful sideboards and bookcases, the neat boots and shoes, the well-turned kettles and pots, the perfectly printed bills and leaflets which their industry has wrought, involuntarily you ask: "Where would these boys have been, and what would they now be doing, save for Barnardo's Homes?"

A survey of this centre's industry is not our purpose. It must, however, be noted that from the lasts of the boy shoemakers are turned off all the boots and shoes worn by Barnardo children in the various Homes, which means a weekly output of 250 new pairs, and the mending of more than 500 pairs. Here, too, the boys make much of the furniture, and all the pots and pans Barnardo's need: they make every one of the strong, tin-lined trunks with which boys and girls emigrate; in their own station they generate their light and power; on their own land they raise all their vegetables and nearly all their fruits. Even the lorries plying

[1] This need was generously met by a single anonymous gift.

the roads from Home to Home, exchanging product for product, were partly made by these boys; while much of Barnardo's printing is turned off from the "Goldings" press.

But how came this school to be named after William Baker? Here, too, emerges romance. A lifelong zealot for Barnardo's, in 1905, on the Doctor's death, Mr. Baker, who at Dublin University won a "double first", and who at his Law examinations captured the highest honours, gave up a lucrative practice at the Bar to devote his time to the Homes' service. To commemorate his fifteen years of *full-time* voluntary endeavour, together with much previous labour, this Industrial School bears his name. But Barnardo's have unknown as well as known helpers. One of the charming sights at "Goldings" is the chapel, which seats the 300 boys in residence, and many visitors besides. Yet the donors of this edifice chose to remain secret. On a modest tablet inside the doors you read:

> "To the Glory of God
> This Chapel is given by a Few Friends
> In the Hope that the Boys who Worship
> Here may learn to know the Lord Jesus
> Christ as their Saviour, Master and King."

Even a racing glimpse at the Barnardo system dare not overlook the Watts Naval Training School, where boys are equipped for the Royal Navy. This school, situated at Elmham, Norfolk, was built as a County Agricultural School, and as such was opened by King Edward VII, then Prince of Wales. In that capacity it failed, and finally was closed. But in 1901 Mr. Edmund H. Watts, a ship-owner, after conference with Dr. Barnardo, bought the school with its fifty-four acres, and having expended upon it thousands of pounds, thus converting it into a "ship on land", he gave it to the Doctor as a naval training centre. And under Barnardo's genius it flourished. A few days' association with this school will reveal the secret of Barnardo boys' success on the high seas. Its Governor, a charming Christian gentleman, and an old captain of the Royal Navy, had thirty years' experience at sea, and every man on his staff is a practical seaman. Here every nook and cranny is charged with the wonder of ocean life. Deep-voiced bells proclaim the time of day; bugle-tones ring out the names of lads and issue forth commands; a superbly trained boys' band makes the air to tingle with martial strains; ropes, boats, life-belts and anchors are all prominent; while naval uniform, worn always by officers and boys, completes the impression of life at sea.

But try to enter into the details of the place, and unless you be a sailor trained you will find them bewilderingly complex. The school itself has been so recast as to present the illusion of a huge ship with decks and quarter-decks, bow and stern, bridge and helm; while, as for the crew's activities, they seem legion. Roused from slumber by the sound of bugles, while yet the lark proclaims the dawn of day, these Jack Tars have completed morning ablutions and devoured breakfast ere most of us are awake. Then, before the duties of class and drill commence, governor, officers and crew assemble in the Great Hall for prayers; and there, led by the Chaplain, a Cambridge graduate, two stirring hymns are sung, a brief Scripture lesson is read, and a seven-minute Bible talk is given. Devotions over, like a flash the lads betake themselves to their respective quarters for school or drill. And now, as you wander from deck to deck and cabin to cabin, admiration deepens. Push into this room and you find a class exploring the mysteries of algebra or geometry; in that they are pursuing arithmetic or draftsmanship; in a third they are engrossed in history or geography; in another they are battling with grammar or composition. "Ordinary school routine," you say. Perhaps. Though even in the classroom the Barnardo Spirit is active. But go now to the gymnasium, and as you see the lads performing on swing and bar, rope and ladder, track and mat; as you note their brawny arms, sun-burned faces, well-kept teeth, sparkling eyes and, above all, their irresistible good nature, you will be less than human if you fail to catch the contagion of their merriment.

The swimming-pool presents a scene not less captivating than "the gym", while the drill-room's spectacle of gunnery and team-work makes the uninitiated gasp with awe. Here is revealed the Barnardo sailor in embryo. But push on! This school has a hundred charms. Its chapel is almost as fine as "Goldings" chapel; its library, containing books presented by the Queen, is well stocked with tales of sea-life, travel and adventure; its magazine is one of the finest in the Barnardo series; its bank and tuck-shop are run in orderly manner; its "old boys' room", furnished by old boys at sea, and the "bed" maintained by them, suggest one of the links between present and past students; while the flattering reports of the school's status by Admiralty officials prove its high efficiency.

After finishing at Watts, the boys, at fifteen or sixteen, go to Shotley, the Government Naval School with over 1,000 students, for final training; and the success of Barnardo boys there is outstanding. In 1923 the Government established a system of prizes for the best entries, and up to the present Barnardo boys have won three-quarters of the first prizes, a large percentage of the second, and, some years, both first and second. The signed Report of Captain Noble, "Commanding Officer of the Royal Navy Training Establishment, Shotley", June 15th, 1926, states that one Barnardo boy, Hardaker by name, won "the highest marks ever obtained by a Signal Boy in Final Examination".

Remarkable as is Watts Naval Training School, its wonder is almost duplicated at the Russell-Cotes Nautical School, a Barnardo branch at Parkstone, Dorset, designed to train boys for the Mercantile Marine. Here too, bells, bugles, naval uniforms, nautical drill, martial music, wireless and the mysteries of seamanship are ever present. But most alluring is the school's *esprit de corps*. The joyous fellowship between staff and boys is wondrous to behold. It reveals a spirit that most public schools might envy. Yet this *esprit de corps* is not peculiar to the Russell-Cotes School; it represents the soul of the Barnardo system.

The above are typical of Barnardo's larger centres. Yet some of the most astounding of their achievements are wrought in the dozens of smaller branches.

At Liverpool they have a Migration Home, where all the year round 150 lads are in residence undergoing three or four months' training, to test their fitness for frontier life in Canada or Australia. Here, alongside many interesting, are some unique endeavours. Two are especially impressive. One is an arrangement with the Liverpool Corporation, whereby the boys daily spend hours in the city's stables learning to feed, bed, clean, harness, and generally care for horses, while also they are taught to ride and drive; the other is an arrangement with the Liverpool Cow Keepers' Association, whereby boys go to different cowsheds and there learn to clean stables, tend calves, milk cows and separate cream, as well as perform a score of incidental duties. And what success has attended this scheme? Everywhere I went, both in stables and cowsheds, the keepers were emphatic in its laudation. All said that the lads were willing and quick to learn, that they were kind to the animals, and that a more chivalrous lot of chaps one could never hope to meet. But the finest tribute to this work comes from Overseas. Barnardo's have many letters from Canadian farmers alone, who express delight at the knowledge these boys had acquired about horses and cattle, before ever they saw a Canadian farm.

Another of the smaller Branches is the Musical Home for Boys at Clapham, where 150 budding minstrels are always in training. People all over the Empire have been thrilled by the concerts of Barnardo protégés. Yet every one of these highly trained lads was once destitute; his every attainment he owes to the Homes. All Barnardo Branches teach music and teach it efficiently, but Clapham is the finishing centre for talented youths; and it speaks well for the thoroughness of the musical education imparted, that "old boys" are leading orchestras the world over. Some have played solo parts in both Queen's Hall and Royal Albert Hall Concerts, London; while the present Musical Adviser to the London County Council, Mr. Walter Reynolds, who arranges and directs all park concerts for that august body, is proud to proclaim himself a Barnardo boy.

In the Barnardo family are more than one thousand babes, most of whom are cared for through an ingenious system of Boarding Out. Others are placed in "families" at the Girls' Village Home and kindred Branches. But all these must be healthy babes, whereas Barnardo's always have a number who are neither blind, deaf, dumb, paralysed, nor deformed, but simply delicate. Hence, for such, in Hawkhurst, Kent, amidst exquisite surroundings, Barnardo opened his picturesque Babies' Castle. Here always you find about seventy babes, who, under the care of trained nurses and kindergarten teachers, are gradually finding robust health; and the sight of these "tinies" in cradles and hammocks, on swings, delving in the sand, rolling on the grass, or playing at school, affords entertainment which only Babydom could supply.

These sketches are only a bird's-eye view of a few Barnardo centres. They can but vaguely suggest the proportions of this many-sided work. The importance of the system is best seen in the extent to which its methods have been copied. In England, the Established Church, the Salvation Army, the Methodist and the Baptist Churches, as well as the Roman Catholic Church, have established child-rescue schemes on Barnardo's lines; and the Quarrier Homes of Scotland have learned not a little from this source. Again, the present governor of Knowles Rescue Home, Canada, is an old Barnardo boy; while different countries, East and West, boast child-rescue systems which admittedly are Barnardo's progeny. And still the influence spreads, for, in every month of every year, Barnardo Branches are inspected by child experts and Government officials from all continents. Indeed, decades ago, Governments themselves began to admit their indebtedness to Barnardo's genius; for, in 1896, a prominent Cabinet Minister, after labouring for two years as Chairman of a Royal Commission appointed to investigate the whole status of Poor Law Schools and kindred institutions, declared that "much as the Government owed Barnardo for what he himself has done, it owed him more for what he has *taught the State to do*".

Such is the significance of this child-rescue system. But what of its Founder? Who was "the Father of Nobody's Children"? How came he to catch his vision? In what circumstances did his work begin? In what atmosphere was it carried forward? Whence came its support? What principles directed its evolution? What to-day is the Homes' goal? Wherein do Barnardo's set an example to the modern world? These and a hundred co-related questions must now engage our thought.

CHAPTER III

BIRTH AND REBIRTH

IF ever a man had a mixed pedigree, Dr. Barnardo was that man! The blood of at least seven nationalities pulsed in his veins; and it is possible this was reinforced by that of as many more. His own formula for his ancestry was—"a bit of all sorts".

The earliest records of the Barnardo family go back to the fifteenth century, in Alexandria, whence, owing to Turkish persecution, they fled to Spain, changing meanwhile their Hebrew name to its Spanish equivalent. A century's habitation in Spain witnessed the mixing of Barnardo blood with that of the native race, thus assimilating a Moorish strain. But persecution again drove them hence. When the terror of Inquisition and Index darkened the horizon, the Barnardos were suspect, and calling in what credits they could fled incognito to Italy. Here one branch of the family acquired eminence, as is instanced by the erection of the Palazzo Bernardo, standing to this day on the Grand Canal, Venice. But our subject's forbears were not destined to permanent association with the Queen of the Adriatic. After the passing of several generations, political turmoil in Italy, together with business opportunities in Germany, induced them to emigrate to Hamburg, where, becoming established as international bankers, they helped to finance both Napoleon Bonaparte and the Hudson's Bay Company of Canada.

Here, in 1800, was born John Michaelis Barnardo, the Doctor's father. But Germany was not to be the seat of the family he established. As a young man he founded a prosperous business in Dublin; and settling down to manage it he there courted and married Mary Drinkwater, daughter of an English Quaker family, long resident in Ireland. On July 4th, 1845, in Dublin, the ninth child of this union, Thomas John Barnardo, was born.

The omens of the moment were bad. On the day of Tom's birth occurred the bankruptcy of the Wicklow-Wexford Railway, a crash involving John Michaelis Barnardo in the loss of thousands of pounds. But more intimate troubles were at hand. Thomas John was born a puny child; and for days it seemed improbable that either he or his mother would long survive the ordeal of his birth. The mother, however, soon rallied and was restored to health; but Tom, for years, remained fragile.

When two years old he was smitten by a serious illness, and after lingering for weeks on Eternity's brink, he finally was pronounced *dead* by two physicians. The coffin actually was in the house, and the undertaker was embalming the body for burial, when, to his amazement, he discovered a flutter of the heart. The "corpse" was alive! Every remedial measure was forthwith applied; and in time Tom Barnardo developed into a sturdy lad.[1]

If, however, this child was snatched from death in fulfilment of Providential purpose, that purpose left little immediate impress; for Tom was neither angel nor saint. Family records present quite the opposite impression. He was hot-tempered, self-willed and highly imperious; and whereas his brother Harry, slightly younger than he, had curly hair, finely chiselled features and a heavenly singing voice, Tom had wiry hair, plain features and a voice better adapted for shouting than singing. Hence, these two occupying the nursery together, many a storm ensued. A member of the family recalls that Harry, because of his voice, was frequently taken into the drawing-room to entertain guests; and as, on these occasions, he generally was regaled with chocolates, Tom, left behind, stamped and fumed. Once when Harry returned to the nursery munching his last sweet, Tom's fury overleaped bounds. Rushing

[1] Incredible as the coincidence may appear, Dr. Barnardo's widow informs me that one of their own sons, as a babe, was pronounced dead by the attending physician; but hours later, in his grandmother's arms, he rallied, as from a trance.

forward before anyone could intervene, he smacked him furiously on the face, crying, "Take that for showing off in the drawing-room!" Then, pushing the howling brother into a corner, as he delivered another blow, he roared: "And that, you pig, for eating all the chocolates yourself!"

Schooldays developed little more of the saint than emerged in the nursery. Evidence accumulates that Tom was a problem at school; and certain it is that he was to the fore in causing his section of his Form to be dubbed "Praters' Row". His brother, Dr. Frederick Barnardo, has left a graphic pen-picture, part of which reads: "He never was one of those goody-goody boys. . . . He was full of fun and mischief, thoughtless and careless. Do not suppose he was born a saint and always a saint. He gave a good deal of trouble at home and had a very strong, determined self-will. . . . At his first school he gave no end of trouble . . . and subsequently, when at the Rev. J. Dundas' School . . . he was no better." From other members of his family we learn that Tom was little attracted to any sport save swimming; but at this he excelled, for, while yet in his teens, he saved two men from drowning. As a child, however, his favourite amusement was the reading of imaginative stories; and on his widow's evidence, one of his lifelong regrets was that never could he find time to write a volume of fairy-tales. Yet, years before leaving school, Barnardo developed a taste in reading which carried him far beyond the story form of literature. Any volume which came to hand he dipped into, and all except schoolbooks retained his interest. Not always, however, were his books adapted to his age. When fourteen, he blatantly was declaring Voltaire, Rousseau and Paine to be his favourite authors. And, as a counterpart to this boast, he assumed a cynical attitude to all Christian doctrines, announcing himself an Agnostic.

But these facts are in advance of our story: the out-standing impressions of Barnardo's schooldays are his aversion from the curriculum; his distaste for routine; his feeling that personality was, in school, more frequently crushed than developed; his love of mischief; his incurable talkativeness, and his passion for reading. Examinations he treated with contempt: this probably being a pose resulting from Rousseau's influence; but, be that as it may, Barnardo left school at sixteen without special attainment, although he was recognized as a "bright chap", if only he would stick to his proper work.

One other impression of schooldays should not be overlooked. In later life, an experienced educationist, reviewing his own memories, he said that in one school he had sat "under the thraldom of one of the biggest and most brutal of bullies—the most *cruel* man, as well as the most *mendacious*, that I have ever in all my life met". Recalling certain "victims" over whom this master tyrannized "with monstrous sway", he added: "Had I been one of them, I could never have returned to school and awaited the torture he was ready to apply." This brutality left its mark: "Such intense loathing and disgust . . . were awakened in my heart . . . that I went to the opposite extreme in my detestation of anything having the least appearance of cruelty or hardness."

So much for school and its impressions; but what of young Barnardo's spiritual life? As an infant he was baptized in St. Andrew's Church, Dublin, where his father was an office-holder and his mother a member. He attended Sunday-school, too, in this church, and at fifteen was confirmed by the Archbishop of Dublin. His earliest religious influences, therefore, were according to the rites of the Church of Ireland, which at that time meant the Church of England. But there is no evidence that these ministrations left any abiding mark. Certain it is that the example of his godly mother, with her Quaker traditions, he always revered; but equally certain is it that the sacrament of Confirmation was entered into without regard to its significance. He accepted it in a formal manner, impelled by external

D

influence, not conviction; for, at this time, he was more interested in Agnosticism than Christianity. Indeed, for a year before Confirmation, he had been airing his sceptical views, and for nearly two years following, his chief idols were Voltaire, Rousseau and Paine. And whatever inspiration these writers provided for "Radical" reformers on the Continent, they developed in young Barnardo only a cynical priggishness, which made him sceptical of all regenerative power. But this was soon to change.

On leaving school Barnardo, through his father's influence, secured a good business post, whereat he exhibited ability and method. But his heart was not in business. Reading was still his master-passion; and the arguments of the Agnostics still captivated his mind. On all sides he emphasized his "rational" outlook, scoffing equally at the Bible and at organized Christianity.

At this time Ireland was in the grip of a revival which caused thousands of twice-born men to enlist for service in the Kingdom of God. This awakening began far North in 1859, and the following year reached Belfast, where its influence was profound. Then, proceeding South, a tidal wave of spiritual power passed over Dublin. The Metropolitan Hall, previously a circus building, was the centre of operations; but auxiliary meetings were held in other quarters. And as enthusiasm spread, several members of the Barnardo family, including two of Tom's elder brothers, one of whom became a medical doctor and the other a civil servant in India, accepted the Lordship of Christ. But although these brothers told Tom of their newly found joy, and pleaded with him to consecrate his life to Christ's service, he still scoffed. Finally, however, he agreed to attend the revival meetings and judge for himself.

Here he witnessed striking demonstrations of spiritual power. But his masters had taught him subtle arguments wherewith to explain away religious experience. Was not all this emotional hysteria? The revival results were psycho-

logical phenomena, and destined to no permanence. Watch
and see the newly proclaimed "saints" revert to all their
former sins! But though this stripling scoffed, he was set
thinking; and—awkward thought—his explanations did not
quite explain things to himself. Therefore, much as he
disliked the ordeal, he decided to go with his brothers to
some of the smaller meetings in private houses. Attending one
of these gatherings, in the home of William Fry,[1] he was
besought to surrender his life to Christ. But apparently in
vain! The cynical attitude was still uppermost. A letter,
written years afterwards, to Mr. Fry explains the youth's
conduct. Referring to this meeting, Barnardo confessed:
"I did not half like to go, but nevertheless I went; and in
that meeting Rocheford Hunt spoke to me, and so did you.
I behaved very badly. I was just as cheeky as a young fellow
can be, and I thought you looked at me as if you would say,
'If I had that young fellow alone for five minutes I would
take down his conceit, I'd give him a good hiding.' But
somehow your words were very *kind*, and not at all in
harmony with what I thought your *looks* meant; that was
the beginning."

Barnardo's recollection is significant: this gathering in
William Fry's home was the beginning! From that day a
sense of doubt invaded his mind; he felt compelled to test
the efficacy of his Agnostic creed. Was his superior attitude a sham? Were those at whom he smiled right—and he
wrong? Regularly now he attended the meetings, and
gradually he learned that there was more reality in the
revival than he had permitted himself to believe. Finally,
some weeks after the experience in the Frys' home, he heard
a trenchant address by John Hambleton, the one-time
tragedian. Conviction of error pierced his soul. He knew
now that he was wrong; he knew also that peace and power
could never be his until he found God. But before the dawn

[1] William Fry was the father of Sir William Fry, Vice-Chairman of the
Barnardo Council.

of another day Light broke. One of Barnardo's brothers, referring to Hambleton's address, says: "That was the turning-point!" Then, relating how Tom, long after midnight, entered the bedroom of two of his brothers "in great distress of soul", he continues: "Many tears did he shed . . . for he was in great agony of heart; so the three brothers knelt together and cried to God . . . and He graciously heard, and light and joy and peace there and then . . . filled his heart. We all rose from our knees rejoicing and thanking God."

Such was the manner in which Thomas John Barnardo, on May 26th, 1862, five weeks before his seventeenth birthday, had revealed to him the Light of God. That date marked for Barnardo a rebirth. From then on he, as much as Wesley, Wilberforce or Shaftesbury, was a Christian to the bone!

Scarcely could one imagine a more complete reversal of attitude than Barnardo's. Paine, Rousseau and Voltaire were now forsaken. Henceforward the Bible was to him the Book of books. The scoffer had turned Evangelist! And to this new task he consecrated every fibre of his being. Immediately he enlisted as a teacher in a Dublin Ragged School, a service which plunged him into the midst of much abandoned life. This challenge, however, acted as no damper to his zeal: rather it spurred his spirit to restless energy. Scarcely was he installed in Ragged School work when he felt impelled to visit the homes of his pupils; and in doing so he was shocked: "Had I a dog, I would not kennel it where I found these immortal souls, destined to share the glories of eternity!"

But even after conversion Barnardo had his "ups" and "downs". In fact, to the end he showed little of the negative serenity of proverbial saints. One day in company with Mr. Owens, a helper in Ragged School visitation, he asked why his friend always carried a stick? "Oh, habit," replied Owens; "I like a cane or an umbrella in my hand." "So used I," returned Barnardo, "but I had to give it up, because one day, when I began to come here, the boys so annoyed me . . . that I lost patience and had all I could do to keep from striking them with my stick. If I had, it would have killed my work for the Lord; so I left it at home after that." Here was an attribute of the later man. If, in pursuit of his Purpose, his right hand offended, he was prepared to "cut it off and cast it from him".

Of the nature of these visitations, Owens has left a brief account. Recalling a visit through Marrowbone Lane, a winding alley in the "Liberties", Dublin's vilest slum, he states: "There we went from house to house and room to room, and, as we got access, spoke, read and prayed with each family and left a tract. At the end of the lane was a widows' almshouse; there Barnardo loved to go. He often gave the old women tea, and helped others in extreme cases of sickness and poverty." From Owens we learn, too, that always before setting off on such visitations Barnardo prayed earnestly, "not only for those we were to visit, but for wisdom and grace for ourselves". From another co-worker we get a glimpse of the seriousness and sympathy with which he gave himself up to this labour of love. Calling at the house of an afflicted family, shortly after Barnardo had paid a visit, this missioner was told that the previous visitor "had wet the floor with his tears, as he prayed by the bedside of the invalid".

The influence of the revival upon the vilest districts of Dublin was not insignificant; augmenting the labours of Ragged Schools and other missions, it sent a band of noble workers to grapple with the ghastly problems of slumdom. Twelve years after conversion, Barnardo, revisiting the worst haunts of his native city, wrote: "For unswerving faithfulness, real loyalty to Christ and earnest, aggressive, philanthropic effort, perhaps few cities in the world are to be compared with Dublin, when its size and the small number of its Protestant population are considered." But still he pronounced the situation bad: "The fact is that whisky-drinking, added to the vicious tendencies of the people who dwell in these wretched hovels, have demoralized them to the lowest degree." Then comes the vehemence of the mature Barnardo: "The Corporation of Dublin have reason to be utterly ashamed that such fever dens and loathsome sources of moral contagion are allowed to remain in a city which boasts so many noble streets and imposing public buildings!"

Ragged School endeavours, strenuous as they were, did not monopolize Barnardo's zeal. Simultaneously he started a Bible Class for children of the well-to-do: the revival having proved that they were often as ignorant of the Bible as slum children. And of the six members of his class, one to-day is an eminent Christian barrister; one a trusted Civil Servant in India; one a Church of England clergyman, who, more than once, lifting high an inscribed Bible, has exclaimed: "Were it not for the influence of Dr. Barnardo, my old Bible-teacher, who presented me with this copy of Holy Writ, I should not be standing in this pulpit to-day!"

But Barnardo's conversion enthusiasm carried him into wider ministrations than teaching and visitation. Soon he felt called to *preach* the Gospel to the poor. So, dropping none of his Ragged School work, and continuing his Bible Class, he, along with his brothers, rented two rooms in the "Liberties", and there conducted Evangelistic Services. This was up-hill work. Barnardo's quaint description of the district is suggestive: "There are some Protestants here; but the majority of the population are deeply affected by superstition, ignorance and whisky." Nevertheless, despite difficulties, and in the face of opposition, the Barnardo brothers continued for months these Evangelistic services: and evidence remains that their labours bore fruit.

From now on Barnardo gave up all his spare time to Bible study and Christian endeavour. Sunday found him engaged in four or five religious services; five week-nights

saw him employed in Christian activity; and the "off" night
was spent in study and meditation. Religious endeavour
was now not only his recreation, it was his life. With un-
flagging zeal, service was heaped on service. He became a
member of the Y.M.C.A. and was active in its endeavours;
he joined the staff of Swift's Alley Mission and helped
there; he entered into fellowship with the Open Brethren and
laboured in certain of their missions. Again, when, through
the munificence of William Fry, Evangelical services were
started in Merrion Hall, he was an ardent supporter.

Before he was out of his teens, Barnardo was an avowed
"Open Brother". A catalogue of his library at this period
contains only books on Brethrenism and the Bible. It
is notable, therefore, that in middle life he declared:
"Brethrenism is an excellent street through which to pass,
but a bad street in which to abide!"

One aspect of Barnardo's spiritual development demands
special notice. Shortly after his conversion, on reading the
Scriptures, he was troubled by the question of Believers'
Baptism; and the more he pondered, the more was he
convinced that through this solemn sacrament it was his
duty to show forth to the world the burial of his old body
of sin, and his resurrection, by faith, to newness of life with
Christ. Accordingly, despite his infant baptism, he now
decided to be rebaptized, by Immersion.

An old diary, filled in from day to day by Barnardo's
hand, reflects, as a mirror, his state of mind at this juncture.
On October 16th, 1862, three days before his Immersion,
appear five entries, all revealing a state of ecstasy. *On rising*,
he wrote: "O Almighty Father, I praise Thee for Thy
mercies of the past night. . . . Make me ever grateful to
Thee for Thy continued kindness and care of this Thy
servant." A Bible text, chosen as the day's motto, is: "Blessed
is he that considereth the poor." An *eleven o'clock* entry
speaks of his "holy calm", adding that, on awaking, he had
prayed the Lord to permit him "to *feel* His presence";

then follows: "Up to this hour He has answered me abun-
dantly . . . grant that this day, I may, by my walk and
conversation, testify Christ to all around me, and that I,
Thy humble servant, may be a living epistle to be read
and known *of all men for Thy Glory.*" *Six o'clock*: "On coming
home from business I could not help feeling grateful to
Thee, O my Father, for having sustained me so graciously
throughout this day." An *eight o'clock* note states that along
with two of his brothers he attended a prayer meeting in
a Baptist Chapel, where his "soul was very much refreshed".
After this meeting he informed "dear Mr. Giles", the
minister, of his determination to be baptized the following
Sunday. Home again, we find him, with his brothers,
reading and discussing several chapters in St. John's Gospel:
"Truly, there is nothing so comforting and soul-refreshing
as reading the '*Word*' *after prayer*. Blessed be God for having
placed such ample means at our disposal." The closing
entry for the day was made at *12.30 a.m.*: "I at last got into
bed in the most happy frame of mind imaginable, happy
that I am able to say with David, at least for one day,
'That I have kept God always before me.' "

Next day, if not a day of ecstasy, was one of peace. Three
entries record his experiences. *Before breakfast*: "Thanks be
to God for having spared me to see the light of another
day. O Lord grant that it may be spent in Thy service and
for Thy glory." His Bible text reflects again his passion to
help the poor: "The needy shall not always be forgotten."
But the day was not so well started as its predecessor, and
its "joy was less": "In consequence of rising late, I was not
able to devote a proper length of time in prayer to the
Lord, and to this I attribute my want of vigour throughout
the day, for although I was neither miserable nor unhappy,
yet I did not experience that degree of happiness which I
did yesterday." A *six o'clock* note praising God for "everlasting life", adds: "O Lord! I can never thank Thee enough
for all Thy kindness and mercy to me, who am so unworthy

to receive the very least of them." *Eleven o'clock*: "I have
passed a most delightful evening at home reading the
Word of God. My Heavenly Father has indeed been with
me whilst reading the sacred volume, for my soul is as a giant
refreshed with wine. . . ." This same entry contains prayers
for the unconverted members of his father's household and
for friends, that, "by the effectual application of the Holy
Spirit", their minds may be prepared "to receive with
meekness Thy Word".

Saturday, October 18th, was again a time of rapture.
9.0 a.m.: "This day I awoke with a most lively feeling of
God's presence with me. May this continue throughout
the day, for Jesus' sake. In consequence of getting up earlier,
I had more time to spend in sweet communion with the
Lord . . . it gave me a great feeling of calmness and con-
tentment." A *3 p.m.* entry returns to the forthcoming
ceremony: ". . . asked the Lord to bless the ceremony of
Baptism, which I am to undergo to-morrow, in token of
my willingness to bury the old body of my sins in my
Saviour's grave, and rise therefrom in newness of life."
Fervent petitions follow to the end that God give him
"courage to declare before *all worlds*" his resolution "of
putting on Christ"; that he be made more ready to do God's
will; that grace be granted him to declare to his father his
determination of being baptized; and that the Almighty
would so "soften" his father's heart, "that he may not
merely give his consent, but accompany me to Thy house
when the Baptism is being accomplished." An *8 p.m.* note
says that his "dear brother George" and he had just taken
his "grave clothes" to the Baptist Chapel. All was now in
order for his Baptismal day.

Sunday, October 19th, 1862, was, in Barnardo's spiritual
experience, a red-letter day. Many diary pages are given
up to its events. Rising early, instead of choosing one text
he chose *three*, the first being: "Neither pray I for these
alone, but *for them* also which *shall believe* on Me through

their word"; the others referred to the significance of Baptism. There follows a brief prayer: "Grant, O Lord, that this day may entirely be spent in Thy service." A *10.30 a.m.* jotting states that, after breakfast, he went to St. Ann's Sunday School; but he complains that "the entire inquiries in the Scriptures are there *very cold*", while "the tumult caused by the Charity boys" created "a bedlam-like scene", disturbing temporarily his "calmness and peace"; but, school over, before he had gone half-way to the Baptist Chapel, "peace again visited" his "troubled soul". At the chapel he heard a "beautiful sermon on the necessity of Believers' Baptism", after which he partook of the Lord's Supper: "Truly I felt what a privilege it was for me, who am not worthy to partake of the very crumbs which fall from the Lord's Table, thus to be graciously provided with the very best and choicest. . . ." At *three o'clock* he was off to attend to Ragged School duties at Fishamble Street; but here again his rapture was perturbed by the noise of the overcrowded school. What with the "bawling of babies", the "calling of men and women", and the "hooting and hurrahing of boys and girls", a scene was created which, to a soul requiring calm, was exasperating. "Another day I might not have minded it at all; yet to-day, when I needed much calmness and quietness to prepare me for the evening, I felt very distressed."

Six o'clock: "I am now . . . going to the Baptist Chapel. May the Lord keep me and comfort me." At *12 midnight* comes a long, exuberant record of the whole experience: "On leaving home, I fell into a very happy state of mind, my thoughts being on Jesus, remembering how He loves me, comforting me with the assurance, 'He who declares Me before men, him will I confess before the Father'! Blessed Saviour, I will declare Thee before the world; and, O Lord, do aid me to keep this solemn vow made in the presence of the assembled multitude, that unbelievers may have no cause to scoff and revile Thy Name, but rather to fear it.

Lord Jesus, be with me in my daily avocations, that I may testify Thee in my walk and conversation." Arriving at the chapel vestry before the minister, he opened a large Bible, and after reading for some minutes, jotted down his reaction : "O Blessed Word of Truth! O Fatner, how can we ever thank Thee enough for the blessed privilege of going to this Thy written Word and finding comfort !"

Dr. Hunt, a warm friend, having now arrived, the youth and he engaged in prayer. Then the minister, Mr. Giles, appeared and spoke a few words "about the importance of the ordinance", after which Barnardo, accompanied by his "dear brother Fred", took a front pew in the chapel. The sermon, from the text, "Repent and be baptized every one of you in the name of Jesus Christ . . ." is pronounced "most impressive". Next the diary describes the ordinance. Entering the vestry, both Mr. Giles and Barnardo robed themselves for the Immersion, the latter in "grave clothes". Then, reappearing in the church, and standing by the baptismal pool, they joined the congregation in singing, "Ashamed of Jesus".

Barnardo's notes present a vivid record of his emotions : "Oh, I felt so happy, I cannot describe the joy which pervaded my heart at thus being enabled to testify Christ before all here. God grant that my example may be blessed to someone there." As for the act of Baptism, he says : "I surrendered myself passively to Mr. Giles and he immersed me completely in water ; I never moved ; I felt I was in the arms of Jesus. . . . Oh! the joy and happiness I felt in thus obeying my Saviour. And now, O gracious Father, help me to keep in remembrance that I have buried the body of my sin in my Saviour's grave, that I am risen to newness of life, that I must endeavour in everything to please Thee, and with Thy aid to remember that now I am dead to all the world, and all the world is dead to me. . . ." After chapel, Dr. Hunt dropped around to Barnardo's home, where, following an evening meal, a "happy time" was spent in singing hymns, in prayer, and in reading "the Word". Finally, after private meditations, wherein he "enjoyed sweet communion with the Lord", the enthusiast "retired to rest, to think and dream of Jesus".

Such was the nature of Barnardo's conversion and baptism. His whole being overflowed in rapture before God; and if, in mature years, his enthusiasm was tempered by broader experience, deeper knowledge and more comprehensive charity, it none the less is certain that the ecstasy of this experience remained with him—a priceless possession to the end.

For nearly four years following his conversion, Barnardo continued at his business post; but although he won promotion his soul was elsewhere. So finally—as was inevitable—there came a "call" which, striking the deepest chords of his spirit, caused his whole being to leap up in response. No business prospect in the world could hold him now! He felt he had "been laid hold of by Christ" for a peculiar work. Henceforth, not only on Sundays and in the evenings, but during all the hours of every day and every week, Christian service must claim his time.

The manner of this "call" deserves attention. Among the meats on which Barnardo nurtured his spiritual life, was attendance at a Young Men's Class held by Dr. Grattan Guinness.[1] There, one night, Guinness told "his boys" about a remarkable man. He had been to Liverpool to hear the founder of the China Inland Mission tell of his work, and so passed on his impressions, adding that he had made arrangements for "this great man"—Hudson Taylor—to come to the Merrion Hall, Dublin, and speak. Would his boys like to invite Mr. Taylor, while in town, to address the Class? Unanimously this suggestion was accepted.

Well before the hour arranged all members of the Class

[1] Dr. Guinness was a man of remarkable gifts. Several times he travelled around the world on evangelistic campaigns, and finally he established a missionary training centre in London, which has sent over 1,000 missionaries to different parts of the Foreign Field. See *Dictionary of National Biography*.

were assembled in Dr. Guinness's drawing-room; the atmosphere was electric with expectation. What would "the
great man" be like? Soon there appeared the athletic figure
of their teacher; and behind him, overshadowed by his proportions, was a diminutive figure, of youthful countenance.
Were they to be disappointed? Had "the great man" failed
to appear? At this moment Guinness, stepping aside, introduced the Rev. Hudson Taylor; and Barnardo, himself no
bigger than Taylor, turning to a class-mate, whispered:
"There's hope for me yet!"

In preparation for this visit the young men had read
Taylor's booklet, *China's Spiritual Needs and Claims.* They
expected great things; but the heights to which they
were lifted exceeded those to which their imagination had
soared. In conversational manner, Taylor told of China's
"teeming millions", of her national disintegration, her
staggering social problems, her dearth of spiritual leader-
ship, her gross superstitions—her need of the Gospel of
Christ.

The result of that meeting is memorable. Four boys
volunteered, there and then, as missionaries to China;
and all four became faithful builders of the Kingdom of
God. Three were destined to mighty service in China: the
fourth to even greater missionary achievement, though in its
fulfilment he never saw the land of his dreams.

CHAPTER IV

CHINA CHALLENGED BY EAST LONDON

WITHIN ten weeks of the memorable drawing-room meeting in Dublin, Barnardo found himself established in Coburn Street, East London, training for missionary endeavour among the Chinese. On setting forth from Dublin he carried letters of introduction both from the Open Brethren and the Y.M.C.A., commending him to fellowship among Christian workers in London. And although his missionary curriculum was exacting, he nevertheless found time to embark immediately on Christian service in East London. Was not *the world* God's vineyard? How, later, could he minister faithfully in China if, meanwhile, he closed the bowels of his compassion to the needs of East London? Such was the logic of his position, and he took it to heart. Scarcely had he discovered his new landmarks when he discovered also the location of Ernest Street Ragged School; and to its staff he at once volunteered his aid.

Of the academic side of Barnardo's first months in London, scant record remains. One point, nevertheless, stands out. When he left Dublin he left solely to train as an Evangelical missionary, the idea of studying medicine never entering his mind. His purpose was to take two or three years' training in Bible subjects, and then set forth to China. But of the practical side of those early days the evidence, from the start, is clear. Into his Ragged School endeavours he threw himself with zest; and so great was his power over rough lads that in a few weeks he was urged to accept the superintendency of the institution. This he did, with results indicating that he had his own ideas as to how a Ragged School should be run. So, as later will appear, it was not long before his aggressive—perhaps imperious—innovations, conflicted with the conservative procedure of his colleagues; and chafing under their yoke he finally jumped the traces—to "try out" his cherished ideas in a free field.

Meanwhile, as in Dublin, the labours of the Ragged School by no means monopolized his zeal. Here, too, he felt himself called upon to *preach* the Word in the highways and by-ways; and among his early London experiences none is more illustrative of the man than his street-preaching exploits. The challenge of open-air preaching roused all the energy of his being; and the fact that he had done obeisance before Agnostic shrines helped him to understand and refute the arguments of his rationalistic opponents; for however proud he had once been of his "philosophical" doctrine, he now adjudged it an empty husk. One debt, nevertheless—whether he recognized it or not—Barnardo owed to his youthful allegiance to rationalism. It taught him the value of cogent reasoning; and although, after conversion, he came to esteem other elements of personality more illuminating than pure reason, he never despised the faculty of reason as such. To the end, he defended by rational argument the position to which he was led by faith. All he now demanded was that reason work in harmony with other attributes of personality—especially faith, intuition, imagination and spiritual experience. Briefly, Barnardo's quarrel with the rationalistic attitude was that frequently it strove to subjugate faculties with which it should have co-operated on a basis of mutual respect, while, not infrequently, it became the defender of social wrong. Therefore, in all his preaching, he advocated the symmetrical development of the whole personality.

The indomitable spirit of this street preacher is illustrated by an incident which occurred shortly after his arrival in London. One evening, seeing a throng of boys and girls entering a "penny gaff", Barnardo, desirous of ascertaining the nature of the entertainment, followed them. But soon his blood was boiling. "As I looked down from a side box", he says, "upon their eager faces drinking in the abominations of the place, I stipulated with the proprietor for permission to go upon the stage during the interlude, and address a few words to the lads." The proprietor would agree only on condition that Barnardo pay him £5. Yet, extortionate as was the charge, the enthusiast consented, and handing over half the fee in advance, demanded that he be permitted to finish his speech without interference from the management. To this the proprietor agreed, believing that the audience would quickly terminate the address.

Accordingly, when the curtain rose, the young student, "instead of the highwaymen who were to have appeared", occupied the stage. At once he was recognized by hundreds, some greeting him with cheers, others with jeers. When the first uproar subsided, he shouted that if the crowd were quiet he would sing a song.[1] Silence ensued: the song was sung; and "having gained complete attention" he "spoke forcibly of the wrong and harm they were doing themselves by being present in such a place", pointing out "in simple terms the joy . . . of the Christian life".

The audience was dumbfounded. Barnardo was now master of the situation; and, seizing the opportunity, he bearded the lion in its den. But when his denunciation was at its height, the lessee rushed furiously upon the stage, demanding that he leave at once. "Not for ten times £5", he shouted, "will I permit such an address!" The stage was now a storm centre, while the auditorium resounded with shouts. Barnardo's speech was abruptly terminated; but the enthusiast was unabashed. Turning to his interrupter, he rejoined: "Well, I will leave if you insist upon it; but in that case, as you have broken your bargain, you must give me back my money and allow me to tell the boys why I leave." This point the proprietor reluctantly conceded;

---

[1] Up to the time of his conversion (1862) Barnardo exhibited no talent for, or interest in, music; but immediately following that event his emotions responded to music's call, and realizing its value in worship he set to work and developed a strong, melodious singing voice.

and Barnardo, depositing in his pocket the returned £2 10s., shouted out: "My lads, I am not allowed to finish . . . but if you care to listen I shall be outside in front of the house, and will talk to you afterwards." Then, "the curtain coming down amidst 'Kentish fire' and three cheers", he disappeared.

But the scene was not closed, and the next episode Barnardo himself must tell: "To my surprise, in a twinkling the benches were emptied; the whole house poured out after me. Gathering the crowd around me in front of the 'gaff', I stood upon a costermonger's barrow and spoke more plainly and fully than I had done before, reasoning of 'righteousness, temperance and judgment to come', while finally I commended all of them to God in a brief prayer. 'Good night, sir,' 'Thank you,' 'God bless you,' 'We wish you'd come again,' mingled with more quiet but not less sincere expressions of gratitude, closed this interesting scene as the youthful crowd dispersed and I retired homeward, thankful for the fresh opportunity afforded me of speaking the word 'in season' and 'out of season' as the case might be."

Not always did this enthusiast find himself master of such situations. One evening, for instance, when visiting the public-houses in a notorious quarter to sell Bibles, he found himself in a sorry plight. Entering a certain beerhouse, he sold what copies he could at the central bar and was passing toward the parlour, whence issued "the sounds of riotous mirth", when the publican begged him to desist, declaring that if he entered dire consequences might ensue. Barnardo, however, was not to be deterred. Believing his mission a sacred one, he pressed on. Inside the door, his vision was obscured by a cloud of tobacco smoke which "completely filled the room"; but soon he discovered himself to be in a "long, low, narrow" den, crowded with "lads and girls of from fourteen to eighteen", most of them intoxicated. Two huge fellows, moreover, had backed against the door, thus

E

cutting off retreat. Nothing remained but boldly to fulfil
his task; and from it he did not flinch.

"Advancing to the centre of the room," he says, "I
declared that I came to sell them the Word of God, and
announced that I could give the whole Bible for threepence
and the New Testament for a penny." But these revellers
would hear of no payment. "Come, old fellow, chuck 'em
out!" shouted one. "None of yer palaver; let's have the
books!" roared another. Barnardo was adamant: "I was
determined not to part with the books unless I received
payment; and leaping upon the table in the centre of the
room I appealed to them to deal fairly by me, adding that
these books cost me exactly double what I was selling them for,
and that therefore they ought to pay like honest men for
what they wanted." Argument was futile. In answer came
another chorus: "Chuck 'im down!" "Bonnet 'im!" "Put
'im out!" Yet, temporarily, presence of mind saved the
situation. As at the "penny gaff" he volunteered a solo;
and all joined uproariously in the chorus. But such ex-
pedients could not long stave off the madness of this drunken
crew. Crowding around the table, they tumbled it over,
plunging their victim headlong on the floor.

This proved the signal for further ribaldry. Before Barnardo could gain his feet, several youths grabbed the table,
and, placing it, legs upward, on his body, began to dance
upon it a "devil's tattoo". The result may be imagined.
The Bible-seller was removed to his lodgings unconscious:
examination showed that everywhere his flesh was bruised;
and two of his ribs were broken. Yet, from his own description,
no ill effects ensued: "I was not dangerously injured and
after the exhaustion of the shock had passed, and firm
bandages had been applied, I felt but little inconvenience
from the fracture, although it was quite six weeks before
I regained my strength."

On recovering consciousness, Barnardo was waited upon
by a policeman to know if he would prosecute the ring-

leaders; but the inquiry was met by a categorical negative: "I have begun with the Gospel, and I am determined not to end with the law."

This reply was noised abroad, with results of which Barnardo little dreamed. Next night, in the same "parlour", his assailants met again, now sober; and there they decided that henceforth no one should injure a hair of his head. But their gratitude found other expression. Every day, during his convalescence, there called at Barnardo's lodgings a deputation from this gang to inquire about his condition, and so assiduous was their attention that it became "almost a nuisance". The net result of the experience was, nevertheless, all to the good, for concerning it Barnardo wrote: "I believe this incident . . . gave me a greater influence over the rough lads and girls of that quarter than I could have attained had I been preaching or teaching among them for years."

Up to this time, there is no evidence that Barnardo intended to study medicine. But as month succeeded month, Hudson Taylor, a rare judge of men, divined in him the special gifts required for a *medical* missionary; so it was arranged that he enter upon an abridged course of medical study to fit him for fuller service abroad. Accordingly, on October 1st, 1866, Barnardo, now twenty-one, entered The London Hospital.

His impression upon student associates was not favourable. He was older than most students commencing medicine, and the crude horseplay so characteristic of medical freshmen, was highly repulsive to him. But while fellow-students sneered, Barnardo was winning the esteem of those destined to prove his lifelong friends—the East End poor. Scarcely was he established in The London Hospital when the cholera epidemic of 1866 broke out, and East London proved its chief seed-plot. Frantic with alarm, the authorities called for volunteers to stay the plague. Barnardo at once proffered his services, and during the weeks of that struggle

few laboured more valiantly than this street-preacher—
"dropped" by "the smart set" amongst his fellow-students.
The experiences of those cholera days stood Barnardo in
good stead. Then, more closely than ever before, he met
face to face the ghastly problems of poverty and destitution;
for during those weeks he witnessed as many as sixteen
deaths in one day—the result of dire neglect. Of the thousands
of cholera victims in London, more than sixty-five per cent.
were cut down amidst East End slums.

The horror of those days Barnardo's memory could not
efface. The stampede of terror-stricken souls; the sight of
corpses "piled up" awaiting burial; the spectacle of old
and young writhing in agony; the anguish issuing from
desolate hearths: above all, the vision of little children
orphaned and destitute by the ravages of a preventable
plague.

This pestilence over, Barnardo returned to a life more
eventful than before. His new experience made him dream
of the vast possibilities of East End Mission work. Hence,
into the superintendency of his Ragged School, into his
street preaching and Bible distribution, he threw himself
with renewed zeal. But his path was not smooth, and often
he encountered humiliation. Once, when he was conducting
a street service, a clever imp decided "to distinguish himself".
Before the meeting there had been a downpour of rain; so
the youngster, soaking street dirt in water, kneaded pellets
"about the size of small eggs", and thus armed, awaited
his prey. Let the victim conclude the tale: "With my hat in
my hand, I had just opened my mouth in prayer when,
lo and behold, it was neatly and tightly plugged, so . . . that
I could neither shut my mouth nor eject the missile! Of
course I instantly opened my eyes and found everyone
around me convulsed with laughter! The boy was gone!"

On such occasions Barnardo's sense of humour won
the day, for even as a youth he possessed that rare gift
which permits one to laugh heartily at one's own expense.

Gradually, therefore, by dint of perseverance, he came to win the confidence of even the roughest classes. On a certain evening, for example, he arranged to hold a cottage service in Hope Place, a blind alley in a rough part of Stepney. Invitations to attend were circulated in different quarters, including several "pubs"; and a group of half-drunken rowdies, led by a local "bruiser", decided to attend—intent on giving the preacher "some fun". At a signal from the "bruiser", the meeting was to be interrupted and the preacher carried bodily into the street, where a "jolly good hiding" would be given him.

Such was the plan. At the hour arranged, the "pub" party stumbled into the room, filling half its space. But imagine the leader's thoughts when gradually it dawned upon his half-stupefied mind, that the preacher he had come to molest was none other than the medical student who, risking his own life, had attended him during his cholera illness. How could he assault this man? He was no such cur as that! But Barnardo, too, recognized "his man", and although he never dreamed of the gang's purpose, he preached to their leader as though his own soul depended on that one man's conversion. The ruffians, however, soon grew restless. Why was the bruiser delaying his signal for "the fun"? Had he lost his nerve? Was he cowed by the preaching of this "little man with the big head"? Finally one fellow broke out: "Hey, bruiser! Wat abart th' fun?" The leader, sobered by the situation, now jumped up and, turning to his pals, exclaimed: "If any o' you chaps touches this man, you settles wi' me!"

Some of the gang, disgruntled at this rebuff, filed out of the house; some stayed with their leader. But before the termination of that cottage service, the notorious fighter requested Barnardo to pray for him. He went home that night a humbled man, determined, at any cost, to find peace with God. Thus, groping in darkness, he sought the Light; and later, after a desperate struggle, and under Barnardo's influence, he entered into the consciousness of a twice-born soul.

This "bruiser", so dramatically converted to the service of God, was William Notman: one of the best workers Barnardo's cause has known.[1]

But ere the year 1866 had run its course an event, more pregnant with consequence than anything related above, thrust itself athwart Barnardo's path, and carried captive his heart for life.

After months of service at the Ernest Street School, and while continuing his labours as its superintendent, Barnardo, supported by two or three students, opened a new experimental ragged school. Yet, often as he chafed under the stereotyped ideas of his Ernest Street colleagues, his new venture was in no sense a counterblast to that institution. On the contrary, it was initiated as a sort of supplement, its chief labours being undertaken at hours when the Ernest Street School was closed. In short, the project was designed as a testing-ground, wherein Barnardo was free to experiment with ideas peculiarly his own.

This tiny school, situated in Hope Place, was a humble affair. It was housed in a dilapidated cottage which for years had been used as a donkey-shed, and which Barnardo rented at two shillings and sixpence a week. Without delay he and his friends had put it in order for human habitation. This meant laying a floor to cover the earth, whitewashing walls and ceiling, and repairing a fireplace which had long been out of gear. Finally, late in 1866, the donkey-shed, now transformed, was opened as a Ragged School.

With the ups and downs of this school we are not concerned. One co-related incident, however, is historic. Shortly after its opening, on a wild winter's night, there passed through its doors a peculiar character. He entered with no desire to be taught; he wanted shelter, warmth—

[1] Two of Notman's sons became ministers of the Gospel and wrought a noble work among the East End poor.

if possible, food. During school proceedings, he wormed his
way close up to the blazing fire, and there, perched on a
box, stared into the vivid flames, a wild content written
on his face.

But the last session of the school now over, it being time
to bolt the doors, Barnardo, looking around, observed this
youngster lying on the floor, crouched like a dog before the
glowing coals, and half hidden by the box on which he
previously had sat. Feeling that almost by chance the lad
had escaped imprisonment in the school, Barnardo accosted
him sharply:—

"Here, my lad! Wake up! And off home to your mother!
You've nearly been locked in this place overnight."

"Well, that w'd suit me foine, sir!"

"What! You young rascal! Away home to your mother!"

"Ain't got no mother, sir."

"Well, then, off to your father."

"Got no father neither, sir."

"Away then to your home, wherever it is."

"Oi've got no 'ome, sir."

"Well, off then to your friends, wherever you live."

"Ain't got no friends, sir! and *Oi—don't—live—nowhere* !"

Barnardo was incredulous. Hundreds of urchins had
tried to hoax him before; he was no easy prey. Yet this
youngster told his story with a ring of sincerity. Could there
be any truth in it? Was he, in fact, a street-arab without
friends or abode? The medico turned up the gas and called
the boy to his side. With "slow, heavy steps" the urchin
drew up—"as though his feet were weighted". Barnardo
scrutinized him. Neither shirt nor underclothing protected
his spare frame: his feet and legs were bare, although the
weather was freezing. His only apparel consisted of a
jacket, short trousers and cap; all worn to rags. His chief
covering was a thick coat of dirt.

Here was a strange case, and Barnardo determined to
ferret out the truth.

"How old are you, my lad?"

"Ten, sir."

"What's your name?"

"Jim, sir. Jim Jarvis they sometimes calls me; but oi only knows o'im Jim, sir."

The lad's physique suggested a child of seven, or at most eight. But "his face was not the face of a child". It bore "a careworn, old-mannish look, only relieved by the bright, keen glances of his small, sharp eyes". But, as Barnardo peered at him, his problem grew more perplexing. The child's countenance was "sadly overwise"; and his pathetic appeal—eloquent even when mute—together with his "querulous, high-pitched tones", produced in his questioner "an acute sense of pain". But sentiment was no substitute for fact, so the examination went on. Either the lad was lying or Barnardo was on the threshold of a revelation.

"Now, my boy," he demanded, "do you really mean to say that you have no home at all, and that you have no father or mother or friends?"

"That's the truth, sir. I ain't tellin' you no lies!"

"Where, then, did you sleep last night?"

"Down in Whitechapel, along o' the 'ay market, in one o' them carts filled with 'ay, sir."

"How was it you came to the school?"

" 'Cos, sir, I met a chap as I knowed, and he tell'd me to come up 'ere to the school to get a warm; and 'e sed p'raps you'd let me lie nigh the fire all night."

"But you must know we don't keep open all night."

"Yes, but I won't do no 'arm, sir, if only you'll let me stop! Please do, sir! It's so cold outside!"

Now, "with overwhelming force", there rushed across Barnardo's mind the thought: "Is it possible, that in this great city there are others also homeless and destitute, who are as young as this boy, as helpless, and as ill-prepared as he to withstand the trials of cold, hunger and exposure?" Surely, he reflected, it was unthinkable that London, with

THE ORIGINAL DONKEY-SHED RAGGED SCHOOL IN WHICH BARNARDO
"DISCOVERED" JIM JARVIS

its "vast wealth, open Bibles, Gospel-preaching and Ragged Schools", could be harbouring such inhumanity. There followed, therefore, a piquant question:

"Tell me, my lad, are there other poor boys like you in London without home or friends?"

A "grim smile" lighted up the urchin's face, as promptly he replied:

"Oh yes, sir: lots—'eaps on 'em; more'n I could count!"

Barnardo stood aghast. Jim Jarvis was an enigma! Almost he had believed the lad's story. But this last statement was surely a fabrication.

One thing, however, must be done; the youngster must be fed and sheltered for the night, and his strange story explored. Meanwhile, as Barnardo led the way to his rooms, a further query was made:

"Now, Jim, if I give you some hot coffee and a place to sleep in, will you take me where some of these poor boys are, as you say, lying out in the streets . . .?"

"That oi will, sir, and no mistake."

Barnardo led the way to his "digs", where Jim proved his prowess before a jug of coffee and a formidable pile of bread and butter. "I almost feared to supply him," says Barnardo, "with such voracity did he swallow the food."

Now warm, and better fed than he had been for months, Jim became verbose. His father he "never know'd nor heerd of"; his mother was always sick, and died in the " 'firmary"; he himself was in the workhouse for a while and ran away; later he was the slave of a drunken bargeman, "Swearin' Dick", who beat him atrociously; while, after escaping from this wretch, he had been wandering about London "pickin' up what he cu'd". Almost daily he was buffeted from pillar to post by the police; once he was locked up for sleeping out. When specially fortunate he had tasted the luxuries of threepenny lodging-houses: but such indulgence had its disadvantages, for generally he left with a load of vermin more hungry than himself.

This, and much more information of like sort, the youngster volunteered. But when he paused, Barnardo interrogated him again:

"Jim, have you ever heard of Jesus?"

"Yes, sir; I knows about Him a' right."

"Well, who is He? What do you know about Him?"

"Oh, sir," he looked sharply about the room—with a timorous glance into the darker corners—then, dropping to a whisper, exclaimed: "He's the Pope o' Rome!"

"Whatever do you mean, my lad? Who told you that?"

"No one, sir; but I knows I'm right. 'Cos, mother, 'fore she died, always *did that* when she spoke of the Pope"—a clumsy sign of the cross was made—"and one day, when she wor a-dying in the 'firmary, a gent wor there in black clothes a-talkin' to her, an' mother wor a-crying. They began to talk about Him, sir, and they both did the same."

"Then because your mother made the same sign . . . when she spoke about the Pope and about Jesus, you thought she was speaking of the same person?"

"Yes, sir, that's it." The boy gave a nod of pleased intelligence.

Shocked by this revelation, Barnardo lost not a moment in relating to the urchin the story of Bethlehem's Babe. He told him of Jesus' tenderness and compassion, of His sympathy and mercy, of His love for children, of His miracles of healing, and of how He preached the Gospel to the poor. Then he explained in simplest terms the growing jealousy of scribes and pharisees, the traps laid to catch Him, His trial before Pilate, His scourging, His crown of thorns. Tears trickled down Jim's face; but when he came to the Crucifixion, the lad, breaking into sobs, exclaimed:

"Oh, sir, that wor wuss nor Swearin' Dick sarved me!"

The story concluded, Barnardo put his arm around the boy's neck, and both knelt in prayer.

It was long after midnight when the two, hand in hand, sallied forth on their quest. The urchin, proud in the consciousness that he was leading, kept tugging ahead. Soon all important streets were left behind, and passing through a maze of alleys they came at length upon "a long, empty shed", used by day as a second-hand-clothes market. For some minutes they stopped to examine its dark recesses; but no child was found. Doubts again entered Barnardo's mind; was the youngster hoaxing him, after all? Jim was unperturbed: "All right, sir; don't look no more. We'll come on 'em soon. They dursn't lay about 'ere 'cos the p'licemen are werry sharp all along by these 'ere shops. Wunst, when I wor *green*, I stopped under a barrer down there . . . but I nearly got nabbed, so I never slep' there agin."

He led his companion through narrow lanes till they entered a blind alley; and, nearing its end, putting a finger to his lips, he whispered: "Sh! we're there. You'll see lots on 'em, if we don't wake 'em up." A high wall confronted them: looking around, Barnardo could see no trace of life. "Where are they, Jim?" he queried.

"Up there, sir!" The lad pointed aloft.

But to get "up there" meant scaling a wall ten feet high: and how was that to be achieved? Jim solved the problem. Pointing out certain interstices between the bricks, he gripped them with fingers and toes, and in thirty seconds had mounted the wall. Barnardo watched with amazement; how could he follow suit?

His calculations were quickly interrupted. Again the lad's fingers went to his lips.

"Quiet! Sh!—ther' 'ere a' right!"

Jim disappeared, but a moment later was again on the wall. Leaning over and reaching down a stick, he enabled his benefactor to ascend.

Once on the wall, Barnardo was dumbfounded.

"There, with their heads upon the higher part, and their feet somewhat in the gutter, but in a great variety of postures . . . lay a confused group of boys on an open roof—all asleep. I counted *eleven*."

"No covering of any kind was upon them. The rags they wore were mere apologies for clothes . . . as bad as, if not worse, than Jim's. One big fellow who lay there seemed to be about eighteen; the ages of the remainder varied, I should say, from nine to fourteen."

As the Ragged School teacher gazed upon this spectacle, "the moon, which previously had been obscured, shone clearly out"; and its pale light gleaming upon the faces of those sleeping boys, he realized "the terrible fact that they were all *absolutely homeless and destitute*". But more staggering, the thought haunted him: Are not these boys *"but samples"* of many others, bereft of home or friend? Again he drank in the challenge of the scene, and peering into these pitiable faces, it seemed "as though the hand of God Himself had suddenly pulled aside the curtain" and revealed to him "the untold miseries of forlorn child-life upon the streets of London".

Jim experienced no such emotion: Barnardo's meditation was rudely disturbed:—"Shall I wake 'em, sir?"

But to what purpose? Unable to offer help, he dare not rob them of heaven-sent sleep. One thing, nevertheless, he must do. Jim Jarvis he must care for "at all costs". Ere Barnardo descended from that wall, iron entered his blood: the mute appeal of those "upturned faces, white with cold and hunger", burned itself into his soul, where, for weeks on end, it was to haunt him, until at last he could find "no rest except in action on their behalf".

A final glance, and Barnardo, breathing "a silent prayer of compassion", clambered down the wall, to be met by the interrogation:

"Shall we go to another lay, sir? *There's lots more!*" But for one night he had seen enough!

*   *   *   *   *

What the spectacle of New Orleans' slave-mart was to Abraham Lincoln, "the Emancipator of America's Slaves";

what the spectre of a pauper-funeral at Harrow was to Lord Shaftesbury, "the Emancipator of Industrial England" —*that* the sight of those homeless boys, sleeping on a winter's night upon an iron roof, was to Dr. Barnardo, "the Emancipator of the Outcast Child".

Not yet was Barnardo himself aware of the fact; but, from that hour, the Chinese mission-field was challenged by East London's waifs and strays.

CHAPTER V

SCEPTICS DISARMED

THE more Barnardo pondered over that roof-top revelation, the more persistent became East London's challenge, while the call of China became less personal. Could it be that "his China" was right at hand? When first this idea asserted itself, Barnardo thought it the guile of a demon to be exorcized at once. Had he not volunteered for missionary service in China? And dare he take his hand from the plough? But whether that challenge represented the voice of demon or angel, it would not be hushed. Hand from the plough? it persisted; surely God has other furrows to plough as important as any in China! Must not the true missioner be content to serve wherever his talents will bear best fruit? Might it not be that his hand was better fitted to hold the plough in East London than in China?

Meanwhile, his most pressing duty was discharged without delay. Keeping Jim Jarvis a few days in his own "digs", he solicited help from friends; and Jim was found a home with a humble Christian family near by. So, boarded out, he tasted for the first time the privileges of family life. Now, too, for the first time, he went regularly to school, where he proved studious and alert. But after a few years at school, a craving for adventure asserted itself. He had heard much of the lure of Canada's vast spaces, and his ambition was to own a Canadian farm. This ambition, if we may anticipate Jim's history, was fulfilled; for fifteen years after leaving England he was a prosperous Canadian citizen, proprietor of a good farm, and a man highly respected throughout his community.

But returning to that fateful night, it will be remembered that when Jim Jarvis blurted out, "Shall we go to another lay, sir?" and volunteered the information, "there's lots more", Barnardo was too sick at heart to see more. When, however, the first shock had spent itself, he felt it his duty to investigate more carefully the problem he faced. Were these conditions accidental? Could such a sight be seen *any* day of the week? Where else, if at all, were "lays" to be found? How large was this tribe of outcast boy life? Were any girls similarly circumstanced? Above all, how could the shame of such neglect be laid upon the consciences of Christian men and women?

With Jim's help, Barnardo pushed his inquiries into other districts; and true enough, *"lots more"* were found— " 'eaps on 'em"—more than he himself could well count! Barnardo was staggered by the nature of the problem confronting him. But what could he do?—he, a missionary student, with little capital and no income save an allowance from his father. He was in no position to offer these lads a home, or employment, or even friendship worthy of the name. Yet one or two things he could do. Through his Ragged School connection he offered what little succour was possible. But, more important, in season and out of season he impressed upon his every Christian acquaintance the disgrace of these conditions.

At this juncture there was convened in the Agricultural Hall, London, by the Rev. Dr. Thain Davidson, a popular rally to stimulate interest in foreign missions. Barnardo, a candidate for China, was invited, and allotted a front seat on the platform. At the hour of opening, the hall was packed; but the chief speaker, a well-known public man, had not arrived; and later, during the singing of a hymn, came a message stating that the "big man" had been taken ill and could not come. Consternation overwhelmed Dr. Davidson. What could he do? This great assembly could not be sent home without a message, and upon whom could he call?—An inspiration! Had not the medical student by his side told him a stirring tale about East London's waifs? Was not this a missionary challenge? And could not this

Irishman speak with a missionary's zeal? In dire extremity
Dr. Davidson called on Barnardo.

The youth was flabbergasted. Never before had he
addressed an assembly one-fifth the size of that before him.
But while Dr. Davidson was introducing him, he offered up
a silent prayer and strove desperately to collect his thoughts.
A moment later he was standing in the centre of the platform, the eyes of that vast company riveted upon him.
With no attempt at rhetoric, he told in simple words the
story of Jim Jarvis and the experiences of that memorable
night. He told, too, of later investigations, thus proving
the proportions of the problem at stake: for certain intervening visits had revealed "lays" even more deplorable than
the original.

For the better part of an hour Barnardo laid bare his
facts. Several times he had attempted to stop; but the
audience urged him on: and when finally he sat down
the hall was reverberating. There could be no doubt as to
the effectiveness of his appeal. He told only of what he knew
by experience: and his every word and gesture bespoke his
earnestness. His message pierced as an arrow to the souls of
hundreds, and many went home glad that the "great man",
whom they had come to hear, had not arrived.

Among those deeply stirred was a young servant-girl,
who, staying after the meeting, asked if she might speak to
Mr. Barnardo. Shyly she related how for weeks she had
been saving all her farthings "to help the missionaries
abroad". But after hearing this speech she desired to give
her savings "to help the waifs on London's streets"; so,
before Barnardo could utter a word, she pressed into his
hand a little bag, saying: "Surely to help these homeless
lads is missionary work!" Then, leaving Barnardo speechless,
she disappeared. He had not even learned her name; yet
the incident was significant: this was the first donation he
had received from a stranger, and he considered it not only
a "public subscription", but a call to greater service. On

JIM JARVIS SHOWS BARNARDO A "LAY" OF HIS PALS SLEEPING
ON A ROOF

reaching his "digs" he opened the package; it contained twenty-seven farthings.

Next day Barnardo's statements were reported in the Press. Immediately they evoked letters of censure, and although at that time Barnardo took no newspaper and for days knew nothing either of the report or the attacks, his speech became a topic of heated discussion.

Among those who read with deep concern the report of Barnardo's speech and the replies was Lord Shaftesbury. For twenty-three years the Ragged School Union's army of voluntary workers had been labouring among the children of the half-submerged classes; and during those years Shaftesbury had been not only their President but their leader. Could it be that a whole tribe of street waifs, without home or abode, was slipping through their net? The thought seemed incredible. But Shaftesbury knew too well the elusiveness of the social problem to dogmatize or condemn. No categorical denials passed his lips. He refused to stigmatize this youth as a deceiver. Had not he himself, on a hundred occasions, been confronted by the incredible? And, after all, was not this young man one of his Ragged School superintendents? His duty was to ascertain the facts; and to this end plans were laid. He would invite this enthusiast to dine with him at his London home, to meet some friends interested in social questions, among them certain of his critics.

A few days after the Agricultural Hall meeting, Barnardo was Shaftesbury's guest. The party worked out as arranged. Accusers and open-minded gathered around the Earl's board, and soon conversation centred around Barnardo. A torrent of questions drew forth all the salient facts of his life: Where was he born? When did he come to London? What led him to train as a missionary to China? How long had he been teaching in a Ragged School? How came he to speak at this Agricultural Hall meeting? Were the reports of his speech exaggerated? Was not what he had seen something accidental? One gentleman even asked, was it not possible that these youngsters had organized a clever hoax? Finally, after a long and searching conversation, came a challenge: "If these statements are true, will you pilot us into the East End and show us the sights described?" Barnardo replied that he would be glad to do so, whenever they wished.

Shaftesbury stepped into the breach: "It may be difficult to assemble our party again. Why not to-night?" Barnardo agreed; so, midnight drawing near, cabs were summoned: and soon this strange company, fifteen to twenty strong, was passing West End revellers to seek out East End waifs. On and on the cabs rolled, Barnardo having directed them to "Queen's Shades", near the Billingsgate Fish Market. It was now after one o'clock, and the night was biting cold. The place Barnardo had in mind was protected from the raw East wind, and on such a night was dark as pitch. Under like conditions he had there discovered a score of urchins.

After driving through a maze of narrow, dirty streets, Barnardo ordered the cabs to stop; and the party jumped out. A bleak wind caught them full in the face: "Surely on such a night", cried one, "no children are sleeping out"; his words expressed the thought of his companions.

Leaving the cabs behind, Barnardo led the party through muddy by-ways to an open area where, out of the darkness, emerged piles of boxes, barrels and crates. In or around these piles, Barnardo assured the group, homeless youngsters were sure to be found—unless they slipped off unseen. Here, accordingly, the search began. Matches were lighted, boxes and barrels were overturned, barrows and crates were heaved about; but not a boy was found. Whispers began to arise. Meanwhile Barnardo kept to the centre of the yard, where a large pile was covered over with tarpaulins, which at intervals were staked to the ground. Under these tar-paulins Barnardo again and again thrust his arm and felt about. But to no effect! Could it be that, on this night of all nights, he had struck an empty "lay"? That thought he quickly dismissed; he felt certain that boys were sleeping here, and find them he must.

So, striking another match, he discovered the spot where two tarpaulins overlapped, and thrusting in his hand felt carefully about—but in vain. Going to the opposite side he repeated the process. Soon his hand fell upon the foot of a sleeping lad. "Gently but firmly", he says, "I threw my weight upon my prize and presently drew down a poor, ragged, half-starved looking boy!"

Tumbling at Barnardo's feet, "his eyes still blinded with sleep", the youngster thought he was caught by the police, and immediately began "to whine a remonstrance". But assured that he was among friends he quickly brightened up, realizing that out of this rude awakening something "might come his way". When asked: "Are you the only lad sleeping here?" he replied: "No, guv'nor; *there's a sight more chaps up there!* "

The whole party surrounded the waif: "Will you try to get the others out if we give you sixpence?" His answer was emphatic: "In course I will!" And forthwith he clambered up the side of the tarpaulin, toward the flatter surface on top. This reached, he began to jump wildly about, as if dancing a savage tattoo. For a moment the party gazed in wonder, not realizing the purpose of this display; but when one shouted out: "Why are you dancing around like that?" he replied: "I'm roofin' 'em! This 'ere 'll wake 'em up foine! "

His spectators looked closely: the surface of the tarpaulin was seething; the youngster was jumping squarely on the bodies of his companions. At once Shaftesbury besought him to desist. His method, however, was not without effect, for before he reached the ground five or six of his companions had poked their heads outside the canvas to ascertain if the road was clear. But being only half awake most of them were caught.

The problem now was how to induce the boys still under the tarpaulin to come out; but this difficulty was solved by one of the captive lads: "Promise to give 'em all somethin', and they'll come out!" Shaftesbury accordingly offered a penny and a free meal to every lad that appeared, and with magical effect; for a stampede ensued. "The tarpaulins," says Barnardo, "hitherto stretched tightly over so large an area, began to collapse in parts for want of the human stay that kept them up, and soon we had, as we arranged them in a single line before us, a strange army of homeless childhood—a terrible proof, as Lord Shaftesbury remarked . . . of the need of such work as I was then beginning to do."

"When these street-arabs were placed in line *they numbered seventy-three*: their ages ranging from seven to seventeen years. Few had any covering on head or feet, and all were clad in vilely smelling rags." Yet they were a typical regiment in the army of outcast boy-life inhabiting London's streets.

Barnardo knew of a coffee-shop near by, which kept open all night—"Dick Fisher's". So he led the way toward the promised feast; the urchins, meanwhile, shouting with delight. Cold, hunger and nakedness meant nothing to them now. Were they not about to partake of a "big feed"? And had they not been promised by these "swells" a penny each? On arrival at "Dick Fisher's" this strange company packed the place; yet all ate till they could eat no more. At first the proprietor was annoyed to see his shop besieged by ragamuffins, but when he discovered that Lord Shaftesbury was their host, he "fell over himself to do the thing grand". More than once he sent off to a neighbouring night-shop to replenish stores, and when his task was done every urchin in the gang felt that he had partaken of a Christmas feast. And certainly in quantity, at least, they had a feast; for the coffee and sausages, together with the bread and butter they consumed, would have fed twice their number of men.

The "banquet" over, Shaftesbury requited Dick Fisher for his pains, at the same time procuring from him change in pennies for a half-sovereign. Then, the youngsters passing by in single file, the "Good Earl" gave to each the promised coin. As the last received his prize, there arose a roar of thanks, and for several minutes shouts of joy filled the air. This over, both Shaftesbury and Barnardo addressed a few words to the boys, promising further help. Then, after much urging, the lads returned to their lairs.

It was now 3 a.m., and Barnardo, being within walking distance of his "digs", did not join the others in their Westward course. But before the cabs started Shaftesbury called him aside, and spoke to him as a father might speak to a son. Placing his hand on the youth's shoulder, this veteran apologized that he, or any of his guests, should have doubted the veracity of his statements. But now the truth was established; and sad as the revelation had been he was glad the facts were known. "Public opinion alone", he exclaimed, "can cure this ghastly ill . . . I will see that all London knows of what we experienced to-night."

Then, in intimate tones: "I thank God, sir, for your work! These children must be saved from the horrors of their lot! . . . You hope to go as a missionary to China. That is a noble ambition; God needs many labourers in China. But pray earnestly over the events of this night. It may be that God is calling you to labour as His chosen missionary among the homeless children of this Metropolis!"

These words spoken, Shaftesbury clasped Barnardo's hand, and gripping it tightly, added: "God bless you and lead you, young man!" Then, turning away, he joined his guests. A minute later the cabs were dashing Westward.

To appraise the significance of that night is impossible. If Jim Jarvis was the emissary of the underworld who revealed to Barnardo the challenge of his life-work, Lord Shaftesbury was the emissary of God who inspired him to attempt great things as a *missionary* to the slums.

As Barnardo pondered the events of that night, all seemed to stand out in providential light. In accepting the challenge of Shaftesbury's guests, he felt certain that twenty or thirty homeless youngsters would be found. They roused seventy-three. This was the largest, and most pitiable, band of outcast children Barnardo had ever seen. Long afterwards, he exclaimed: "I pray God that never again may I look upon such a sight!" And it is doubtful if he did. He, therefore, not only disarmed his critics; actually he revealed to them conditions worse than he had described.

But more: Lord Shaftesbury, a rare judge of men, had advised him to consider prayerfully the call of God in East London. And could this advice be lightly set aside? Was not Shaftesbury President of the British and Foreign Bible Society? Was he not, too, a potent figure behind the greatest Missionary Societies in Britain? Yet this arch-enthusiast for *foreign* missions had suggested to Barnardo that his peculiar talents were more fitted for missionary work in London than China. The Ragged School teacher pondered and prayed; and increasingly he seemed to hear in Shaftesbury's suggestion the voice of God.

Admittedly, later, in his *First Occasional Record of the East End Juvenile Mission*, Barnardo still referred to himself as a candidate for China, if someone could be found to pilot his London mission. But none of his helpers had his vision; and none felt able to wear his mantle. Nevertheless, though Barnardo remained in London, before his death he had the joy of bestowing his blessing upon seventeen of "his children", who sailed as *foreign* missionaries in his stead.

CHAPTER VI

A MUSTARD SEED

In mature years Barnardo reflected upon the importance of his early missionary training and marvelled at the way his footsteps had been led. "I now saw clearly revealed", he says, "the wisdom and goodness of God in what had already happened, and how unconsciously I was being prepared for this Home Mission enterprise. I now realized that the call to Medical Missions in China had been absolutely necessary for the work in England. . . .

"1st. It had thoroughly detached me from home and from family claims.
"2nd. It had kept alive and fresh in my heart the missionary spirit, which in ordinary business or professional life I might have lost.
"3rd. Without it I would never have settled in East London, and probably never would have met my first homeless child. . . ."

Then, significantly, he adds: "If at any subsequent moment I looked wistfully away from the slums of London to China, it was but to beseech the Lord that as I could not myself go forth . . . I might still be instrumental in directing the steps of others of His servants thitherward."

This missionary fervour was typical of Barnardo to the end: first, last and always he was a missionary. He pulled up stakes in Dublin and came to London, to prepare for foreign missionary work. He began teaching in a Ragged School and preaching at the street corners because, like Wesley, he believed "the field was the world"; and his decision to study medicine was motivated by a yearning to fit himself for fuller missionary service abroad. Again, his cholera experience, his superintendency at Ernest Street and his donkey-shed Ragged School, had all deepened his missionary zeal when Jim Jarvis introduced him to a tribe of street-arabs as much in need of missionary endeavour as any benighted race. But still other missionary voices flung echoes across his path. The warm reception given to his Agricultural Hall address, and the memory of that servant-girl's gift, fired his imagination and extended his horizons: while the debate over Shaftesbury's dinner-board, the apocalyptic spectacle of those seventy-three homeless urchins, and Shaftesbury's suggestion regarding missionary work in London bound cords about his soul too strong to break.

Now, of the peculiar Missionary Movement which Barnardo built up, all the world knows something to-day. But few have followed the romance of its development, and fewer have familiarized themselves with the tiny "mustard seed" from which it sprang.

Ernest Street Ragged School initiated Barnardo into the mysteries of child-life among East London's slums, and bred in him his first desire to forge out new schemes for grappling with the problems he met. Among his colleagues, however, were teachers who shuddered at any sort of divergence from their own beaten tracks: so, when Barnardo suggested radical innovations, they refused consent; and under pressure of their restrictions he itched for the boon of a freer atmosphere in which to try out new plans. In this restless mood, but without resigning the "Ernest Street" superintendency, Barnardo, supported by one or two student helpers, opened up for experimental purposes the donkey-shed Ragged School; and here it was he came upon Jim Jarvis and the distressing problem of homeless boys.

Jim, however, had to be housed, and a tribe of street-arabs stood in equal need. Hence the necessity for a "Home". But encouraged by Shaftesbury's interest, Barnardo was soon dreaming of something more than either a "Home" or a "Ragged School", though it included both. Already there was looming on his horizon, the vision of a Christian Mission which would minister to all the pressing necessities of slum children and youths: and to such proportions did that vision grow that finally all else was dwarfed by its range.

The first glimmer of Barnardo's dream was given to the world on July 25th, 1867, in a letter to *The Revival*,[1] which emphasizes the urgent need of Mission work among boys and girls who nightly were prowling about the streets, or frequenting the vilest beer-dens. A few paragraphs from this letter will make clear Barnardo's case: "Shortly after I came to this great metropolis, I began, in company with a dear and highly honoured servant of God, to preach in the open air in some of the narrow streets, lanes and alleys of the parish of Stepney. Though frequently we met with a measure of opposition, we were not discouraged, but looking above for results, we sought in weakness, and oft-times in much fear and trembling, to sow the precious seed of the Kingdom. . . . In this way we laboured chiefly on the Lord's Day, sometimes giving four or five addresses in different localities upon the same day. We were deeply struck with one fact, that whilst about one-half of our audiences were children, and perhaps only one-fourth their parents, etc., the other fourth and sometimes even a larger proportion consisted of that class which, in the lower ranks of society, goes far to fill our prisons with inmates and to supply the ranks of those lost women who nightly parade our streets, viz., boys and girls whose ages varied from thirteen to twenty-eight years. These were they who came about us and listened with open mouths as well as ears to our story of love."

Then, referring to Ernest Street Ragged School, and mentioning that always he invited his street-corner audiences to attend its classes, he proceeds to illustrate the character of its pupils: "A policeman one Sunday evening stepped into

---

[1] *The Revival* a little later changed its name to *The Christian*. Always it was a warm supporter of Barnardo's work; Mr. R. C. Morgan, its editor, rendered Barnardo valiant personal aid.

the School, and having looked around . . . drew the superintendent aside and asked him if he had any conception
of the class of beings by whom he was surrounded. Upon
receiving a reply in the negative, the policeman said he
knew at least one-third of those present as having been in
gaol once, and many of them twice or more."

Next Barnardo informs his readers of the conditions
under which he and his staff were compelled to work.
Even in summer, "upwards of one hundred persons" were
squeezed into "a low, narrow, small and badly ventilated
room which contained sittings for only eighty-six"; while
in winter they "frequently had to close the door for lack
of room", thus "leaving as many outside as within"; and
those excluded found "a willing shelter and welcome in
the low beer-houses and tap-rooms of the neighbourhood".
But another class incited Barnardo's pity. Besides those who
in vain sought admission to the Ragged Schools was "a very
large number who never enter a Church, Chapel or School,
and who, with none to care for their spiritual welfare, pass
the Sunday in all imaginable manners and haunts of vice".
To this class, outside the pale of every moral influence,
Barnardo felt a special call: "I want to reach *these*. They
are laid upon my heart. I yearn over these poor souls who
are as sheep going astray, having no shepherd. But what is
to be done? How can they be effectively reached?"

The solution Barnardo offered the readers of *The Revival*
was as follows:

"After much thoughtful consideration and prayer the following plan
has been laid upon my mind, and from my experience with this class I
believe it, with God's blessing, likely to be extremely practicable. To
procure a large building, room or shed, capable of holding about six
hundred persons. To obtain the personal and voluntary aid of about
forty or fifty earnest Evangelical brethren and sisters from the various
Churches, Chapels, etc., in the neighbourhood. To commence our efforts
by a large tea-meeting service, the tickets for which will be carefully
distributed amongst those only whom it is intended to reach. Afterwards
to throw open this room on Sunday evenings at a given hour for boys
and girls, young men and women, of the class described. To get about

six or eight large banners made, inviting them to this room, each of these banners to go out about two hours before the service, borne by some of my present school singing hymns and parading the parish, to return at the hour of service, bringing their crowds with them. And then, having once got them inside, seeking wisdom from Him who is its source, so to set Christ and His boundless love before them as may, with His blessing, result in leading many to Himself. . . . Of course we shall seek to have addresses every Lord's Day from different brethren or sisters whom the Lord may have blessed or used in such work."

The above was the first printed suggestion of Barnardo's mission scheme. But from whence would come finances for breathing into it life? This problem did not bother young Barnardo. He himself was but a student, and few of his Ragged School associates were more blessed with this world's goods; but he had faith in God, and already he had the promise of £25 from sympathizers. Hence, with no apology for so doing, and with confidence as to the result, he called upon "the Lord's stewards", who might read his letter, to advance him £200 with which to *begin* this mission work: his statement implying that later they would be privileged to give much more.

Now, remembering that at this time Barnardo had been in London barely fifteen months, and that, save for his association with Lord Shaftesbury, he was all but unknown in influential quarters, this appeal may strike one as an instance of colossal "nerve"; yet, to Barnardo, it was as natural as breathing. Since his conversion, he had used his time, talents and means as God's property, of which he, temporarily, was steward. And did not *The Revival* circulate among Christians professedly of like mind? Therefore, why should not they be as much interested in furthering this missionary proposition as he? They, too, were God's stewards! And was not this obviously God's work? Such being the logic of Barnardo's thoughts, it never entered his mind that he was "begging"; he was simply opening up a new field of Christian opportunity.

Consequently, after pointing out the "immediate neces-

sity" of the work, and reminding his readers of the importance
of getting it under way "before the cold season" set in, he
continues:

"I beseech those brethren and sisters whom the Lord has blessed with
abundance, prayerfully to consider the real necessity that has induced
me to bring the God-glorying work before their notice. Shall we be
stopped in the outset by lack of pecuniary support whilst many of
God's dear children, who may read this, 'have enough and to spare',
and yet practically withhold the Word of Life from thousands who are
not in Africa or India, but in the East of London and are now perishing
for lack of knowledge?"

Shortly after the appearance of this letter Barnardo wrote
to *The Revival*, informing his readers that "rather suddenly"
he had been offered "large and suitable premises, capable
of accommodating one thousand persons". So now he
awaited only the receipt of "further aid, both in money and
in personal help", to begin the work. Again he called for
"the contributions of God's people", and invited "forty or
fifty evangelistic brothers and sisters *of all denominations*,
whether rich or poor", to proffer "personal and voluntary
aid". His concluding petition implies that personal assistance
and money were not forthcoming as rapidly as he had
hoped: "May God Himself press the deep spiritual need
of the young 'roughs', and poor girls and children of this
neglected district, upon the hearts of all who read this!"

The receipts from this initial appeal were £90; and
though Barnardo had asked for £200, he decided to commence operations, trusting that as the work advanced
more support would arrive, and it did: within twelve
months well over £200 had been committed to his trust. But
meanwhile he cut his pattern to fit his cloth. The quarters
offered him, The Assembly Rooms over the King's Arms
public-house, at the corner of Mile End Road and Beaumont
Square, he engaged; but being handicapped for funds his
programme was severely curtailed. Although his appeal
centred around the need of Sunday endeavour, and called
for Sunday workers, there is evidence that, had the desired

support come in, he had planned to supplement Sunday efforts with week-night endeavours.[1] As it was, receiving scarcely half the funds for which he had asked, he decided, *pro tem.*, to concentrate on the Sunday programme.

But before the doors of the mission were opened, Barnardo was confronted with a misunderstanding on the part of certain colleagues. In his letter to *The Revival* he had referred to the work of the Ernest Street School; so some of its teachers maintained that either that school should control the new venture, or it was entitled to a proportion of the *funds* which Barnardo's appeal had brought in: it being maintained that certain subscribers had sent money in the belief that the new mission was under the direction of Ernest Street Ragged School.

Some friction resulted, the upshot of which was that Barnardo resigned the superintendency at Ernest Street and wrote again to *The Revival*: "If any subscriber has misunderstood my letter and would wish to apply the money sent for the old school, if they will kindly communicate their wishes to me I shall at once comply with the same." A perusal, however, of the "List of Contributions" and the "Balance Sheet" appended to Barnardo's *First Annual Record* shows that only one subscriber—"Mrs. H. G. G.", who had sent £5—asked to have any money transferred: she desired that *half* her subscription be given to "Ernest Street" and half remain with Barnardo for his special work. All other subscribers granted Barnardo a free hand to move as he felt led. But although this misunderstanding caused Barnardo to resign the Ernest Street superintendency, it engendered no ill will. The very letter containing the announcement of his resignation contains a pledge of good will toward the old school. That institution, he writes, "still retains my warmest sympathies, my earnest prayers, and, God willing, as far as possible, my earnest aid".

[1] See *The First Occasional Record of the Lord's Dealings with the East End Juvenile Mission (July 15th, 1867, to July 15th, 1868)*, by Thomas John Barnardo, p. 10.

When Barnardo engaged the Assembly Rooms, he knew well that he was launching upon a scheme much more adventurous and difficult than any he had piloted before. His pioneer work in Dublin, though strenuous, had been conducted on a small scale. "Ernest Street" was packed when one hundred children found shelter within its walls: while, as for the donkey-shed school, its size may be gauged from the fact that it was rented for two shillings and sixpence a week. Indeed, as an experiment, there is no evidence that the donkey-shed school, *per se*, was a success; its life seems to have been brief, and had it not been instrumental in discovering Jim Jarvis, it probably would have been obliterated from the record of Barnardo's work. Looking back, it is memorable only as a stepping-stone toward better wrought-out schemes.

The opening of the Assembly Rooms, however, Barnardo considered a great missionary venture, and the inaugural ceremony was planned with care. On November 5th, 1867, the scheme was started by a free tea-meeting attended by "no less than 2,347 rough lads, young men, girls, young women and children, a large proportion of the older ones being thieves and poor lost girls". The filling of these hungry stomachs had to be executed in relays, but Barnardo had around him a valiant body of voluntary workers, and by united endeavours all were provided with "a plentiful tea"; yet so economically was this feat performed that an examination of the Balance Sheet shows the total expense to have been £27 3s. 11d.—just under threepence per head. This achievement illustrates Barnardo's organizing genius. All the tea was made on the premises, all the labour was voluntary, and the huge supply of bread, butter, jam, cake, etc., was provided by friends at cost price. Every penny was made to do double work.

The feeding of this multitude was an unconditional success; but, of the deeper purpose of the undertaking, the same could not be said. In his *First Occasional Record*, Barnardo made no attempt to paint the picture in rosy hues. All considered, he pronounced the tea-meeting "not very satisfactory". "Such a rough lot" he did not think were ever before assembled in Stepney. "The noise and the tumult were terrible"; so he was "not permitted" to say all he desired. Yet he "was not discouraged"; "for after the larger proportion had withdrawn, many of the elder ones remained seeking salvation".

So much for the inaugural event: the Sunday following, the mission's real work began. Barnardo and his helpers, an hour before the time of opening, paraded the streets, singing hymns and carrying banners, inviting boys, girls and young people to attend the mission; and though this method of invitation had its drawbacks, as was proven by the hurling of missiles at the paraders' heads, it achieved its purpose. Within ten minutes of the procession's return the Assembly Rooms were filled, and this procedure continued for six weeks. Then came a new proprietor at the King's Arms, and the following Sunday, when Barnardo arrived to make ready for the procession, he was denied access to the hall. The mission had begun to affect the habits of many youths, who previously had been liberal customers at the King's Arms bar; so in no circumstances would the new management permit the use of the hall.

This intelligence fell like a bomb on Barnardo's plans. Had he not "been assured of the Lord's guidance hitherto", he would have stayed his hand, for his path "seemed closed". Soon, however, these events appeared in a different light. Within a week of this blow, Barnardo was taken "seriously ill", and "for nearly two months" was "prevented from engaging in any service". Hence, looking back, he reflected: "Had not the work been hindered as it was, *we would in any case have had to close the schools* because at that time there was no brother with us who would willingly have undertaken the supervision. . . ." Furthermore, in retrospect, Barnardo perceived that positive conquests sprang out of this apparent defeat. The overthrow of all his plans uprooted every vestige of self-conceit: it proved his own "exceeding weakness" and threw him completely, in faith, upon God. But, in another respect, it proved a blessing in disguise: with his small income and his heavy expense in running so large a hall, it was impossible properly to develop the *week*-evening aspects of his scheme, which later grew at an amazing pace.

If, however, in the perspective of later days, Barnardo came to look upon the forced closing of the Assembly Rooms in providential light, he never felt any doubt that in opening them he was divinely led. One of the most indefatigable of his lifelong helpers was, in this mission, converted to the service of Christ; while the huge tea-meeting, and the daring processions, helped greatly to advertise the mission's purpose in quarters where later it took root and grew.

The Assembly Rooms venture, like the donkey-shed Ragged School, is important only because of its association with greater things. It is easier to recognize ultimate values in retrospect than when suffering apparent defeat: hence, for the moment, Barnardo was downcast. He had centred all on one big scheme, and, like a house of cards, it had tumbled. His finances, too, were sorely depleted: and now, with broken tools, he must begin to build afresh. That was sufficient to test any zealot's faith. But just as his plans for reconstruction were maturing, severe illness stayed his hand.

The new beginning, therefore, of necessity, was of the humblest. With Barnardo laid up, a nucleus of helpers, at his request, to "prevent complete cessation of the work", hired "a small room in a poor street"; and there—Barnardo directing operations from his bed—was laid the "foundation" of his week-night programme. On different evenings this room was utilized for a Free School, a Reading Room, and a Sewing Class, each being opened "under many inconveniences, but with encouraging results".

Late in January, 1868, Barnardo was sufficiently con-

valescent to be searching in person for larger premises.
Already the mustard seed had sent forth shoots requiring
more soil, more sun, more air; and so rapidly did they
grow that on March 2nd, 1868, the mission was moved to
more commodious quarters, in Hope Place, where "two
small four-roomed houses" were acquired—one for boys,
the other for girls. Here the mission was duly baptized,
the name given it being "*The East End Juvenile Mission*",
an appellation ever dear to Barnardo. Indeed, his earliest
printed report, dated July 15th, 1868, is mainly a survey of
his first four and a half months' labour in these cottages.
Yet so comprehensive had that work already become that
the *Record* fills fifty-six closely printed octavo pages, brim-
ful of interest from first to last.

A perusal of *The First Occasional Record* is essential to an
understanding of the mustard seed from which Barnardo's
work sprang. Within nineteen weeks the activities of the
East End Juvenile Mission included regular Church services
at which Barnardo, as "Shepherd of the flock", had baptized
by Immersion thirty converts, and a Sunday-school which,
averaging an attendance of over 300, taxed every inch
of space. These were the nucleus of the Mission's work,
but every day of the week had its programme. Around
Church and Sunday-school were organized Bible Classes
for children, young people and adults—the sexes meeting
separately—prayer meetings on Sunday mornings and three
evenings a week, night schools, a penny bank, a free lending
library, a reading-room, a reading circle, an employment
bureau, a shoe-blacking brigade, a sewing class, and a tract
brigade, plus a series of special meetings to satisfy peculiar
demands. For instance, on Good Friday, Barnardo, with
his colleagues and converts, held an All Night Prayer
Service, when, from 10 p.m. till 5 a.m., the "entire time,
with the exception of an interval for refreshments", was
occupied in pleading "at the Throne of Grace" God's
promises and the Mission's needs.

Such was the programme of The East End Juvenile Mission in the middle of July, 1868. True, this Mission was a Ragged School; but it was more. From his earliest association with the Ragged School system, Barnardo had felt the need for a wider programme. None more than he appreciated the work which Ragged Schools had done for Britain's neglected children; yet he criticized their labours as partaking too exclusively of the nature of schools, and lacking the adventurous spirit which should characterize a vigorous Christian mission. Often he had complained that most Ragged Schools were open only on Sunday and two or three week-evenings, whereas he had long dreamed of a mission with an Ever-Open Door and a programme for every day of the year; and now, after many perplexing vicissitudes, the embodiment of that dream, though still in embryo, was pulsing with life.

These labours, to recapitulate, were all conducted from two small cottages in Hope Place. But already Barnardo was directing another branch of "mission" work, destined to even greater importance. With private aid from a few friends he was holding himself responsible for the upbringing not only of Jim Jarvis, but of several other street-arabs, for whom he had found "homes" with humble Christian folk.

The day, however, was soon to dawn when Barnardo's "family", now growing at an astounding pace, was itself to find shelter under the roof of the East End Juvenile Mission. Many of his boys had been on the streets so long that they were scarcely amenable to the restraints of ordinary family life. They needed discipline and instruction in some trade; hence there arose the necessity of bringing them all under one roof, where the influences of school, mission, workshop and home, might be blended together, thus enabling them to face the world equipped for an honest career.

But the romance of up-building Barnardo's *Homes*, as such, must not detain us just here: enough now to remember that they were part of a great missionary dream. By 1868 the mustard seed had germinated sufficiently to make its properties known: (1) The soul of the whole organism was a Christian mission. (2) That mission was designed primarily to minister to juveniles. (3) It was based squarely on Jesus' teaching that it is "not the will of our Father in Heaven that one of these little ones should perish". (4) The mission must include Homes for destitute children. (5) Those Homes must be based on the principle that the most unfortunate child, whatever his parentage, if not mentally defective, could be so reared as to honour both his country and his God.

These features were all latent in the work of the East End Juvenile Mission by 1868; but the phenomenal development of that mission during the next few years is without parallel in the history of benevolent achievement.

CHAPTER VII

CREATIVE EVOLUTION

As the New Year heralds drew back the curtain upon the
year 1869 and peeped down upon the East End Juvenile
Mission, they beheld a child which had quite outgrown its
clothes. Never a nook or cranny could be found but was
crowded out; and in fine weather the backyards of both
cottages, together with the blind-alley on which they
opened, were filled with benches, tables and forms.

"Teacher, they're squeedging of me!" shouted one
youngster in the schools. "Teacher, I can't *breave*", whined
another; and these complaints were no jests. Barnardo
expressed doubt if children ever were so closely packed
together, "in any room, before or since"; often he himself
"could hardly 'breave'!" Nor was this congestion peculiar
to the schools.

Turn to the "Fellowship". It first met in "a small upper
room", eighteen being present, all but two of whom had
been converted under Barnardo's influence. But so rapid
was its growth that month by month it was compelled to
seek more space. From the "small upper room" it moved,
by stages, through every larger quarter the Mission could
boast, till within four months it was occupying the most
spacious room, seating seventy people; but it, too, was
soon crowded out. With the advent of the year 1869, when
the "Fellowship" assembled on Sundays at 3 p.m., Barnardo
was standing in doorways or on stair-steps, that his voice
might be heard as he led the worship of people packed in
different rooms. Yet many were unable to gain admission.

The growth of this "Fellowship", moreover, was due to
no sensational means. Its members were known by no name
save "Christian"; and they were at liberty to establish
concurrent membership in any Church. They held that
"no difference of judgment or experience ought to hinder

communion and visible unity amongst those who love the Lord Jesus Christ". They acknowledged "no creed, narrower or wider, or other, than *the Whole Word of God*"; and "esteeming the 'communion of saints' to be of great value", they met "every Lord's Day afternoon" to "break bread and worship". They desired, "by the Grace of God", to cleave to "the simplicity that is in Christ, not only in outward matters, but also in spiritual things; avoiding 'strifes of words', yet earnestly contending for the faith once delivered to the saints". Their one High Priest was Jesus; their one sacrifice "a finished and completed one"; and they, "with all the people of God, in every place", desired "to offer spiritual sacrifices well-pleasing unto God". . . .

This Fellowship had "no stated minister". It was leavened by Brethrenism and Quakerism; by Baptists and Methodists. But though Barnardo was not ordained as its minister, it did "not reject the Christian ministry", and the young zealot had towards the flock "truly a pastor's heart". Two hindrances, however, to the complete exercise of pastoral care stood in his way—"lack of ability and want of time". "I am persuaded firmly of my call to do the work of an *Evangelist*," he writes, "but I am not at all clear as to the pastoral vocation." Soon, however, the day arrived when others were appointed to the pastoral charge, leaving Barnardo free to concentrate on his special "calling".[1]

With the Mission, then, like a chrysalis, defying confinement, more property was imperative: and thanks to admiring friends it soon came to hand. First one adjoining house was added, and then a second; but by the close of 1869 overcrowding was as pronounced as when only two cottages housed the Mission's work. Yet, meanwhile, the intersecting walls of the four backyards had been torn down; and over the boundary walls a roof had been built, thus providing an assembly hall seating three hundred. All such arrangements, however, proved inadequate. Extended quarters had

[1] See *First Occasional Record*, pp. 38-40, for an account of this "Fellowship".

been accompanied by an extended programme; an extended programme caused the Mission to be besieged by a still greater throng; and by spring, 1870, neighbours were complaining that it was impossible to enter their houses without climbing over tables, benches, stools, chairs and forms.

A new and bolder advance step was now imperative; and already the "hat was being passed" among friends. The management accordingly of these schemes, one might have thought sufficient to fill every waking hour of an able, vigorous man. Yet besides looking after all this work himself, Barnardo, at twenty-four, was still prosecuting his medical studies, while also he found time, once a week, to go to Annie Macpherson's "Home of Industry", Bethnal Green, and drill boys whom that remarkable woman was training for emigration to Canada.[1] This interest, too, is significant, for in July, 1868, Barnardo had laid down the principle that emigration of suitable persons to the British Colonies, particularly Canada, must be accepted as the chief remedy for unemployment; and before he began to organize migration parties of his own, he sent to Canada, under Annie Macpherson's guidance, hundreds of his lads.

But, reverting to Hope Place, further expansion was there impossible; so looking around for additional premises Barnardo discovered at 18, Stepney Causeway a large property reasonably adapted to his needs, and forthwith he procured it "on lease" at £45 per annum plus taxes, which were £12.

This property was intended to do more than simply relieve congestion at Hope Place: its cardinal function was to act as a "Home" for destitute lads. True, Jim Jarvis and certain other of Barnardo's protégés, at their own request, had in May of this year (1870) sailed with Annie Macpherson to Canada, thus helping to make up her original party of

[1] See *The Children's Home Finder* (1913), by Lilian M. Birt, for an account of Annie Macpherson's work.

one hundred lads; but Barnardo still had a large "family" boarded out, and these lads he felt should now be brought together where their training could be carefully supervised; besides, he knew of more homeless urchins whom he yearned to succour.

But, faced by acute financial problems, he felt the time not yet ripe to receive only *destitute* lads. The expense of such an undertaking would, at this stage, have been prohibitive; and he knew well that he would have to experiment, testing methods by results. The original plan of the "Home" was to cater for three types of lads : *first*, the "wholly destitute", who would be "fed, clothed, housed and taught trades"; *second*, "lads desiring work, but for whom no opening could at present be found"; *third*, "good, steady, respectable lads in work", but sorely needing a Christian home, for which they could pay a modest fee.

Barnardo's first published intimation concerning this "Home" was contained in a letter to a friend. "Our Boys' Home, when completed," he says, "will contain five dormitories, capable of accommodating sixty lads." Carpenter, plumber, painter and gas-fitter already were fitting up the premises. Lavatory arrangements, basins and baths were all being installed, while also a good kitchen, a washhouse and a private apartment for the "father and mother of the family" were being duly arranged : all being executed "as plainly and economically as is consistent with *permanent* usefulness".

So much for the lads' housing; but Barnardo recognized, too, their need of sport, for the letter points out that "space for healthful recreation" was provided. The first Home, then, was now procured; and necessary alterations were so far under way that Barnardo believed all might be ready for occupation in "three weeks' time". But his eternal bugbear stood in his way: "You will, I am sure," he concludes, "sympathize with me when I add that, for want of funds, I fear I shall be compelled in a few days to call off the workmen and suspend operations, as I am quite determined not to go into debt."

Had Barnardo's expectations been realized, the opening could have taken place in September, 1870. But owing to a shortage of funds it was deferred for ten weeks; and when finally the ceremony was observed, its simplicity was almost austere. A letter from Barnardo published in *The Christian*,[1] December 8th, 1870, reads:

"Beloved Friends, Our 'Home for Lads' has at length been formally opened. We asked no outside friends, invited no subscribers, but, getting our dear fellow-labourers, the father, the mother and the school-master of the Home together, we, with the dear boys, solemnly dedicated this new undertaking to Him under Whose gracious auspices the design originated and has been carried out. But it was a precious time, such simple, childlike pleading with God, such earnest, heart-broken cries for mercy upon as yet unsaved fathers, mothers and friends."

With this "Home", then, opened as a branch of the East End Juvenile Mission, Barnardo's programme was quickly extended. Wood-chopping, shoe-making and brush-making, were soon flourishing industries inside the Mission's walls; while outside shoe-blacking and city-messenger brigades, in distinctive uniforms, rendered a public service which demonstrated the practical effects of Barnardo's work. Again, the Home's programme tolerated no idleness. Every moment of every day had its preoccupation. Between 6 a.m., when all arose, and 10 p.m., when lights were extinguished, the Time-table included morning and evening prayers, two periods of school, a span of industrial training, three meals, physical drill, open-air sports, an interval for reading and meditation, and time for attending to household duties; for the boys were taught to make their own beds, sweep and scrub floors, wash their own clothes, and attend to many household needs.

With "Stepney Causeway" open twenty-four hours of every day, and with the "father and mother of the family" in continual residence, it is not surprising that gradually

[1] This is the same paper as *The Revival*, which has now changed its name.

"the Home" came to be considered the nucleus of the Mission's work. Indeed, soon Stepney Causeway was the acknowledged Headquarters and "Hope Place", where the Mission was baptized, though it lost none of its energy, came to be regarded as an auxiliary. Yet for years to come the work in all its ramifications continued to be known as the East End Juvenile Mission; and under that name it rose to national fame.

From April, 1866, when Barnardo came to London, till December, 1870, when "the Home" was opened, the strides of this young enthusiast appeared rapid enough; but later his work leaped forward like a thing possessed of supernatural strength. A glance at its finances reveals the extent of the Mission's growth. Up till July, 1867, Barnardo made no appeal for *public* funds; after that date he furnished annual reports; and their perusal reveals a miracle. The first Report, covering July 15th, 1867, till July 15th, 1868, shows the Mission's income to be £214 15s. During the succeeding twelve months it had mounted to over three times that amount; the next year it was more than trebled again; while the year following the opening of the "Home" it was nearly £7,000. And, for the twelve months ending March 31st, 1877, it reached £30,000.

These figures suggest the remarkable growth of Barnardo's work within ten years. But more remarkable is the fact that all this money was entrusted to a student zealot, who himself had sole charge of finances, and who during those years had no Council to co-operate with him in directing the Mission's policy. In his *First Occasional Record*, Barnardo states plainly that he was in absolute control: "Fellow believers desirous of helping the Mission's work should remember, ere they do so, that their donations or subscriptions are to be forwarded to a *private individual*—that I have no Committee, Treasurer, Secretary or other than myself in the management of the financial affairs of the Mission— that their names will never appear in print; but that they will be written to, and their subscriptions or donations privately acknowledged by me."

In another paragraph, emphasizing that he desired to avoid everything which "might savour of the praise of men", he continues: "To this end the *names* of contributors will be suppressed, the *initials* only being given. The prevailing habit of publishing in full the names and addresses of donors cannot, I think, be too strongly reprehended as unscriptural, leading as it must do to giving 'to be seen of men', and to the entire disobedience of the exhortation, 'But when thou doest alms, let not thy right hand know what thy left hand doeth; that thine alms may be in *secret*, and thy Father, which seeth in secret, shall reward thee openly.'"

But though Barnardo maintained autocratic control, he nevertheless "solicited" the "fullest scrutiny of the Mission's affairs"; for "the books containing the accounts" could be seen "at all times by any donor desirous of doing so, *without the necessity of giving previous notice*". Regularly, too, he published the *initials* of all known subscribers together with the months in which their subscriptions were made; and before these initials, if any indication had come to him, he invariably printed Mr., Mrs., Miss, Rev., etc., while anonymous gifts were published with whatever information he could obtain. In a word, every subscription was reported, and any contributor could easily verify his own donation. Hence, none could reasonably have complained at the manner in which Barnardo rendered his account.

The day, however, was to come when, by the assaults of his enemies, Barnardo's peremptory methods were brought to task; and although from the "valley of humiliation" he emerged unscathed, he learned the folly of autocratic control by any individual over the funds of a charitable work. But that is a future story. From this excursion into financial affairs we now return to the year 1870, to trace the evolution of the Mission's work.

When Barnardo leased the Stepney Causeway property, he was granted an option on the adjoining premises, if needed later on. And well it was that this precaution had been taken, for soon Number 18 overflowed into 20, while these in turn absorbed 22, till within a few years Barnardo had all Stepney Causeway from 18 to 26; while simultaneously he opened in other quarters more than a dozen different centres for specialized work.

But what necessitated this vast expansion? Just here lies both tragedy and romance. Early in the Homes' history there came one winter's day to "Stepney Causeway" a half-naked, half-starved boy, eleven years old. His mother, when he was seven, had turned him upon the street to fend for himself, and henceforth John Somers, nicknamed by his street-pals "Carrots", because of his freckles, never saw his mother except when she caught him on the streets and rifled his pockets in search of money—for gin. Now "Carrots", being cold and hungry, pleaded for admission to the Home.

Barnardo listened to the child's tale with aching heart: but every bed was full and no lad would be leaving for a week. He comforted the boy as best he could; gave him a hot meal and half a crown, and promised him that a week hence *room would be found for him*. So "Carrots" left with a lighter heart. But for days following the weather was wet, stormy and cold. No one wanted the matches "Carrots" tried to sell; and everyone was too busy to observe the misfortunes of a homeless lad. The day before "Carrots" was "banking on" admission, two workmen in Billingsgate, shortly after dawn, on turning over a hogshead, discovered two boys, apparently asleep. One immediately awoke and, agile as a cat, rushed away. The other seemed soundly asleep; so one of the men shook him, but without effect. He was motionless, as if in a trance. Hence the workman lifted him up, and touching his face drew back with a start. "Carrots" was dead!

The coroner's inquest revealed the fact that he "had succumbed to the combined effects of hunger and exposure". The little pinched-up face and fleshless body told their own tale: the verdict was: "Death from exhaustion, the result of frequent exposure and want of food."

This tragedy pierced Barnardo's heart. He was unable to dismiss the thought that he had turned "Carrots" from his door; indirectly he felt responsible for his death. The past, however, was irreparable, and remorse of no avail. One thing Barnardo could do. He resolved, by God's help, never again to turn away a destitute child. So across Headquarters he swung a large sign: "NO DESTITUTE CHILD EVER REFUSED ADMISSION."

The acceptance of this motto was a tremendous declaration of faith. Yet ever since, it has remained the Homes' charter, and though often their faith has been tried, never has their "barrel of meal or cruse of oil" failed.

This process of creative evolution into wider spheres of service was not, however, limited to the Homes. A few months after establishing the first Home, the Mission opened large Ragged Schools in Salmon's Lane, which proved a boon to the inhabitants of a sordid area; while in September, 1871, it opened in North Street, Limehouse, a Tract and Pure Literature Depot, which, providing inspirational reading for the poor, was an oasis in a desert of sin.

But more significant was another development. Late in 1871 Lord Shaftesbury requested Barnardo carefully to study the records of "his children's" histories, and compile statistics as to the *causes* of their destitution. Barnardo gladly complied: "I tabulated in special columns the various traceable causes . . . which led to the children becoming candidates for the Homes; and the astonishing fact emerged (doubly astonishing to me, because I was not then a total abstainer, nor even in sympathy with the Movement) that no less than *85 per cent.* owed their social ruin and the long train of their distresses to the influence, direct or indirect, of the drinking habits of their parents, grandparents or other relatives." [1]

Shocked by this revelation, Barnardo immediately became a teetotaller, thenceforth linking the Temperance Cause with the ethic of Christ—Who willed that "not one of these little ones should perish". Soon, therefore, plans were laid for a concentrated attack upon the liquor traffic. After much prayer and preparation Barnardo, supported by his "Fellowship", invited Joshua and Mary Poole to come to East London and, in co-operation with the Mission, conduct an Evangelistic Campaign. In August, 1872, it began—the scene of operations being a tent seating nearly three thousand people and pitched in front of the "Edinburgh Castle", the vilest "gin-palace" in Limehouse. Barnardo and his associates were set on bearding the lion in his den.

This campaign resulted in hundreds of lasting conversions, among the regenerated being drunkards, prostitutes and thieves. Some who had been looked upon as hopelessly abandoned, became lifelong workers on the Mission's voluntary Staff. But not least remarkable was the Revival's temperance effect. Every convert signed the pledge; and so also did hundreds who never professed conversion.

During the Campaign, Barnardo wrote: "The scenes we are permitted to witness nightly are such as I never remember beholding during any previous period of my spiritual life. Last Lord's Day evening twenty-five hundred persons crowded to hear the Word of Life, and for hours afterwards we were occupied in dealing with anxious souls. . . ." Again: "The result of such work was that large numbers of our dear working-folk took the temperance pledge. Nearly four thousand pledges were taken in the tent from

[1] T. J. Barnardo: *Something Attempted, Something Done*, p. 13. This book, containing 280 pages, and copiously illustrated, provides a series of graphic pictures of Barnardo's work up till 1888. But it makes no attempt to interpret the consecutive history of the Homes.

persons in adult life, and *these pledges were registered, and the persons carefully visited and looked after.*"

But most dramatic of the effects of this campaign was the fact that two public-houses, through loss of customers, were forced upon the market, one being the "Edinburgh Castle".

Prior to the Tent Services, "The Castle" had been visited by Samuel Morley, Annie Macpherson and Dr. Barnardo; they discovered "a flaming gin-palace, with well-lighted and attractive frontage", to the rear of which was "a music-hall of the most unenviable reputation". Barnardo's impression of the visit reads: "The scene that met our eyes burned itself deep upon the memories of all three. Both bar and music-hall were crowded, chiefly with young men and women. A roaring drink-trade was going on, and on the stage songs were being sung which won applause in strict proportion to the filthy *doubles entendres* and questionable gestures with which they were plentifully besprinkled. Round the room were statues of the nude, which I suppose would be considered all the more artistic in that they were disgusting to decent people . . . we were in the presence of a demoralizing agency of the worst description."

When, as a result of the Tent Revival, most "bar customers" at the "Edinburgh Castle" were drawn away, and the music-hall was practically empty, Barnardo felt that his campaign had been providentially led; but when this whole property was forced on the market, he seemed to see clearly the hand of God beckoning him to "go in and possess the land". Accordingly he lost not a moment in challenging "the Lord's stewards" to join with him in capturing this stronghold of iniquity for the service of Christ. A letter to *The Christian* runs, in part, thus:

"As one result of the Tent Services, two large public-houses immediately adjoining are for sale, one being quite closed. The other is a splendid house, containing eighteen rooms: a large, well-ventilated apartment seating 200 persons; another great concert-room with seats for 1,100; and ground surrounding the same sufficiently large to enable us, if necessary, to hold open-air tent services in fine weather. Already many intending bidders at the forthcoming sale have looked at it and we hear of its being reopened as an attractive concert and music-hall.

"I tremble at this and cannot but pray that the Lord will enable some of His stewards to lay this at His feet for His holy service. Most thankfully will I receive and reply to communications upon this subject, earnestly hoping that our gracious God will fill the hearts of His stewards with willingness and ability, as also with sympathy for the poor dwellers in the East End, so recently brought under the sound of the everlasting Gospel."

This call to "God's stewards" aroused the desired response. A few weeks later the Mission included "Edinburgh Castle". Tuesday, October 22nd, was the date fixed for the public auction; but Barnardo learned that a West End music-hall had designs upon it; so "an hour before the time arranged for the auction", he bought the place "by private contract" for £4,200—£840 being paid as a deposit until the Deeds could be examined.

When the day dawned on which final payments were due, £110 was needed to reach the grand total. But not a penny was borrowed; at 11 a.m. a friend called "to have a last shot at the citadel. It was a 100-pounder!" Another gave £10, and "by twelve o'clock the entire sum of £4,200 was in hand, and about £100 more promised towards the fittings!" Recording the result, Barnardo wrote: "How good is our God; how faithful are all His covenants! Beloved friends, unite with us in a song of praise and triumphant hallelujahs!"

This money was sent to Barnardo himself. He had neither treasurer nor committee and no names were made public; yet so great was confidence in his integrity that among his donors were Lord Shaftesbury, the Hon. Arthur Kinnaird (afterwards Lord Kinnaird) and Lord Radstock, who alone gave £1,000.[1]

Over this "enlarged branch of the East End Juvenile

[1] This intelligence was conveyed to the author by *private* information.

Mission" Barnardo maintained "active management";
but the property was vested in seven trustees, "selected
from various sections of the professing Church".

The day Barnardo bought the "Edinburgh Castle" he
was offered an advance of £500 on his purchase price.
But such overtures fell on deaf ears. Six days after the
conquest, a huge tea-meeting in "The Castle", followed by
a jubilant service in the great tent, marked a new advance.
Much renovation, however, was necessary before the old
gin-palace was in condition to render the Mission full service,
so the *official* opening was postponed until alterations were
complete. Meanwhile, there was no marking time. Within
a fortnight the "Fellowship" was organized into "The
People's Mission Church" with deacons and elders; and
Barnardo was unanimously "elected" pastor over the
flock, which at its first meeting in "The Castle" numbered
over two hundred and fifty members, together with fifty-five
candidates for membership.

During the Tent Revival, Barnardo sought after some
scheme whereby to offer a social substitute for the public-
house; but it was not till the renovation of "Edinburgh
Castle" had begun that he hit upon his plan. Decorators
were at work in the central bar-room when Barnardo,
gazing at its flashing mirrors, flaming chandeliers and
brilliant colours, thought to himself: "Are not these the
attractions which allure working-men into the public-house?
And could they not all be maintained without the sale of
intoxicating drink?" There and then he decided to leave
bars, mirrors, chandeliers and other "attractions"; so,
removing only what was obnoxious, he determined to make
this one-time centre of debauchery the citadel of his temperance work. Hence the gin-palace was transformed into
a coffee-palace, where all forms of non-intoxicating drinks
were sold; where meals were served at the cheapest rate;
where papers and magazines were supplied, and where
dozens of innocent games were at hand. Barnardo's outlook

is summed up in a sentence: "The working-man is caught with guile by the publican; why should he not be diverted by similar means into better ways?"

The *official* opening of "The Castle" was anticipated as a triumphal event, so preparations were thoroughgoing. The place was re-decorated inside and out; Scripture texts were painted on the walls; inspiring pictures, tastefully framed, were hung about; and after much cleansing and fumigation this one-time "gin-palace" was made to radiate beauty, serenity and peace.

On February 14th, 1873, a strategic date in the evolution of Barnardo's work, "The Castle" was formally dedicated. One man, above all others, could make this ceremony ring with significance; and his services were procured. Lord Shaftesbury declared "The Castle" open to fulfil its "new and glorious mission"; and in his address he uttered words Barnardo loved to quote: "The Churches and Chapels", said Shaftesbury, "no doubt do a very good work in their own way . . . but they are sadly deficient in the aggressive spirit, and far too much taken up with looking after their own people. They seem to imagine that it is sufficient to open a building and let it be known that religion can be had there; whereas that has never sufficed, and never will suffice, to bring the masses to religion. Now, as of old, *you must go into the highways and byways, and compel them to come in.* The working classes have never come in, and will never come in, while things are as they are to-day. . . . There must be active, aggressive work, open-air preaching, house-to-house visitation; in short, every means must be employed to bring the truth home to the hearts and con-sciences of all. . . . Such", exclaimed Shaftesbury, "is the high task which the 'Edinburgh Castle', under God and through the instrumentality of the People's Church, has set itself"; while, referring to the Coffee Palace, he said he prayed God it might be the forerunner of many such efforts, "to provide fellowship, recreation and social intercourse, without the menacing atmosphere created by the sale of intoxicants".

Tremendous enthusiasm from every part of the crowded assembly greeted this pronouncement, and, the ceremony concluded, hundreds declared they had experienced the most inspiring event of their lives. Nor is it surprising that such depths of emotion were stirred, for among Shaftesbury's hearers were those who, by his efforts, had been emancipated from the early barbaric conditions of factory, workshop and mine; among them, too, were ex-chimney-sweeps and those whom, as children, he had freed from the ghastly horrors of brick-fields, calico-printing works and agricultural gangs; while scarcely less deeply stirred were such as remembered their debt to this veteran for the Saturday Half-Holiday, Public Parks, Ragged Schools, Workmen's Institutes, decent housing, the Y.M.C.A. and other *aggressive* reform steps. Moreover, when he referred to the temperance design of the Coffee Palace, many remembered that it was he who, by Act of Parliament, had stopped the atrocious custom of paying wages in public-houses; that he had set the first great example of conducting an election without free beer or gin; that he had shortened the hours for the Sunday sale of liquor; and that, when he inaugurated Britain's first model-housing scheme of 1,400 houses, with gardens, in Battersea, he had stipulated in the Deeds that the property be "for ever free" from the menace of the liquor traffic within its bounds.

The Coffee Palace, both socially and financially, was a success from the start. It attracted large numbers of working-men, and, as a social centre, out-rivalled public-houses round about. But, most important, it created an ideal atmosphere in which to nurture the temperance sentiments of the multitude who, during the Revival, had signed the pledge. The People's Church, moreover, was not less successful. Every Sunday evening the transformed music-hall was packed with worshippers, while following the enlargement of the "Edinburgh Castle", in 1884, the new hall, seating 3,200, was as crowded as the smaller one had been.[1] Yet for fifteen years Barnardo, besides all other duties, retained the honorary post of chief pastor, and preached to this multitude once, twice or three times a week. So great, too, was his power as a preacher that many advised him to concentrate on this work, leaving other branches of the Mission to other hands. To this proposal he could never agree: "I feel that my Master has called me and given me as my life-work my children; *for nothing can I desert them.*"

Yet, even after pressure of labour forced Barnardo to resign the pastorate of The People's Church, he remained active in its work, preaching frequently and supervising all its activities. "I unhesitatingly assert", declared Barnardo, "that those who tell us that the working classes are inimical to Christianity, are wholly misinformed; I am persuaded that the Gospel, if faithfully preached with strength of personal conviction and in plain Saxon, will prove now, as ever, powerfully attractive to the working classes and the Poor generally. At the 'Edinburgh Castle' we have a crowded morning congregation of decent, respectable working people, at an hour when all such are popularly supposed to be either in bed or at the public-house corner. . . . On Sunday afternoon we have usually 2,500 in attendance. In the evening the full capacity of the hall is tested, and I know no more hopeful and inspiring sight than is afforded by a visit to 'The Castle' between the hours of 7 and 8.30, when every one of our 3,200 sittings is occupied."

It must not, however, be imagined that the People's Church was a preaching centre alone. Soon, for example, it had around it a splendid body of deaconesses, who conducted Bible Classes, Mothers' Meetings, Young People's

---

[1] In 1884 "The Castle" was rebuilt and enlarged; at the reopening the Lord Mayor of London attended with the Sheriffs in state.

Guilds, etc., and few knew East End homes better than they. Moreover, the Copperfield Road Ragged School, which sprang from "The Castle's" work and whose Staff was manned by converts of the People's Church, became the largest Ragged School in London; and so effective was its teaching that almost every year it was recommended by Government inspectors for the highest State grant.

Not to Barnardo's efforts alone, however, was traceable the power that flowed from this Church. Its debt to Joshua and Mary Poole was immense; to special services by Moody and Sankey in 1874 and 1883 it owed much: and not least important among its milestones was an evangelistic campaign conducted in 1875 by "Uncle Tom", immortalized by Harriet Beecher Stowe in *Uncle Tom's Cabin*. This lovable negro, who bore upon his body deep scars from the manacles of slavery, went right to the heart of East End audiences, and profound was the impression he left on the People's Church. Nevertheless, it was chiefly to Barnardo that the Church owed its driving-force.

* * * * *

But while the Mission advanced apace into more and more creative spheres, its founder made "the great advance" in his private state. Up till 1871 there is no suggestion of any love-affair in Barnardo's life. He seemed so utterly in love with his work as to be immune from Cupid's spell; but that ingenious imp finally has his day; the person through whom he conveyed his shafts being Syrie Louise Elmslie, only daughter of William Elmslie, a wealthy City business man residing in Richmond.

Miss Elmslie was raised in a fashionable environment. Luxury had surrounded her; private tutors had conducted her education; her every whim had been gratified. Religion had formed little part in her upbringing, and Sunday in her circles was scarcely different from other days of the week. When eighteen, however, under the influence of Lord

Radstock [1] and Dr. F. B. Meyer, she underwent a soul-stirring religious experience, which changed her life. Immediately she began Ragged School work in Richmond; and into it she threw all her powers.

After some years of this work, in the autumn of 1871, Miss Elmslie organized a large tea-meeting and entertainment for all poor lads of the district; and having heard much of Barnardo's achievements, she invited him out to speak. He came; and after having tea with the lads delivered an address which riveted the attention of all. But not till his talk was over did he meet Miss Elmslie. Up till then she had been too busy even to receive the speaker; but when they did meet both were impressed. Barnardo admired the skill with which Miss Elmslie had organized the event; she admired the magnetic influence he exercised over her roughest boys; but each also admired the other for reasons they could not have defined, even to themselves.

So much for their first meeting, but fate decreed that they meet again next day. At Paddington Station, Barnardo had booked third class for a destination two hours from London, when he ran into Miss Elmslie and her father, bound by the same train for a more distant station. They, however, were travelling first class. So, rushing back, he changed his ticket and joined the Elmslies to his destination. This chance meeting increased "admiration" on both sides. Barnardo admitted afterwards that Cupid then directed a dart at him, while Miss Elmslie confided to friends that the little rascal had robbed her of her accustomed calm.

But Barnardo was engrossed in his work; he had no time even to think of love, so Miss Elmslie and her charm he tried to dismiss from mind—but in vain. Her vision haunted his dreams. Not, however, for eighteen months

---

[1] Lord Radstock's life was a source of blessing to thousands. He devoted his means to religious and humanitarian ends; at his own expense conducting evangelistic campaigns in different countries.

did he see her again, and that meeting was as accidental as the previous one.

In the spring of 1873 Miss Elmslie, amidst the crowd at the Rev. Pennefather's funeral, got lost from her friends; and behold she and Barnardo "ran into one another" again. The search for her friends ceased; Barnardo volunteered to see her home; and before they parted both knew they were "in love".

A few days later they pledged their troth, Barnardo making a special trip to Richmond to plead for Mr. Elmslie's consent. But so rapid had been developments, and so little did Barnardo know about the Elmslie family that, when met at the station by his fiancée and her youngest brother Harry (a boy of nine, perched high on the cab alongside the driver), he inquired if this "nice little lad" was the cabman's son.[1]

Despite such indiscretions, all went well. Four weeks later the Metropolitan Tabernacle was crowded to overflowing to celebrate the nuptials of the happy pair, who, in the absence of the Rev. C. H. Spurgeon, were married by three close friends—Dr. Gratton Guinness, Lord Radstock and Henry Varley—an evangelist.

There followed a six weeks' honeymoon; but Barnardo's life was so wrapped up in his work that not even during those memorable days could he detach himself from his Mission and "his boys". Nor did his bride desire that he should. Scores of letters were now written and happy hours chased one another, as bride and groom read aloud together and mused aloud concerning united plans for greater things to be. Those musings, moreover, were not vain, for soon was born one of the most important branches of Barnardo's Homes.

The honeymoon over, the couple were given a rousing

---

[1] This incident was related to the author by Mr. Harry Elmslie himself, who, with his wife, has already spent more than three decades in the service of Barnardo's Home.

"Welcome Home". For this function every sitting in the great hall of "Edinburgh Castle" was occupied; and when Lord Shaftesbury, on behalf of the People's Church, presented to Mrs. Barnardo a silver tea-service, emotions could brook no restraint. The assembly, jumping to its feet, rent the air with cheers. Barnardo seemed the hero of the East End, and now that he was married, admirers expected of him still greater things.[1]

[1] The whole story of Barnardo's courtship and honeymoon was told me by Mrs. Barnardo; and many letters, which through her courtesy I have been privileged to read, show that as a lover, both before marriage and till death, Barnardo was scarcely less ardent than as a friend of the outcast child.

CHAPTER VIII

FAITH AND ADVENTURE

BARNARDO's life was one of ceaseless adventure, inspired by faith. One night, when making a round of lodging-houses in a notorious district, he was pounced upon by "roughs" who relieved him of hat, coat, watch, chain, fountain-pen and every penny in his pocket. Next moment the thieves dashed out of sight. Barnardo knew it was useless to give chase. Though loath to part with his belongings, being powerless to recover them, he proceeded with his calls. To his amazement, a little later, he was confronted by one of the robbers, who, handing all back, exclaimed: " 'Ad we know'd ye was Dr. Barnardo, we would niver ha' touched ye. We begs yer pardon, sir!"

This experience is suggestive of scores which befell Barnardo around the lodging-houses of East London. In 1851 Lord Shaftesbury brought forward a Bill for the "Registration and Inspection of Common Lodging-Houses", which Dickens pronounced: "The best Act ever passed by an English Legislature." But though this Act forced registration and inspection, limited the number of occupants, and compelled certain sanitary measures, conditions were still bad. When Barnardo began his Mission, scores of London's lodging-houses were still spreading mental, moral and physical corruption. And certain of those frequented by lads of from twelve to twenty were among the worst.

Into one of these lodging-houses, well known as the resort of young thieves, Barnardo tried for years to gain admission, but without success. It was closely guarded; the deputy, a burly giant, allowing no stranger to pass its inner doors. More than once Barnardo, pausing at its entrance, was gruffly warned to "pass on about his business". But a time came when things changed. One night, in scouring the Drury Lane district, Barnardo was approaching this

"Thieves' Kitchen" when he noticed the deputy standing outside, his face shrouded in gloom. Instead of scowling as the medical student drew near, he obviously was relieved. Immediately he beckoned him to the doorway, and in agitated tones related his fears that a regular lodger was smitten down with fever: "Will you examine him, Doctor? And for Heaven's sake keep us out of quarantine!"

Barnardo's long-awaited chance had arrived; at once he was conducted to the sick lad. Many boys were in the room, none seemingly more than nineteen. The patient was a wiry lad in his early teens, and the fever, being mild, quickly yielded to treatment; so quarantine was unnecessary. But the lad had to remain in bed a fortnight, and Barnardo visited him once or twice every day. Soon, therefore, he came to know something of the secrets of the place; and the appellation "Thieves' Kitchen" proved apt. The house was a den of thieves, where frequently stolen goods were sold to accomplices at a seventh, or even a tenth, of their market price.

Soon also Barnardo realized two things which proved significant; first, that most of the house clientèle could neither read nor write; second, that if he visited his patient late at night he would find nearly all the boys "at home". This information he put to account. On his third visit he had brought a copy of *Uncle Tom's Cabin* to read aloud to his patient, thus helping him while away the hours in bed; but, to his surprise, he had scarcely begun to read when all the boys in the room gathered round him, "with open ears and open mouths". So, realizing his opportunity, he postponed his visits till later at night; and when, after attending his patient, he continued the story, nearly every lad in the house was listening.

On the fourth night he arrived specially late, and, passing through the kitchen *en route* to his patient, noticed a tall, lithe youth about seventeen toasting a herring before the grate. The lad's appearance made Barnardo pause. He had a finely shaped head, classic features and an athletic frame. His bearing marked his presence in this haunt as a paradox. The furtive glance and twitching mouth, so characteristic of thieves, were foreign to him; he seemed perfectly at ease, completely master of himself.

Leaving the kitchen, Barnardo turned to a boy following him and inquired who this youth was. "Why, that's Punch!" came the reply. "He's king o' the place, he is! There ain't another chap in London what knows his trade like Punch. He lifts more 'an a dozen ordinary chaps, he does. And he's niver been pinched!"

That night Punch joined his pals around the patient's bed, and as the story proceeded none was more spell-bound. From then on he missed no word till the book was closed; and later, when Barnardo read *The Pilgrim's Progress*, Punch's interest was no less keen.

Finally, the patient having recovered, when Barnardo announced that he would no longer be coming to read, several lads desired admission to "The Home", where they could learn to read for themselves. Punch wavered. He was overcome by a burning desire to learn to read; but imagining The Home "a regular prison", he nibbled warily at the bait. At last, after a hundred queries, he requested permission to enter for a year only, expressly stipulating that, if then he had not learned to read, he be allowed to leave just the same. Realizing well the metal of which Punch was made, Barnardo without compunction agreed; so this "king o' lifters" entered "The Home".

For obvious reasons Barnardo kept a watchful eye on this lad's progress, frequently bringing him into his office to attend to odd jobs; and gradually certain facts came to light. Punch never had known either father or mother. His first memories were of a Poor House, where he was abominably treated and from which, when nine, he ran away. For some time he tried to "make his way" by selling matches; but this was difficult, for often he had "to sleep out" and do with one meal a day. Then one night in a lodging-house "a clever chap", laughing at his simplicity, promised to teach him to "prig": "Why, it's aisy at this 'ere gaime to make 'alf a crown, or, if ye're lucky, five bob, in no time. But sellin' matches, it takes yer all day long to make a tanner or two!"

Punch agreed with his pal's "philosophy", so forthwith he began training for "the profession"; and so proficient did he become that in three years he was recognized by his mates as their "king". But even after he had been several weeks in the Home he seemed to develop no conscience regarding the ethic of stealing. To him it still remained a clever game.

So one day, while tidying Barnardo's office, on being questioned regarding his past, Punch began to brag stoutly of his achievements as a "lifter" who "never was copped". Barnardo, on hearing his "tall tales", rebuked him warmly for his exaggerations. Punch was silent; and both resumed work. About twenty minutes later the lad asked what time it was. The Doctor felt for his watch; it was gone! So also were his chain, wallet, pen-knife and pocket-handkerchief! Punch grinned; and lifting a blotting-paper from a table near by, revealed all the missing articles.

Following this incident, Barnardo spoke to Punch about the inherent wrong of theft, but without effect; so he tried new tactics. Punch, he knew, had formed a strong attach-ment to a boy in the Home called James—a lad of sterling honesty. Hence he told him that if ever James learned he was a thief their friendship would cease. This brought a puzzled look to Punch's face; and there the matter was dropped.

A few days later Punch, with downcast countenance and swollen eyes, entered Barnardo's office, declaring that he must leave the Home *at once*. The Doctor inquired the cause of this peremptory demand, and like a shot came the accusation: "You've been a-blowing on me, you have! James 'as called me a thief."

Barnardo assured Punch that he was mistaken, and soon both were on their knees. First the Doctor prayed; then Punch prayed; and before they arose the lad had lost all pride in his old exploits. From that day thieving was a closed chapter in his life.

In seven months Punch could read well, so Barnardo presented him with a Bible and *Uncle Tom's Cabin.* At the end of a year, when he was free to leave, he pleaded for permission to stay longer and master his trade. Within two years he was a proficient shoemaker instructing other lads. Then, three years after his admission, there came a request to the Home for an expert shoemaker to establish and supervise a shoemaking trade in another institution. It was a fine opportunity; and Barnardo called for Punch. To his amazement, tears welled in the youth's eyes: "I'm sorry, sir, you want to get rid of me."

Barnardo disillusioned him on that score; and the one-time thief went forth to this responsible post, where he gave eminent satisfaction and set a Christian example to the boys he taught.[1]

Not all Barnardo's doss-house adventures ended so happily. Experienced fisherman as he was in these murky waters, sometimes the "human eels" whom he set out to catch, caught him. One night, in a notorious doss, a girl of about seventeen, spying him, shouted out: "Molly! Molly! Here's the bloke as has taken away our pals!" A minute later, Barnardo was surrounded by a ring of infuriated girls who pulled his hair, slapped his face, tore his clothes and tumbled him over on the floor—several holding him down, while others "slippered" him. And when finally he succeeded in shaking off his assailants and dashing

---

[1] See "Rescued for Life: The True Story of a Young Thief," by T. J. Barnardo. Scores of these early pamphlets dealing with Barnardo's experiences in doss-houses, streets, etc., may be seen in the British Museum Library.

away, his glasses were broken, his body bruised and his clothes tattered.[1]

The reason for this punishment was that just previously Barnardo had persuaded some lads to leave this doss-house —where every night abandoned girls came to dance with them—and enter a model lodging for working lads conducted by Quintin Hogg.

The above incidents are representative of scores; but one doss-house experience stands out in the Doctor's life-story as unique. Only once did Barnardo *sleep* in a lodging-house; and the memory of that adventure remained with him always a nightmare.

After long association with lodging-house life, Barnardo determined to sample a "doss" himself; so with the help of Mick Farrel, an effervescent little Irishman of thirteen years, who had slept in nearly all the "doss-houses" of East London, his plans were laid. For days no razor touched his face, and the resulting beard, along with "a little dust and mud judiciously distributed over face, head and hands", formed the first essential of his "make-up". Tattered coat and trousers, a battered "billy-cock", a filthy red handkerchief, dilapidated boots and a bit of rope for suspending his trousers, completed the disguise. So, with the dauntless Mick as pilot, the exploit began.

All the way to K—— Street, Mick bragged of the particular "doss" for which he headed. It was frequented only by "swell chaps", "fellows as did big business, an' no mistake"; yet for fourpence you got "lily-white sheets" and accommodation withal "fit for a king".

In a street both "narrow and foul", Barnardo stood at length before this wonderful "doss". It was a grimy edifice, several stories high, and above the door was a sprawling sign, "Beds for single men, 4d." Barnardo removed his spectacles, slouched the torn "billy-cock" over his eyes, pulled tighter the rope around his trousers, and followed

[1] For a racy account of this incident, see *Night and Day*, August 1st, 1877.

Mick. Soon they were standing before the deputy, who, recognizing Mick, cried: "Hello, youngster! W'ere 'ave you bin to all this time? Stoppin' at yer country 'ouse, I shouldn't wonder!" The "nipper" assured him that such was the case; and, banter over, the deputy directed them to beds 17 and 18, "the werry splendidest anyw'ere to be found!"—one of them "w'ere Gladstone allus sleeps w'en 'e wants to be fashionable!"

On reaching his "bunk", Barnardo put on his glasses and carefully surveyed the scene. The room was grimy and mean; the air was laden with smoke, dust and stench: in the dusky light appeared thirty-four beds, nearly all of them occupied by boys between ten and seventeen. Apparently the fashion was to remove every stitch of clothing before "jumping in", for on all sides protruded bare arms and chests. A search alongside the beds, moreover, increased bewilderment, for in no instance was any clothing in evidence.

This mystery was solved by Mick, who explained that "the fellers" put their clothes under the pillows and took their boots into bed "to keep from gettin' 'em pinched". But shirts received special attention, as Mick now demonstrated. Pulling off his own, he rolled it into a ball and stuffed it under the tick, explaining that this protected it from verminous attack. Such precaution, he announced, was always taken by those initiated into "doss" mysteries. This information vouchsafed, Mick, now divested of every stitch of clothing, cried: "Here goes!" and jumped between his "lily-white" sheets. Then, snugly nestling down, he added: "This is what I calls a proper 'doss', and no mistake!"

Barnardo could not bring himself to follow Mick's example. Most of his clothing he did remove; but at jumping into bed stark naked he drew the line. Curiosity, too, compelled him to examine his "lily-white sheets"; they were of "tick-like calico, as yellow as well could be". But

worse: they were covered with "indelible marks", proclaiming "many a past conflict with insect life".

Yet finally Barnardo plucked up courage and popped
into bed. "The smell of the sheets and pillow" was "over-
powering", but setting his teeth he resolved to brave it
through: and the hour being late and the air steaming hot,
ere long he fell asleep.

"How long I slept I do not know, when I awoke suddenly out of a
horrible dream, in which I thought I had been discovered by my bedroom companions and denounced as a spy, in punishment for which
they had each inflicted vengeance by pricking pins all over my body
and then rubbing in pepper. I appealed against their cruelty; I struggled,
but in vain, and now the pins came to my face, and it seemed as though
in my eyes and nose the pepper was pushed, smarting, burning, almost
maddening me! Aiming a blow at my assailant, I rolled out of bed and
suddenly awoke . . . to find horrible reality in the brief vision, for while
I now lay wakeful in bed, to which I had returned, the sensations which
I had just experienced in my sleep were found to be no mere fancies!
The gas was still burning; I looked at my hand and arm, which were
pricking intolerably. They were covered with blotches and weals.
Alarmed, I sat up in bed. . . . The simple truth is that the sheet was
almost brown with myriads of moving insects which seemed to regard
my body as their rightful property. I called for Mick. He did not hear
me. Leaping from bed and turning the gas-jet on full I noticed that the
floor, the walls, the ceiling were equally discoloured. The place teemed
with them. I was now suffering frightfully; many of the creatures were
perambulating over my person, feasting upon me at leisure. I could
have shouted in my agony. . . ."

Turning to Mick, Barnardo "shook him lustily", crying:
"Get up, get up at once! I must go out, or I shall go mad!"
With difficulty Mick was roused, and learning of his pal's
anxiety piped out: "Why, 'taint nothing! I've seen 'em far
worse . . . there wor twice as many!" Barnardo, almost
beside himself with pain, was in no mood to argue. Quickly
he persuaded Mick to don his scanty clothes, and without
delay sought refuge outside. But before gaining liberty
they had to appease the deputy, disgruntled at being disturbed. Mick was equal to the task. His "pal", he explained,
"turned sick and couldn't stop. But 'any'ow, we've paid
our browns, and don't want none of your jaw!"

Once outside, Barnardo "again and again" inhaled "fresh draughts of the cool night air". The street was narrow and mean; but it seemed "paradise" compared with the "steaming fumes of that vile den".

Reaching home, he immediately took a hot bath; then, looking in a glass, he had a shock: "I write soberly when I declare that none of my friends would have recognized the face I saw reflected there. Puffed and swollen, red and livid . . . a more professionally belligerent-looking countenance could scarcely be imagined. Quite three weeks elapsed before I was in a state to be visible. . . ."

Mick, however, still contended that Barnardo's experience was second-rate: "Why, sir, I've know'd bugs that cute they'd run up a wall and get on the ceilin' and drop down 'andy on a feller when they couldn't climb up a bedstead."

But Barnardo's adventures of faith were in no sense limited to the precincts of lodging-houses and "pubs". In the early days he was known as "The Young Man with the Lantern"—and with reason; for between midnight and 3 a.m., by the light of his "bull's eye", from sheds, stables, barges, barrels and crates, he rescued hundreds of forlorn youngsters, leading them with paternal solicitude to his Shelter of Love. But even when not so employed, rarely did he rest before the small hours, and occasionally not till dawn. His friend, Dr. Milne, said of him: "While others slept, he wrought and studied."

Sometimes, during the Mission's infancy, when Barnardo was preaching in the streets or carrying banners at the head of a procession, buckets of slops were poured upon him from upper windows. Often rotten apples, tomatoes or eggs were shied at his head, and not always could he dodge a good shot. More than once, dead cats, rabbits, or rats were hurled down the skylights of halls in which he was preaching; while the humiliation of having his hat knocked off and kicked into the gutter came his way more often than he could recall. Such experiences, however, never dis-

THE GIRLS' VILLAGE HOME

1. No Signs "Keep off the Grass"   2. A peep at some of the shrubbery
3. Near the Girls' Church   4. A street in the village

OTHER ASPECTS OF THE "VILLAGE HOME"

1. A verandah of the Australasian Hospital   2. Some village girls at drill
3. The village greets the dawn   4. Sunshine treatment

couraged him; they seemed only to purge his spirit and increase his zeal. A fellow-medical student, who himself smiled at Barnardo's "too rigid sense of duty", admits that on his return from Christian exploits his face "wore its happiest expression—not that of triumph, but of the joy of battle that remains with the resourceful and strong".

*   *   *   *   *

Among Barnardo's early ventures none was more courageous, or more latent with future significance, than his rescue work among *girls*. His Homes started their labours solely among boys; and until 1873 no provision was made for the reception of girls. But experience forced upon him the conviction that until facilities were provided for the rescue of homeless girls his task was but half done. Repeatedly, when visiting common lodging-houses, he discovered girls of thirteen and fourteen with illegitimate babies, and time after time he had been implored by rescued boys to help their destitute sisters. The very titles of certain of his early pamphlets reflect the complexity and evasiveness of the girl-problem he faced. *How I Stole Two Girls. . . . They Never Had a Home, How I Fished for and Caught Her.* These are suggestive of scores of pamphlets in which he sets forth the problem of rescuing destitute girls and those in immoral surroundings.

How, then, was this problem met? Under what conditions began his Girl-Rescue Work?

These questions lead us back to Barnardo's marriage. During his honeymoon there appeared in *The Christian* a forceful letter from Mr. Cheyne Brady, suggesting that the best wedding-present which could be bestowed upon the bride and groom would be the creation of a Fund to establish a "Girls' Home": to which suggestion Barnardo replied that "to open a Girls' Home . . . has *for two years* been the desire of my heart".

After this, developments were rapid. Mr. John Sands

presented "Mossford Lodge", a small estate in Barkingside, Essex, as a seat for the new scheme, while other friends donated funds sufficient to remodel and furnish the buildings. Barnardo and his bride accordingly returned from their honeymoon to live in Mossford Lodge; and by October, 1873, renovations were sufficiently advanced to admit the first twelve girls.

A year later, about fifty erstwhile destitute girls were living at Mossford Lodge; and still the Institution grew. But perplexing problems were in store. The life-stories of the first inmates were "appalling in their revelation of degradation and neglect". One girl had "twice attempted to take her own life"; another, aged nine, "had filled a baby's mouth with sand, and then sat on its face". The Home, too, was at first conducted on the barrack system, which meant the aggregation of many girls under one roof, and the conformity of their lives to an institutional plan. Hence disillusionment!

Ere long there was thrust upon Barnardo a discovery which left no doubt that his Girl-Rescue programme had been ill-conceived:

"One night I overheard some vile conversation in what we thought was our happy *Christian* Home, and then in a moment I realized what were the hidden forces of evil at work, undoing all we hoped had been attained. Indeed, I was made to feel, as I listened with horror, that probably I had done harm, not good. . . . No one can imagine the overwhelming hopelessness of the outlook, which almost seemed to crush me as I realized that the fair plans I had formed were producing such results!"

Barnardo was stunned. All his plans for destitute girls had gone astray. Must he drop this department of his work and confess defeat? He betook himself to prayer: "I told our Father I was willing to give it all up at once and to acknowledge . . . I had been wrong. With that, my peace of mind was restored." But light had not yet dawned; still he sought guidance. Then, one night, with this problem pressing heavily on his mind, he dreamed; and in his dream, as by revelation, his problem was solved.

Barnardo's widow has related to the author her recollections of that memorable night:

"In the small hours, my husband awakened with a start, calling: 'Syrie, Syrie! it has been revealed to me how to deal with our girls.' Then, crying: 'Psalm lxviii. 6, "God setteth the solitary in families" ', he jumped out of bed, turned on the light, and reached for his Bible to verify the words. They were accurate. Returning to bed, he related to me in jubilation his dream. 'I saw', he said, 'an ivy-mantled cottage surrounded by flowers, and a light gleaming from its bay-window. I peeped through. The room upon which I gazed presented every appearance of a cosy, happy home. The furniture was simple, but tasteful; beautiful pictures were on the walls; and in the centre of the room was a large table beside which was seated a happy, matronly looking woman, around whom clustered fifteen or sixteen girls, their faces radiant with joy. I now looked more intently, and perceived that the woman was reading aloud from a Family Bible open at Psalm lxviii. Listening, I heard her read verse six: "God setteth the solitary in families." Arrested by these words, I looked carefully into the girls' faces, and behold every face I recognized as that of a girl in our barracks; but their countenances seemed transformed.' "

His dream told, Barnardo exclaimed: "Syrie, this is a revelation! God means that our girls should dwell in family cottages with 'loving mothers' to superintend their homes!" On arising, Barnardo wrote to *The Christian*, setting forth his vision of cottage homes for girls, and petitioning help to breathe into it life. But days followed the publication of this appeal with no result; and Barnardo, fearing he had acted rashly, felt ill at ease. Had he been unduly influenced by this dream? Was it but the psychological reflex of an overwrought brain? In this perplexed state, feeling the need of spiritual refreshment, he betook himself to Oxford to attend a religious conference.

On the station platform he met "a Christian brother" whom he knew to be one of "the godliest of men"—"a man whose very face told you something of the peace of God which reigned within". This gentleman was setting off for the same conference, so entering an empty compartment he turned to the Doctor and, as though reading his thoughts, asked with "very sincere sympathy" regarding his work. Barnardo made a clean breast of all his doubts; then, poignantly, his companion inquired: "If God shows you that your proposed scheme is too large, and that you should give it up, are you prepared to give it up?"

For a moment Barnardo pondered; but feeling that without "God's approval and blessing" it were better not to succeed from an "earthly point of view", he answered firmly: "Yes, I am quite prepared." His friend replied: "We are going to Oxford for spiritual refreshment. Let us here, in this carriage, alone, kneel down and commit your case to God, and let us ask Him, if it be His will, to show you clearly before you leave Oxford whether you should go on or turn back." Both knelt down and "committed the case of the children to God". They arose "lightened and refreshed". On reaching Oxford it was arranged that this friend breakfast the following morning with Barnardo, in the latter's hotel; and so they parted.

Next morning Barnardo, while dressing, heard a tap on his door. Thinking the servant had arrived with hot water, he cried: "Come in!" A man thrust in his head. "His hair was all dishevelled; he was evidently not yet fully dressed. 'Is your name Barnardo?' he asked. I said 'Yes'. . . . 'You are thinking of building a village for little girls at Ilford, are you not? You want some cottages?' . . . I said 'Yes, yes.' He asked: 'Have you got any?'— never coming in beyond putting his head through the door. I replied, 'No—not yet.' . . . 'Well,' he cried, 'put me down for the first cottage. Good morning'—and away he went."

Barnardo was flabbergasted; he did not even know the man's name. But, recovering himself, he rushed half-dressed down the corridor; overtook the stranger; brought him back to his room; and there were completed the arrangements for building the first cottage in the "Girls' Village Home". This donor had read Barnardo's appeal in *The Christian*, and, discussing the matter with his wife, they decided to erect a cottage to the memory of their own little daughter who recently had died. The man had come to Oxford for the conference, and learning that Barnardo was in the hotel, and that their rooms were on the same floor, without stopping fully to dress he had rushed to announce his gift.

At eight o'clock, in the breakfast-room, Barnardo met his train companion. Before the gift was mentioned, sensing the joy in Barnardo's soul, he quietly quoted the text: "It shall come to pass that before they call, I will answer; and while they are yet speaking, I will hear."

Such is the romance of the first cottage in the Girls' Village Home; but others, whose origin is scarcely less arresting, followed in quick succession. On June 9th, 1875, the foundation-stones of eleven cottages were laid by Lord Aberdeen; and on July 9th of the following year the Village Home, with thirteen cottages and a laundry, was declared open by Lord Cairns.

Thus did Barnardo's dream spring into life; and remarkable was the success of this cottage scheme. Soon there grew up on the green adjoining Mossford Lodge one of the most captivating villages anywhere to be seen; yet the cottage, with the cottage-mother and her family, was the unit out of which the whole village evolved. Moreover, the village plan conformed entirely to Barnardo's dream. Creepers soon mantled the walls; flowers, hedges and shrubs became a prominent feature of the village surroundings; every

cottage was tastefully furnished; each, too, was provided
with its Family Bible; and each had its mother, around
whom clustered a family of happy girls.[1]

The growth of this village was phenomenal. At Barnardo's
death, twenty-nine years after its opening, it boasted nearly
seventy cottages, many of which were, like the first, erected
"In Memoriam". Phenomenal, too, has been its volume of
service, for before its founder "passed on" it had housed,
clothed, fed, mothered, educated and placed in employment—nine thousand girls, while already its lassies in residence numbered far above one thousand. Yet these figures
represent but a fraction of the destitute *girls* rescued by the
Homes before the Doctor's death. Barnardo died at sixty
years of age, having rescued sixty thousand children; and
nearly 40 per cent. were girls.

But returning to the early days, each new expansion
brought with it new challenges, new responsibilities, new
problems; and from none did Barnardo flinch. A pessi-
mist, it has been said, is one who sees danger in every
opportunity; an optimist one who sees opportunity in
every danger. By this standard Barnardo was a thoroughgoing optimist. As early as 1874 he saw that his work had
grown to such proportions he stood in DANGER of losing
personal contact with his helpers. Undaunted, he bought
and edited *The Children's Treasury*, an organ affording him
an *opportunity* of interpreting to them the child-problem he
faced. Shortly after purchasing the "Edinburgh Castle", he
realized the danger to mission work which issued from the
"Dublin Castle", a monstrous gin-palace in Mile End Road;
so, biding his time, he bought it—transforming it into a
Mission Centre and Coffee Palace, scarcely less successful
than the "Edinburgh Castle". Late in 1874, desiring to con-
vene a representative public meeting, he sensed the danger
that neither the Great Hall of "Edinburgh Castle" nor the
Revival Tent would hold the concourse who might attend;

[1] For an impression of the Girls' Village Home to-day, see Chapter II.

hence the opportunity for wider plans : with the Rev. C. H. Spurgeon's support, the meeting was convoked in the Metropolitan Tabernacle, into which crowded five thousand people anxious to manifest interest in the Mission. Again, by 1875, he felt that if continually he was tied to the environment of his own work, it was liable to become stereotyped; consequently this danger in turn he transmuted into opportunity by a visit to Scotland and Ireland, where he studied every effort being put forth in those lands for the nurture of orphan and homeless children. And no point of interest escaped his quick, critical eye.

The vicissitudes of those early years, however, form a story much too long to be recorded here. In March, 1876, Barnardo, despite a hundred pressing duties, faced his final medical exams, and, passing creditably, was made a Licentiate of the Royal College of Surgeons, Edinburgh. Consequently he registered as a London practitioner, and according to medical etiquette was correctly styled "Doctor" Barnardo; though it should be remembered that probably not one medical man in ten has the *legal* right to call himself "Doctor", for but a small percentage ever take the M.D. Degree.[1]

Again, in 1876, Barnardo's work being now recognized by experts, he was invited by the Social Science Congress, assembling in Liverpool, to read a paper on *Preventive Homes* before that august assembly. The same year, "to free cabmen from the temptations of public-houses", he inaugurated the country's first Cabmen's Shelter with cheap meals, free reading material, etc., and it was constructed on the same model as the shelters seen all over London to-day. That year, too, at 19, Stepney Causeway, he opened an Infirmary for Sick Children, which gave birth to several Barnardo Hospitals; while during the

[1] Barnardo, like most medical students, was styled "Doctor" long before he received his medical diploma. Some time, however, before receiving his British qualification, he won a German degree; in 1879 he was elected a *Fellow* of the Royal College of Surgeons, Edinburgh.

same twelve months several Mission centres extended their bounds.

January, 1877, marks the origin of *Night and Day*—the Home's official organ—and from its establishment Barnardo, till death, was editor of this journal, whose thousands of readers were scattered over the world. By this time, too, the Mission's deaconess work, started in 1875, had so grown that two Bow Road residences were occupied by the "Protestant Evangelical Deaconess House", from which eighteen to twenty-five educated women in residence acted as ministering angels to the East End Poor.[1]

But while the East End Juvenile Mission was thus forging on, it, like all aggressive movements, made enemies as well as friends. And whereas some of its opponents were sincere, the majority, following the lead of dismissed servants, enraged publicans, general scandal-mongers, and credulous busybodies, only kindled the fires of malice. But although Barnardo was now forced to pass through the "burning fiery furnace", not a hair of his head was singed; and when finally the embers of controversy had died out, he, like Henry Ward Beecher, learned to thank God for his enemies, because, exasperating as temporarily they were to be, in the end they proved of greater value than many a friend.

Why, however, anticipate? To the facts of this intensely human drama, wherein even Barnardo's honour stood on trial, we now must turn.

---

[1] See *Something Attempted: Something Done*, pp. 219–223.

CHAPTER IX

ON TRIAL

BARNARDO's very success threatened him with shipwreck. Eight years after his arrival in London, and four years after the opening of "Stepney Causeway", the annual income of his Mission had mounted to £23,500. Indeed, by 1874, the Church, the Day and Evening Ragged Schools, the Sunday-Schools, the Temperance Guilds, the Edinburgh Coffee Palace, the Homes, the Industrial Training schemes, the Shoeblack and Messenger Brigades—in short, every department of his activity, seemed thoroughly established. Yet trouble was brewing.

Prior to 1874 many "Jonahs" predicted for the Mission a complete collapse; but now that their predictions seemed remote, certain of them set about to engineer its ruin.

The first suggestion of trouble expressed itself through vague whisperings and rumours; yet so sinister was their effect that soon it was obvious hidden foes were at work. Mrs. Barnardo received many anonymous letters accusing her husband of the most monstrous sins, and stating that among all "whited sepulchres" he was chief; while Barnardo himself received as many, tarring his wife and workers with the same brush.[1]

Now, had slander stopped here, it probably would have killed itself and that quickly, for Barnardo might well have ignored personal attacks, so malicious and insane. But it did not stop here; soon rumours were abroad that he was maltreating and half starving "his children". For instance, although corporal punishment in the Homes was rare, being permitted only to the schoolmasters, gossips asserted that youngsters were often severely beaten; while it was rumoured that underground were dark, damp, vermin-ridden cells into which refractory lads were hurled and detained for

---

[1] These facts were explained to the author by Mrs. Barnardo herself.

weeks on end. And to make these stories more lurid, it was added that rats infested the cells and bit the boys' toes; that mud oozed through cracks of the floor; that "victims" were denied the use of beds; that their only diet was bread and water; and that occasions were known when the door of a boy's cell was nailed up for days.

With these concoctions "going the rounds", open-minded people began to ask if they contained any truth: "Can all this smoke have arisen without fire? Is Barnardo ignorant of these rumours? Or has he no reply?" At this stage, Barnardo felt such stories could no longer be ignored; so with the help of friends he traced most of them to their source. Infuriated publicans, like the Ephesian idol-makers who rose up against St. Paul because his preaching was killing "their trade", proved the chief inventors of these libellous tales. But their diabolical ingenuity stood not alone. Behind them were certain of Barnardo's old employees who, dismissed because of laziness, inefficiency or dishonesty, sought to wreak vengeance on him by circulating reports that "his children" were atrociously treated, and so intimidated as to fear to speak.

But more vicious than any tales started by publicans or dismissed employees were those emanating from bestial parents, whose progeny Barnardo had reared. Parents who had turned their children upon the streets, and would have sold them for a keg of gin, seeing them sturdy, educated, and skilled in a trade, and desiring now to exploit their labour, joined the chorus of abuse, attributing to Barnardo atrocious cruelty toward their "dear bairns".

These attacks, however, were augmented from another source. No sooner had they been whispered about, than they were taken up by scandal-mongers whose delight it is to tear to shreds the reputation of anyone commanding public esteem. And so furiously were the fires of scandal fanned that Barnardo was soon portrayed as an arch-hypocrite and thoroughgoing scoundrel. By "preying upon the public", it was asserted, he was "living on the fat of the land"; and of all his Homes' inmates "none was ever so destitute" as he himself would have been, save for the moneys he pocketed for private use.

Now whether the tongues of publicans, dismissed servants, debauched parents and general scandal-mongers began to wag on their own account, or whether they were encouraged by persons more responsible, is a mystery. But one thing is certain. When absurd stories started up, they were studiously collected by some who should have been Barnardo's friends. Thus the attack was perpetrated from two fronts. And why?

Barnardo had built up a Mission which already was attracting wide attention and winning wide support. Nevertheless, he was not yet thirty years old, and many social workers of twice that age, who had laboured long among the East End poor, saw little harvest for their toil. The temptation to jealousy, therefore, was great; and certain workers succumbed to it. Who was this stripling that his work should be rising to fame while theirs struggled lamely on? Why should he be gaining wide support when their labours remained obscure? These questions asked, the temptation to ask others was strong. Could all the rumours about Barnardo's character be devoid of fact? Would the many stories concerning his maltreatment of children have got abroad unless they contained some truth? If Barnardo was carrying on this charity without fee or hire, whence came his livelihood? Did not the fact that he was his own treasurer look suspicious?

Barnardo, like his patron Lord Shaftesbury—indeed like all great leaders—was a strong personality, whose vehemence intensified all he touched. Most subjects to him were hot or cold; and none in his presence could long remain luke-warm. Hence, possessing this peremptory temperament, together with a remarkable tenacity of purpose, his life demanded a verdict from all who intimately crossed his path. To such, neutrality was impossible; they greatly hated or greatly loved him.

Among the East End social workers in whose breast Barnardo provoked feelings of hatred was one who, signing himself "A Protestant Dissenter", published in the summer of 1875 a ruthless attack on Barnardo and his work. Cruelty, hypocrisy, chicanery and general knavery were all included in his charge; and though the attack stated much, it insinuated more. Barnardo, as reflected in this picture, was a wolf in sheep's clothing.

Stung to the quick by this indictment, Barnardo was unable to hold his peace. The volcanic element in his nature assumed control, and discretion he cast to the winds. Consulting with certain excitable supporters, he quickly collected what information he could regarding the authorship of this libel. Then, neglecting the counsel of cooler advisers that he do nothing to stir further strife, but rather wait patiently till the onslaught had spent itself, Barnardo, on terms of mutual secrecy, passed over this information to a friend of even warmer temperament than himself, on the understanding that he have complete liberty in formulating a reply.

This reply took the form of two anonymous letters, both signed "A Clerical Junius"; [1] and neither was a model of self-control. The first,[2] however, in spite of much petulance, observed some measure of good sense. Personalities were not dragged in, and counterblasts of gossip were not hurled at Barnardo's foes. But the purpose of the letter was not achieved; far from silencing the attack it augmented strife. So "Clerical Junius" hit out again. On September 25th, a fortnight after the publication of his first letter, there appeared in *The Tower Hamlets Independent* his second letter; and, as by this time the temperature had risen substantially,

---

[1] This name was taken from the famous eighteenth-century anonymous letters of 1768–1770, signed "Junius", and attacking the Grafton Ministry.
[2] Published on September 11th, 1875, in *The East London Observer*.

judgment was trampled underfoot. "Clerical Junius" was now almost as violent as Barnardo's assailants, and by vigorously returning abuse for abuse he succeeded only in embarrassing the friend he desired to defend.

Now, in passing, it should be observed that, owing to the vow of secrecy between Barnardo and "Clerical Junius", the authorship of those documents has never been made public, and only two persons alive to-day could penetrate that secret; both of whom are pledged to silence. But this much is now known: the writer was an Irish D.D. of considerable influence, who for years had shown an active interest in the Mission's endeavour. And the fact that he was a warm friend of Barnardo created a delicate situation later on.

Far, then, from silencing the mad onsets upon Barnardo's work, this second letter, by answering invective with invective, inflamed passions to a raging blaze. Immediately Barnardo's opponents threw out the accusation that "Clerical Junius" was none other than Barnardo himself; so forthwith they accused him of gilding his own work and abusing those who criticized him in any way. The valiant champion, therefore, in his attempt to lay low Barnardo's foes, had only stripped from his hero his finest defence—a trustful calm.

Barnardo, on seeing this second letter in print, realized with a shock his defender's lack of self-control, and, though he appreciated the motive behind his friend's reply, he nevertheless felt duty-bound to repudiate the letter. Consequently, on October 2nd, in *The East London Observer*, there appeared a communication signed by Barnardo, in which he not only disowned the authorship of both "Clerical Junius" letters, but denounced the second as "atrocious" and "abominable", adding: "Well may I say, 'Save me from my friends!' For such friends would ruin the best Cause."

* * * * *

To relieve the passionate situation following the publication of the second "Clerical Junius" letter, conciliators got quickly to work; and for a time it seemed as though the storm-clouds had passed. But the problems at stake were in no sense solved; jealousies and animosities were not subdued; and resentment smouldered steadily underground. True, for nearly two years there reigned comparative calm, but it was the calm before the storm; for all the while Barnardo's enemies were searching for missiles of attack.

The vehicle of the new assault was a shilling booklet of sixty-two octavo pages, entitled *Dr. Barnardo's Homes, containing startling Revelations*; the charges being set forth on the title-page:

> "1. Management and Character.
> 2. Appeals grounded upon Misstatements of facts.
> 3. Deceptive photographs.
> 4. Taking credit for other men's Workmanship.
> 5. The authorship of letters written under a forged name.
> 6. Doctor's Degree as a Physician used without a Diploma or Authority."

Under these headings, every sort of indictment was levelled against Barnardo; while the spirit in which the pamphlet was penned may be surmised from a sentence attached as a sort of text: "He who sees not these abuses is *absolutely blind*, and he who attempts to excuse them is *absolutely insane*."

This booklet declared that Barnardo had for years, in spite of the protests of friends, boarded in the home of a drunken, degraded woman, and had recommended the place to others. It stated that more than once he had been seen accompanying intoxicated, immoral women to their homes, walking with them arm in arm; and only one inference was drawn. Never did it enter the author's mind that Barnardo might be following in the steps of One derided as "a friend of publicans and sinners"; One who permitted "an outcast woman" to wash His feet with her tears, and wipe them with the hair of her head; One who moved lovingly among sinners, that He might free them from the bondage of sin, yet kept Himself unspotted from the world.

But reflections upon Barnardo's moral character were among the least savage of these attacks. Some of the Home youngsters, it was affirmed, were imprisoned from three to eighteen days on end in "a filthy underground cellar", which was "perfectly dark, very damp and full of rats". Their boots, it was asserted, were taken from them, and such food as they were allowed was pushed through holes in the cells. Again, parents of children in the Homes, it was averred, would take their oath that their youngsters were being worked to death and half starved; while also, according to this indictment, Barnardo children were being raised as pagans without any training in morals or religion.

The pith of the attack, however, lay in the field of finance. If, as Barnardo had avowed, several of his industries and brigades were practically self-supporting, what need had he for more than £20,000 a year? And how did he spend that sum? These questions were a prelude to charges of swindle. Neglecting the fact that Barnardo, from the first, had told his contributors that the names of no donors would be published, the author threw out the accusation that Barnardo's whole system of finance was designed to permit the misappropriation of funds. Then, to prove his deduction, he asked how Barnardo lived—if not on moneys sent him for the Homes—seeing that when he came to London he had roomed in humble quarters, whereas now he kept up quite a presentable house. In a word, the booklet threw out a dozen suggestions that Barnardo was a thorough-going fraud. So, knowing nothing and apparently caring to know nothing of the fact that every year since his arrival in London Barnardo had an allowance from his father; that in 1871 he had a gift of £1,500 from the same source; that Mrs. Barnardo had a private income of several hundred pounds per annum; and that not infrequently Barnardo was paid for articles contributed to the Press, this pamphleteer trumpeted the charge that the Director of the East End Juvenile Mission was a mountebank, fleecing the charitable public with sentimental tales.

Barnardo's appeals for funds, he maintained, were based on sensational stories, dire exaggerations and gross misstatements; while, as for photographs sent out to illustrate the work, it was charged they were "fakes", designed to prey upon the sympathetic public. Indeed, it was averred that Barnardo habitually ripped children's clothing and bedabbled their bodies with soot, preparatory to photographing them as actual instances of street-arabs admitted to his fold! And such deceptions, the booklet avowed, were typical of the whole system of appeal through which the Mission collected funds.

Another count was based on the printing of certain bills to advertise special Moody and Sankey Meetings. According to this charge, certain posters had been distributed bearing notice that they were printed by Barnardo boys, whereas it was now claimed that really they were produced by professional printers.

As for the "Clerical Junius" letters, most stoutly was it contended that they were written by Barnardo himself; while finally the pamphlet challenged Barnardo to produce credentials entitling him to be known as a Doctor, maintaining that he was masquerading behind an academic distinction to which he had no title—another proof that the said "Doctor" was an impostor!

This frenzied attack could have but one effect. A storm broke, and all hopes of peace were vain till it had run its course. The Charity Organisation Society now placed Barnardo's Mission on its Cautionary List, and until some disinterested investigation was held, Barnardo stood accused before the world.

A libel action seemed the only avenue open; but a pronounced difficulty stood in Barnardo's way. The influence of Brethrenism was still an active factor in his life, and to

Brethren all litigation was sinful. What then could he do? This problem caused him much anxiety, but it was finally solved. The East End Juvenile Mission represented his heart interest, his life-work; it was the child of his hopes, labours and prayers, so if its existence were threatened, even litigation must be endured. Happily, however, intermediaries set to work with despatch, and soon it was agreed that an Arbitration Board, acting under a Rule of Court, be set up with full authority to take evidence and pronounce judgment.

This Board, then, was arranged by mutual consent, the men appointed being wholly disinterested and eminently qualified for their task. They were: Mr. John Maule, Q.C., Recorder of Leeds; the Rev. John Cale Miller, D.D., Canon of Rochester; and Mr. William Graham, ex-M.P. for Glasgow.

In June, 1877, the Arbitration Board began its sittings, both sides being represented by Counsel. The author of the pamphlet, the nominal plaintiff, placed his case in the hands of Mr. St. John Wontner, who was backed by able associates; Barnardo, as defendant, was represented by Mr. A. H. Thesiger, Q.C., and two supporters.

For thirty-eight full days this Arbitration Board sat, during which time all the charges hurled against Barnardo were examined and re-examined. Twenty days were devoted exclusively to the prosecution's assault, forty-seven witnesses being called to substantiate their case; while, following this onslaught, eighteen days were consumed by the defence, who called sixty-five witnesses. Then, on the thirty-ninth day, Barnardo, under cross-examination, refused to reveal the identity of "Clerical Junius"; and that for obvious reasons. "Clerical Junius", he admitted frankly, was a personal friend. He admitted, too, that much material contained in *The Letters* he himself had supplied. The second letter, moreover, which in the heat of the moment he had allowed to be printed, but which, upon due reflection, he described as "atrocious" and "abominable", placed him in an embarrassing position. The writer was a clergyman of the Church of England, who had undertaken the writing of these letters as a defence of his friend, and *absolute secrecy* had been pledged. Then, too, the fact that Barnardo, in repudiating the spirit of the second letter, had written: "Well may I say, 'Save me from my friends!' . . ." made the situation doubly delicate. In such circumstances, to reveal the name of "Clerical Junius", who apparently had repented his vindictiveness, meant to Barnardo the betrayal of a friend; and to such action he would not stoop. The situation was unfortunate; but he refused to reveal the author's name.

Barnardo therefore remaining adamant, his opponents vehemently protested that this information was vital; so a scene ensued. Astute enough to realize that already their case was hopelessly exploded, and desiring an opportunity to save their faces, the prosecutors at this point picked up their papers and walked out of Court, thus striving to create the impression that justice was hampered.

This action brought the hearing abruptly to an end; but already all vital questions had been thoroughly debated. Moreover, it was now the *third* month since the Board began its sittings, and meanwhile all three Arbitrators had visited every Branch of Barnardo's work. Having, therefore, the evidence of all witnesses before them, including the reports of a first-class firm of chartered accountants, who had examined Barnardo's accounts, and having themselves acquired a first-hand knowledge of the Mission's activity, the Arbitrators proceeded to pass judgment.

The marshalling, however, of the arguments upon which their conclusions were based was no mean task; so five weeks elapsed before their verdict was declared: and meantime the disgruntled accusers left no stone unturned. But to little avail. On October 15th, 1877, four months after the Court opened, its Judgment (a closely reasoned document of ten thousand words, signed by all three Arbitrators without reservation or dissent) appeared; and with what effect?

The "Barnardo Institutions" the Arbitration pronounced: "Real and valuable Charities, worthy of public confidence and support." The cardinal charge, misappropriation of funds, was found to contain no shred of truth. Chartered Accountants declared the Mission's finance to be characterized by "thorough efficiency", and the Board could find "no traces" of any mishandling of funds. The "general management" was proclaimed "on the whole, judicious", while the charges of cruelty, semi-starvation and overwork were found to be without the least foundation in fact. Again, the accusation that the Homes were rearing pagans, devoid of religious training, proved absurd; the Arbitrators were "satisfied" with the moral and religious instruction imparted. The general schooling, the system of discipline and the industrial training, moreover, were found to be efficiently conducted and productive of good results; while, as for the attacks on Barnardo's moral character, they were found to be gossip of the most malignant sort.

But, reverting to the crux of the case, namely, the expenditure of the moneys entrusted to Barnardo, the Arbitrators' findings were as conclusive as the Homes' friends could have wished: "The statements of accounts are printed yearly and sent to those donors who supply their names and addresses, and they are requested to receive for any sum they contribute a printed receipt bearing a number, with which they can compare the list in the yearly statements and reports, and there find recorded their respective donations, and thus be assured that their gifts have been duly accounted for. Mr. H. Bishop, of the Firm of Turquand & Young, has, in addition, personally investigated the system of bookkeeping and accounts, and gave evidence before us of its thorough efficiency. There are no traces of any part of these donations and earnings, or of any other such funds, having been, as suggested under this head, expended by Dr.

Barnardo in his own house and in household expenditure, or improperly appropriated to his own personal use and benefit."

On certain minor counts the verdict was not so sweeping. Regarding "deceptive photographs", Barnardo admitted frankly that on rare occasions he had children "made up" for "composite" pictures, but he contended that the results were perfectly true to type, and by no means exaggerated the proportions of his problem. Nearly all the pictures by which he illustrated his work were photographs of children exactly as they appeared on arrival at the Homes; but it had to be remembered that many pitiable applicants arrived by night, when no photograph could be taken; and often desperate "cases" had to be provided with clothes before ever they reached the Homes. Such facts the Arbitrators fully considered; but they contended that *any* sort of "composite" photograph laid Barnardo open to the charge of producing "artistic fiction", and such procedure, they recommended, should in future cease.

As for the Mission's schools, the Arbitrators advised that they be placed under Government inspection, and so receive Government aid. Concerning the charge of brutal punishments, it was found to be so exaggerated and tinged with malice as to lose all contact with reality. For a time the Homes had, in punishment of the worst offences, resorted to a system of solitary confinement; but its conditions bore no discernible relationship to the charges levelled by the plaintiff. The only case, for instance, of a door ever having been nailed up on a boy was on a certain occasion, for half an hour, during the mending of a lock; and other charges of "brutal punishments" were found equally divorced from fact. But, bearing in mind the susceptibility of the Homes to public criticism, the Arbitrators advised that punishments should, in future, be of a still milder type.

On the "Clerical Junius" count the Court expressed a unanimous opinion that Barnardo was *not* the writer of these letters; but, in view of the fact that admittedly he had provided much of the material on which they were based, a measure of moral responsibility for them was placed at his door. The bill-printing charge was pronounced "satisfactorily" answered; while the "*Doctor*" point proved but a storm in a teacup. Barnardo, like most medical students, was known as "Doctor" long before obtaining his diploma, and naturally the load of his Mission labours substantially postponed the date on which he took his final examination; yet more than a year before the Arbitration Court sat, he had won his medical diploma from Edinburgh University, and was registered as a London practitioner, while before that he had a German Degree. Hence this charge carried no weight.

The concluding sentences of the Award express the gist of that document as a whole:

"We are of opinion that . . . the 'Barnardo Institutions' are real and valuable Charities and worthy of public confidence and support. That as regards the conduct and management of these Institutions—the general management has been, on the whole, judicious; but, with a view to obviate the recurrence of controversies; to strengthen the claim of these Charities to public confidence; to ensure their *continued* efficiency and well-being, we recommend that the Trustees should as soon as possible seek to engage the services of a Working Committee of gentlemen, who should be associated with the Director in administering these Institutions, and should take a real and active interest in and oversight of the Homes, as well as afford to the Director their advice and assistance upon the many questions that must constantly arise in the experience of such a work, and that such an alteration be made in The Deeds of Trust as may be necessary to this end. The necessity of such a Committee is enhanced by the fact that the authority and discipline of such Homes appear to be self-constituted and to have no legal sanction in the cases where parents and guardians are not parties to the children's admission."

Such was the tenor of the Arbitrators' Award. But one point we must specially note. The Board expressed an "earnest hope" that its judgment would be accepted as final, and that "all defamatory charges" would immediately cease.

The Award, when time for its perusal had elapsed, met

with warm applause, being on all sides acclaimed an equitable judgment, based squarely upon facts. But to digest this tome of ten thousand words required time; hence four days followed its publication before *The Times* ventured upon even a synopsis of its verdict; then a day later, October 20th, in a leading article a column and a half long, it issued its own reactions.

This lucid and fair-minded article outlined the struggle from its source. Pointing out that early in its development Barnardo's work enlisted the support of powerful patrons, "among them the Earl of Shaftesbury", it traced the remarkable growth of his Mission and the romance of its support. Then, sketching the campaign of attack, it led up to the Arbitration and reviewed the Award.

The "case for the attack", stated *The Times*, was "fully laid before the Arbitration"; and on "all the gravest of the original charges" Barnardo was "*fully* acquitted". There was "no proof of dishonest management or of intentional concealment of the real state of the Homes"; and the Arbitrators were "satisfied with the moral and religious instruction" imparted. Again *The Times* pointed out that the Award proclaimed the Mission a "real philanthropy" with "a real title to public support"; and, appealing to Barnardo's Trustees immediately to accept the Arbitrators' suggestion, and appoint a Committee to confer with The Director in the Homes' management, the "leader" proceeded to call for peace. Now that the Award was given, it pleaded that "the parties who have asked for it" would have "the good sense to acquiesce in it".

In the light of the Arbitrators' Judgment and its reception, the Charity Organisation Society removed immediately the East End Juvenile Mission—now increasingly known as "Dr. Barnardo's Homes" [1]—from its Cautionary List; while

---

[1] The publicity given to Barnardo's work by the Arbitration caused the name "Dr. Barnardo's Homes" to be popularly accepted as the title of the Mission, though, of course, the official name was unchanged.

also certain organs of the Press which, prior to the Arbitration, had attacked Barnardo hammer and tongs, now generously recanted and became stalwart supporters of his work. Nor were these changes of front as remarkable as they may seem; for when the Award is carefully perused, its dominant impression is one of awe that a single individual could possibly have built up such a great rescue-work and made so few mistakes. Admittedly, even after the publication of the Award, a few individuals—cast in the mould of those who "strain at a gnat and swallow a camel"—still attacked Barnardo; but by ninety-nine out of every hundred open-minded people he was now recognized as a national asset—as the prophet and friend of the Outcast Child.

After the storm, therefore, calm reigned once again: and Barnardo's Homes, having like a sturdy oak weathered the blast, stood forth before the world an Institution tested and tried in every branch, yet wholly undishonoured.

CHAPTER X

FROM TRIAL TO TRIUMPH

OFTEN has it been man's experience that out of evil hath proceeded good, and from the mouth of the slanderer hath been established truth.

Scarcely was the Arbitration over when the significance of this paradox dawned upon Barnardo. Having passed through one of the most scathing ordeals to which a man could be subjected, and having fully established his own integrity and the utility of his Mission, he was now in a position to embark upon new and even greater adventures for the destitute child. Not only had the Arbitration acquitted him of every major charge and vindicated his honesty: scarcely less important, it had made plain both the strength and weakness of his work. During the twenty days' assault, every department of his Mission had been subjected to the battering-ram; and wherever a spot proved vulnerable, there the battle raged. Consequently, from the fury of his enemies, Barnardo discovered what he might never have discovered through the kindness of friends—the weak spots in his organization and the breaches in the constitution of his Homes.

Chief among these vulnerable places was the autocratic basis upon which his whole superstructure had been reared. And that, in the light of its origin, was natural. When he began to teach in "Ernest Street", he found himself hampered on every side by the pedantry of certain associates. Hence, when he opened the tiny donkey-shed Ragged School, he took the reins into his own hands and ventured where faith led. The same was true of both the Assembly Rooms and Hope Place Mission. Indeed, in the early days, he had no colleague with an approximation towards his ability, or a tithe of his vision; therefore he determined to avoid all "red tape"; and very probably Lord Shaftesbury encouraged his autocratic course. True, when the "Edinburgh Castle" was acquired, that property was vested with Trustees, as was also the Girls' Village Home. But till the Arbitration, Barnardo remained to all intents and purposes an autocratic dictator over the Institutions his genius had built; for he believed he had been "called" to undertake the work wherein he was engaged; and he felt strongly that, as Director, it was his special business under God *to direct* the Mission's work.

Under this peremptory control, therefore, the East End Juvenile Mission had attained the position it occupied when the Arbitration Board sat. And that its success was largely due to such control, no person, surveying all the facts in retrospect, can doubt; for Barnardo's initiative had left its imprint at every turn. Yet, although this personal authority was essential to initial developments, the day was fast approaching when it might have become a stumbling-block. For every man, no matter how great his talents, ultimately reaches a point where, unaided, he can shoulder no greater load; and that point Barnardo, by 1877, had almost reached. Therefore the Arbitration Board, in recommending the appointment of a Committee to assist in managing the Homes, anticipated a vital need. Already, the Arbitrators realized, the Mission had given evidence of such public utility that its permanence as a National Institution should be secured: and such permanence was improbable so long as it continued under autocratic control; for what would happen if the Director were smitten by sickness or by death? The recommendation, therefore, that a Committee be formed "to assist" the Director proved of real value, and the high tributes paid the Mission by the Arbitrators beyond doubt made it easier to enlist the services of men whose influence would carry most weight.

Indeed, of the fact that the Arbitration was a blessing in disguise there can be no doubt. To take one instance only: Earl Cairns, then Lord Chancellor, followed closely all the evidence; and no sooner had he read the Award than he wrote Barnardo congratulating him on having passed through such an experience unscathed, and suggesting that, if Barnardo desired to appoint a Committee, he would be happy to serve as Honorary President or in any other capacity.

This letter, among hundreds congratulating him upon his defence and proffering personal assistance, Barnardo greatly prized; and its arrival was opportune. No sooner had the Doctor read the Arbitrators' recommendation than he decided to appoint a Committee; already, moreover, he was busy figuring out who should be included in its personnel, when Lord Cairns's offer came to hand; and who could be more appropriate as President than the First Law Lord of the Realm?

Lord Cairns and Barnardo, too, were well qualified to work together. Both were Irishmen born. Both were supremely interested in the social implications of the Gospel; both were sworn enemies of drunkenness, slumdom and vice; both believed that they could best serve their fellows by working continually for the principles of the Kingdom of Christ. Both, too, were true friends of the Poor, who refused to temporize with conditions of poverty, debauchery and sin; yet both believed that the ultimate cure for the most nauseating of social ills must *start* with the child.[1]

With Earl Cairns, therefore, as President, a Committee of sixteen was soon appointed; and on November 15th, 1877, exactly a month after the publication of the Award, its personnel was announced. Among its members were two clergymen of the Church of England; three Nonconformist Ministers; nationally respected philanthropists, such as Lord Kinnaird and the Hon. T. H. W. Pelham; together with Members of Parliament, Y.M.C.A. officials, medical men and such noble representatives of the business world as Samuel

[1] The fervour of Earl Cairns's faith is illustrated by the fact that, even as Lord Chancellor, he found time to teach a public Bible Class.

Gurney Sheppard and John Sands. This Committee represented a broad cross-section of Britain's public life, but its members had much to unify their outlook. All were zealous Evangelical Protestants; all were profoundly concerned with the social ethic of Christianity; all, like Barnardo and Cairns, were sworn foes of the fatalistic interpretation of slumdom, vice and crime; all believed in the infinite possibilities of even the downmost child, if brought into vital contact with the spirit of Christ; and all had been members of Local Committees in connection with Moody and Sankey's first Mission to England.

The first act of this Committee, in conjunction with the Trustees, was to express "deep obligation" to the Arbitrators "for undertaking so comprehensive an inquiry and for prosecuting it with so much assiduity and patience at great personal inconvenience and under considerable difficulties, to a conclusion".[1]

Then the ground was cleared for a new advance, the proportions of which can best be ascertained by a comparison, over a number of years, of the Mission's work before and after the Arbitration Board sat: and, happily, the data for such comparison are all extant.

Barnardo initiated his Mission work *eleven years before* the Arbitration; and, by coincidence, it so happens that much the fullest Report he ever wrote was issued in the form of a 280-page volume—*Something Attempted: Something Done—eleven years after* the Arbitration. Hence the facts are all available for comparison between these two periods, and such comparison is highly illuminating.

During the eleven years between the rescue of Jim Jarvis and the Arbitrators' Award, Barnardo had rescued some

[1] In leaving the Arbitration, it may be noted that a letter among Barnardo's papers from the Hon. Alfred H. Thesiger, dated November 1st, 1877, shows that almost immediately after his duties as Barnardo's Counsel, he was made a judge. The letter expresses gratitude that he was able to complete his Arbitration duties before his "elevation to the Bench" concluded his "work at the Bar".

2,000 destitute children—500 of whom were at the close of 1877 still in the Homes; the Report for 1888, however, shows that he had then rescued 12,653 children—3,000 of whom were then in the Homes. In other words, the total of destitute children rescued during the second eleven-year period was five times greater than during the first eleven-year period, while the Barnardo "family" in the Homes in 1888, was six times greater than in 1877. The increase, too, in finances was equally pronounced. During the pre-Arbitration period the total income received was appreciably less than £150,000. During the immediate post-Arbitration period of equal length, it was well over four times that amount—£655,000; while a comparison of the single years 1877 and 1888 shows that the respective incomes were barely £30,000 as compared with over £112,000.

A comparison of the distinct Branches of the work during these same periods is equally suggestive. At the close of the Arbitration, the Mission included eight separate Institutions, with fourteen cottages marking the dimensions of the Girls' Village Home. Barnardo's 1888 Report shows that during this post-Arbitration period the Branches had increased almost fivefold; for then the Mission boasted thirty-eight "distinct institutions" and the cottages in the Village Home numbered fifty.

Again, though by 1877 these "Homes" had rescued 2,000 destitute children, during this earlier period the Mission partook chiefly of the nature of a glorified Ragged School, of which the Homes were simply a Department; but by 1888 the Homes had grown to proportions overshadowing all else, and this despite the fact that meanwhile Barnardo had initiated new efforts on all fronts. Hence it would appear that the Arbitration assaults, centring as they did around the "Homes", resulted in elevating their position over all other aspects of the Mission's endeavour.

Another point which must be noted relates to finance. During the pre-Arbitration period Barnardo never permitted his annual expenditure to exceed his income; for to him it was a religious principle that he "owe no man anything". But during the post-Arbitration period he was caught on the horns of a dilemma. Up till 1877, and indeed for years afterwards, he was able without financial embarrassment to stand by his pledge to refuse no destitute child; but ere the termination of the second period, the pressure upon the Homes became so great that he found himself confronted by a challenging alternative. Either he must abandon his pledge or keep his doors open with *borrowed* funds. The first alternative he dare not accept, for "Carrots" still haunted his mind; the second he finally reconciled with his conscience on the ground that borrowed money would be used exclusively for *building* purposes, thus representing a mortgage upon freehold property, which he hoped in a few years to wipe off.

Consequently the *actual* proportions of Barnardo's work by 1888 were even greater than the annual income of over £110,000 would suggest.

But returning to the necessity of a mortgage; in *Something Attempted: Something Done* (page 5), we read: "During 1888 the institutions have been reaping in large measure that which was sown in the preceding year. Our doors in 1886 had been pressed wide to the walls by the ever-increasing throngs of destitute children, and I found myself rapidly reaching the limits of accommodation at my disposal. I must either refuse any longer to write upon our walls, 'NO DESTITUTE CHILD EVER REFUSED ADMISSION', or I must face *the immediate necessity of enlarging the Homes.*"

The alternative chosen we know. We proceed to Barnardo's description of the manner in which the extension programme was carried out, remembering that it coincided with the fiftieth year of Victoria's reign, and consequently was called the Jubilee Enlargement.

"Throughout the Jubilee Year, all the Homes rang with the sound of axe and hammer. The Stepney Home had a considerable addition made to it. Leopold House was more than doubled; the Labour House for Destitute Youths was extended; 'Her Majesty's Hospital' was built. I reorganized our Emigration Scheme; the large Manitoba Farm began to be developed; a Rescue Home for young girls was added, as was also The Children's Fold for destitute cripples; while many other extensions and additions took place over all our Institutional economy. To do this added enormously . . . to my already heavy financial burdens. But even as these necessities increased, our Lord put it into the hearts of His stewards to remember His work in my hands more liberally; and though *a great part of the load yet remains unlifted, and has had to be met by the execution of a mortgage,* I am thankful to record the measure of encouragement which followed my efforts to enlarge the gates of these Cities of Refuge for Little Ones."

This catalogue by no means exhausts the developments of the Jubilee Year. During that twelvemonth, nineteen new cottages were opened in the Girls' Village. One thousand additional acres of land were acquired for the Manitoba Farm; three more houses in Stepney Causeway were added to the Main Office accommodation; and five new trades were introduced.

This 1887 programme marked an important milestone, for concerning it Barnardo wrote:

"As a result of these material enlargements . . . I began 1888 with a *wider scope and an ampler machinery* than I had ever enjoyed during the previous history of the Homes, and I have every day since derived advantage from the larger premises thus placed at my disposal. It has been a year of consolidation, of real advances in organization; of steady progress and of much blessing in things spiritual as well as temporal. The extensions have enabled me to *subdivide* and *classify* the various young residents according to age, acquirements and circumstances, more minutely than was heretofore possible; the training imparted has been more thorough, and the supervision closer; while I have personally rejoiced in the greater liberty I thus acquired of keeping the door of opportunity yet more widely open to every destitute little creature who claimed the privilege of being cared for."

In *Something Attempted: Something Done*, Barnardo's survey of his work up till 1888, the chief emphasis is on the "Homes for Orphan and Destitute Children". Other "Branches", including the various Day and Evening Ragged Schools, the People's Church, the Coffee Palaces, the Medical Dispensary, the Deaconess House, the Factory Girls' Institute, the Night Refuges, the Outdoor Relief, etc., had greatly prospered; but the heart of all was now The Homes. And of his huge family, already numbering well over 12,000— many of whom were in distant lands—Barnardo kept a faithful record; each member being to him an individual "child", not a cog in a machine.

What, then, were some typical, pre-entrance histories of boys and girls who took up their abode among what was now "The Largest Family in the World"? Only a few cases may here be cited; but each is representative of hundreds and is vouched for by those whose business was to discover all ascertainable facts concerning applicants' lives.

R. M., admitted to the "Little Boys' Home", Jersey, when six, is described as "a light-haired, blue-eyed little fellow, who has been enfeebled through want of proper food". The facts leading to admission are these: "Father, a lithographic artist, died of consumption four years ago. Mother and son left totally unprovided for, and the former, a respectable hard-working woman, reduced to selling cigar-lights in the streets. . . . Both living in a common lodging-house. Absolutely friendless; addresses of relatives unknown."

The case of W. S. B., also six, admitted to the same Home, the same year (1888), is not dissimilar: "In a state of pitiable distress; the mother begged in person for assistance. The Children's Beadle found her, with eight little ones, in indescribable poverty. Father, a commercial traveller formerly in a good position, now in a lunatic asylum. Mother with no occupation; room almost bare; children wellnigh starving."

A study of records at "Babies' Castle" tells the same sad tale. If we inquire regarding the tinies there admitted in 1888, cases like these confront us on every side: S. E., two months old, was "a tiny female child, with a withered, weird face smaller than the palm of a hand. Mother lying incurably afflicted with dropsy, at *her* mother's house, and cruelly deserted by her worthless, drunken husband, who cannot be traced. Four children, of whom she cannot support one. Her own mother a widow, and wellnigh destitute. Relatives all miserably poor."

"Billy", two years old, was the son of a woman who attempted to drown herself and him and who . . . did succeed in drowning the tiny baby at her breast. Of T. R. (two months) these facts were known: "Mother died of starvation and anxiety four days after giving birth to this child. Father aged; afflicted with heart disease; utterly broken down in health, and unable to work. Another child at home, and all three actually starving. No relatives to assist." Again, the case of J. B. (three months) was equally tragic: "An orphan. Mother died in giving birth to the little fellow. Father, a labourer, slowly dying. . . . No home for this child and a sister of eleven; no relatives able to assist; both children admitted."

Histories associated with the Girls' Village Home, the Stepney Home for Boys, the Boarding-Out Departments, etc., reveal conditions equally heart-rending. The case of J. C. N. (four years), admitted into the Girls' Village Home in 1888, is no isolated history: "A bright, endearing little creature, who comes from sad surroundings. Mother a prostitute, living in a low public-house, in the tap-room of which the little one has been made to stand upon the table and recite low pieces or sing songs. Three sisters of the mother also living a degraded life; grandparents abandoned and worthless." The admission facts for three sisters entering the Village Home are these:

"Actually homeless and destitute with their drunken, tramping father and mother, and all literally without a roof to shelter them. Have been sleeping, at night, for three months under a holly-tree on a well-known race-course. In the daytime they have wandered about where they would. Parents, through drink, have sunk lower and lower and have become so bestial and indescribably filthy that no one will employ them or even let them a room. . . ."

R. M. P. (aged seven) was "A poor maimed little fellow rescued from a wretched home in a Scottish town. Has led a life fraught with misery; was brutally kicked and so severely injured that, after lying for several weeks in an infirmary, his right hand was amputated. Both parents degraded and living apart, the father leading a wandering life. Child found forlorn on a staircase by a benevolent man. . . ."

Or take the case of W. L., admitted to the Stepney Home when thirteen. "A poor little fellow with a diseased jaw. Has been taken about the streets of London by a pavement artist to excite sympathy. Father dead. A drunken and utterly demoralized mother who was found hopelessly intoxicated upon the same bed with her dead husband. She has been turned out of lodgings time after time for drunkenness and non-payment of rent. . . ."

These cases, taken from Barnardo's admissions of 1888, are typical of the 1,768 children received that year. But it must not be inferred that this large figure represents the total of applications; that year 7,298 applications were received, and although scarcely one-quarter of the children concerned were, upon investigation, found really destitute and therefore eligible, nevertheless over 1,200 of those *refused* admission were, by Barnardo's, sent to sea, provided with clothing, found situations or otherwise assisted. Fully half, however, of the total of applications were refused as unsuitable; careful inquiry showing that these candidates had relatives or friends who could be induced to undertake their support. Indeed, from the first Barnardo's resolutely refused to be imposed upon by those who sought to shirk responsibilities and foist them upon the Homes. They refused *no destitute child*; but destitution had to be proved before any child was permanently admitted.[1]

---

[1] In cases of obvious destitution, children were always admitted *at once*, pending inquiry.

L

It is remarkable, too, that among the *applications* received in 1888 were some from every quarter of England, Ireland, Scotland and Wales; while among the *admissions* were children from every city in the Kingdom; and this phenomenon had been increasingly apparent since 1877. Consequently it is obvious that one effect of the Arbitration was to lift "The Homes" to the dignity of a National Institution. Nor is this really surprising; for the Award established the fact that Barnardo dealt with children whom the nation had left derelict, yet his Homes so moulded their lives as to make than an asset to society. Throughout the Kingdom, by 1888, were many young people who had been mothered and trained in Barnardo's Homes; and whatever prejudices against them were first entertained, gradually it became apparent that they were honest, sober, respectable citizens, masters of their craft, generous and co-operative in their conduct—citizens such as form a nation's backbone.

And not only in the United Kingdom were such facts now being observed, for by 1888 Barnardo had migrated 3,773 of his protégés to outposts of Empire, where 98 per cent. had proved themselves pioneers of worth. Nor did these "old boys" and "girls", when far away, forget the Homes which had enabled them to find their feet; for although by 1888 most of Barnardo's Overseas protégés were still too young to have acquired much means, already they *alone* were sending back voluntary contributions of hundreds of pounds a year.

Now, by what alchemy was wrought the transformation of these derelict, destitute youngsters into citizens, bringing honour to their foster-father and his Homes? Foremost among the causes of transformation was a pervading spiritual influence. Barnardo once was rated by a zealous ecclesiastic because no crosses or altars were erected in his Homes. His reply was immediate: "No! But did you not observe the Bible everywhere? That, sir, is not only our

chief text-book; it is the inspiration of these Homes!"
Barnardo and his colleagues entered upon their labour as
a vocation, not a job, and if any instructor found his way
within the fold who was not "in love with his work", he
soon changed his attitude or resigned. For the missionary
spirit in which the Homes were founded, left its imprint on
every branch; and whether at work or play, through a score
of channels, the children were encouraged by precept and
example "to do justly, to love mercy and to walk humbly
with God": while the teaching of Him who summarized
the Law and the Prophets in the Commandment of Love
electrified the air breathed by every Barnardo child.
Religion, therefore, was no appendage to the Homes;
rather was it the bone and marrow of their life.

But though religion was to Barnardo the "be-all and
end-all" of life, never did he despise the so-called secular
pursuits. Indeed, the popular differentiation between the
secular and the sacred he believed tragically misleading;
to him, no honest toil, honestly performed, was ever secular;
while, on the other hand, nothing could be truly sacred
which did not ennoble life. Consequently his schools,
workshops, playing-fields and drill-halls were important
aspects of his scheme—all helping to develop that robust
manhood at which continually he aimed.

The Arbitrators' recommendation that Barnardo Schools
be placed under Government inspection was gladly accepted,
and with gratifying results. By complying with Government
standards, Barnardo's won for their various schools State
Grants, while also they proved that, despite grave difficulties,
they were efficient educational concerns. Here is an extract
from the 1888 Report of Her Majesty's Inspector from
the Privy Council of Education, concerning the Homes'
Schools at Stepney: "The Managers of the Schools are
to be congratulated not only upon the completion of the
commodious new premises, but also on a corresponding
improvement in the quality of the work. . . . Handwriting

receives careful attention and written arithmetic is good. Oral arithmetic shows improvement. Grammar is taught with considerable success; so *the highest grant of efficiency is recommended*. . . ." The Inspector's Report for Leopold House was equally flattering: "This School is in a high state of efficiency as a whole." Its progress he pronounced, "most creditable to the Staff". The exercises in singing by note were "most satisfactorily performed", while the school was "in admirable order". Of the Village Home School, the Inspector reported that, "This large school is, as usual, very ably organized and thoroughly well-disciplined." But, in spite of the 1887 extensions, the Report stated that "the number of children at present on the books is too large for the existing premises, and unless the recent increase is met by an extension of space, this school will be seriously over-crowded in the coming year". Special praise was bestowed upon "the good discipline of the Infants' Class", and the "general correctness of the children in answering questions", while "the effective character of the object-teaching and the care taken with physical exercises" were pronounced "very creditable".

These are representative Reports of Government Inspectors. But Barnardo's system did not limit itself to subjects prescribed by the Government curriculum, and its finest attainments were along lines which drew no Educational Grant. The Bible knowledge, for instance, acquired by the average Barnardo child, put to shame the average Board School; while the same was true in the sphere of music, craftsmanship and physical drill. From an early date, Barnardo's exhibited a genius for instructing children in band music and choral singing, and hundreds of their protégés became bandmasters or choir-leaders in the communities wherein they established themselves; while again every Barnardo lad and lass was instructed in some craft and was taught to enjoy the exhilaration of physical drill and organized sport. Hence, the fact that Barnardo Schools on "prescribed" subjects won such praise from Her Majesty's Inspectors, is doubly creditable.

Other facts, however, lay behind the Homes' success. Their founder, being a medical man, was naturally interested in the *physical* well-being of his children; but this interest was intensified by his devotion to the Pauline doctrine that the human body is the temple of the Holy Spirit. Hence he regarded it a *religious* duty to do everything possible to produce in his children full-blooded health. Wholesome food was a standing rule in all his Homes; and though no luxuries were indulged, the most ravenous appetites were fully satiated, with the result that by 1888 his food bill alone exceeded £100 a day. But this money was well spent; for nourishing food along with regular habits, vigorous sport, occupied minds, and a spiritual outlook on life, contributed largely to the Homes' amazingly low death-rate. In several Branches the annual mortality was less than 4 per 1,000; and what brought the 1888 total up to 12·8 was the large number of under-nourished babies—many only a few weeks old—admitted to the Homes.

Ere the termination of the period under review, a newly established department completed the *National* character of Barnardo's work. The publicity given the Homes by the Arbitration having greatly increased the demands from Churches, Sunday-schools, etc., for "Barnardo Deputations", both the Director and certain members of his Staff were compelled to travel a great deal, addressing meetings and conferences; so by 1888 relief was imperative. Accordingly, that year the Rev. W. J. Mayers (a talented young Baptist minister) resigned the pastorate of a prominent Bristol Church to become the First "Deputation Secretary"; and so successful were his labours that soon other clergymen were appointed; some Church of England, some Nonconformist.

The above are but flashlights on a few of Barnardo's achievements up till 1888, and though they emphasize the rapidly increasing importance of "The Homes", other "Departments" were throbbing with life. A mere glance at Barnardo's programme fills one with awe. In "the briefest possible form," the "ground-plan" of his Mission he thus set forth:

"OBJECTS.
(1) To rescue, educate, industrially train and place out in life, Orphan and Destitute Children.
(2) To evangelize among the masses of the East End.
(3) To heal the sick and relieve the deserving poor.

"MEANS.
(1) (a) Search agencies to discover waif and stray children;
    (b) Free lodging-houses;
    (c) Large industrial homes;
    (d) Small family homes;
    (e) Boarding out;
    (f) Emigration.
(2) (a) Mission halls;
    (b) Deaconess homes;
    (c) Temperance guilds;
    (d) Ragged and Sunday-schools.
(3) (a) Medical missions;
    (b) Free meals;
    (c) General relief;
    (d) Emigration and migration.

"PRINCIPLES: Destitute children are received—
(1) Without any limitation as to age, sex, creed or nationality.
(2) Irrespective of any kind of physical infirmity; crippled children, blind, deaf-mutes, incurables, and even those given over for death are eligible if really destitute.
(3) At any hour of the day or night.
(4) Solely on their merits, without election and without the intervention of wealthy patrons."

This skeleton of Barnardo's 1888 programme suggests but faintly the proportions to which his Mission had grown. Some details of the "Homes'" work at this stage we have seen. The achievements of his Copperfield Ragged School will illustrate one of his many attainments, *quite distinct from the Homes.* The Copperfield "Sunday- and Week-day Bible School" was one of several Ragged Schools run by the

East End Juvenile Mission; and how poor were its pupils may be estimated from the fact that *"30 per cent. of the attendants on a single morning have been known to reach the School without breakfast, that other 30 per cent. had only had a piece of dry bread before leaving home, while 60 per cent. expected no dinner!"* [1] Yet from these pupils whom the Mission had largely to feed, in 1887 this school presented for Government examinations 455 children; and 402—88·4 per cent.— passed in *all* subjects.

These results were far more satisfactory than could have been produced among this type of child by Board Schools; hence gradually, though reluctantly, the Government learned from Ragged Schools the folly of trying to educate a child's mind while his stomach was gnawing with hunger.

The skeleton plan of the Mission's work in 1888 Barnardo has briefly explained:

"I am set primarily for the *saving of the children*; and by God's blessing the Homes under my care may be said to effect this upon a wider basis than any other Institution in the world. . . . But in addition, our East End Mission had from the first undertaken the task of *evangelizing* among the adult poor. It comprises agencies for *visiting the Sick*, the Aged and the Fallen; for relieving and nursing the Sick, both at a Medical Mission and in their own households; for *educating on a Scriptural basis* children of the labouring poor; for supplying *free meals*, or food at a nominal price, to the hungry (both adults and children); for distributing *clothing* of various kinds, boots, etc. For supplying necessitous mothers with bedding and other articles during childbirth; for sending the convalescent Poor to *seaside* or *country* homes; for *paying rents* for the aged and infirm; for *redeeming from pawn* Tools or implements needed to obtain work; for enabling persons out of work—particularly girls—to obtain *situations*; for helping poor women in their struggle with starvation by *loans* of sewing-machines, mangles, etc., and in general, for many like methods of SYSTEMATIC AND CAREFULLY APPLIED RELIEF, designed to raise the fallen, to cheer the faint and to infuse fresh courage into the discouraged warriors in the grim battle of life."

To these proportions had Barnardo's work grown by the termination of the second eleven-year period. But enough evidence has now been reviewed to make it obvious that the

[1] *Something Attempted: Something Done*, p. 178.

Arbitration which threatened disaster, proved a blessing. It disarmed crities and confounded foes. More important—it revealed to Barnardo his vulnerable points and the weak links in his work. Out of it came the Committee of Management, which brought to the Director's assistance some of the noblest souls the realm could boast, thus making the constitution of the Mission less personal and more secure. But another advantage ensued: The Homes became the recipients of a fuller measure of legal protection which, strengthening their foundations, assured their permanence.

Amazing, then, as was the Mission's growth during the eleven years preceding the Arbitration, its development during the eleven years succeeding was at least four times greater. It therefore was by this time transparently clear that Barnardo had passed from trial to triumph; but how great was that triumph will now be seen through the findings of a Royal Commission, headed by one of the most eminent Cabinet Ministers of his time.

CHAPTER XI

BARNARDO GUIDES A GOVERNMENT

ONCE Barnardo was discussing with a colleague the problem of the destitute child, when suddenly the conversation
turned to the State's administration of its Poor Law Institutions. Barnardo jumped to his feet: "My word!" he
exclaimed. "There's one post I covet above all else as a
sphere of National service. I would to God I had control of
all the Poor Law children in the Kingdom!"

Not infrequently during his forty years' experience among
destitute children, Barnardo felt impelled to criticize the
administration of the Poor Law system, root and branch.
But for long his criticism fell on scornful ears. Who was this
egotist who presumed to dictate to Public Officials? What
could he teach the omniscient and omnipotent State? Was
he not a fanatic, beneath the Legislature's contempt? Such,
for years, was the attitude of Officialdom toward Barnardo's
criticism of barrack schools and other of the Poor Law's
machine-like institutions. But the dauntless little Doctor felt
certain that he was right, and that the State, for all its
plenitude of power and despite all its airs, was wrong; so
with his criticisms he persevered, confident that at length a
change would come. And come it did; for, long before his
death, Cabinet Ministers and the State's education Advisers
were praying for "a Dr. Barnardo" to remodel the whole
Poor Law administration.

But behind this change of front, there lies an altogether
unusual romance. How came it about that world-eminent
educationists were led to express such appreciation of
Barnardo's work?

To answer this question we must follow events through
two decades. Even prior to the Arbitration, Barnardo had
criticized, in no uncertain terms, the existing system of
rearing "State" children. And if the whole truth were

known, it is probable that his early audacity in this direction reacted against him and helped create the animosity which culminated in his own trial. But when once he had passed through that ordeal unscathed, the situation changed. Influential people began to ask if his criticisms of Poor Law Institutions were sound. These questions, in turn, incited Press inquiries, and those inquiries revealed conditions no Government Department could excuse.

It was charged, for instance, that Poor Law boys of fifteen or sixteen were frequently thrown upon the world without any means of livelihood, unless perchance they might eke out an existence by washing dishes, darning stockings, sweeping floors or making beds—the only "trades" they had ever been taught. Poor Law girls too, at a similar age, it was claimed, were thrust upon their own resources without even a rudimentary training in house-keeping, or anything else wherewith to earn their daily bread: with the result that thousands drifted ultimately into the streets. In fact, it was suggested that the whole Poor Law System was bankrupt, and that gaols in every county told a sad story of the toll of degradation and criminality traceable to Poor House gates.

These, however, by no means exhausted the accusations against Poor Law administrators. Sanitation within their Institutions was said to be atrocious, while the spread of contagious diseases, especially ophthalmia, which often resulted in blindness, was declared a crying scandal. Then, too, the criticism was directed against Poor Law Schools and allied institutions that their inmates were robbed of all personality, being treated as cogs in a machine and, more disastrous still, that they were cast into the world to shift for themselves without any attempt at supervision. Consequently it was argued that failure was almost inevitable.

These criticisms, too, gained weight from the fact that frequently, within the same family, generation succeeded generation under the same Poor House roof. Thus, Poor Law Institutions being public concerns supported by public funds, a condition prevailed crying aloud for investigation. Yet for years successive Governments turned a deaf ear to all criticisms, side-stepping every demand for an inquiry, till finally the attack became so acute that an investigation could no longer be shelved. Either the State must vindicate the administration of its Poor Law Institutions or admit the justice of criticisms. Accordingly, in 1894, a Departmental Committee was appointed by the Local Government Board with full authority "to inquire into the existing systems for the maintenance and education of the children under the charge of the Managers of District Schools and Boards of Guardians in the Metropolis, and to advise as to any changes that may be desirable".

This Commission is historic. Its Chairman was the Right Hon. Anthony John Mundella, the author of various Education Acts and one of the greatest authorities on Juvenile problems the nineteenth century produced[1]; while behind him, as chief colleague, was the Right Hon. Sir John Gorst, a Cabinet Minister of almost equal eminence; and they were supported by a team of the best child-welfare experts the nation could command. Thus the personnel of this Commission included only eminent authorities, and all were chosen as persons reasonably friendly to the Government's point of view.

For two years this Commission sat, during which evidence was weighed on every aspect of the Destitute Child Problem. Not only were Poor Law Institutions inspected, but so also were those of religious, benevolent and philanthropic organizations; so that before the Commission was dissolved, many scores of schools, homes, barracks and Industrial Training Centres were examined, while hundreds of their

---

[1] See *First Supplement* to *Dictionary of National Biography*. Mundella was Forster's chief colleague in carrying the Elementary Education Act of 1870, while he himself carried several Acts, pushing still farther the victory then won. Note especially Mundella's Compulsory Education Act of 1881.

officers were questioned under oath. No shred of available evidence, therefore, was overlooked; and in the light of that evidence all recommendations were made.

The Report appeared in three volumes, consuming twelve hundred quarto pages, and, to use the Chairman's phrase, it was "very strong". The Commissioners found that nearly all the charges against the Poor Law Institutions were deeply grounded in fact. The barrack system upon which the Poor Law administration was founded, was proven mechanical and soul-destroying; for the human products it turned out were more like "robots" than thinking citizens with personalities and wills. In truth, the routine of barrack life, with its threadbare methods and treadmill procedure, the Commissioners found chiefly successful in crushing out every spark of ingenuity a Poor Law child might naturally possess, and in substituting a sullen moroseness.

Drab, soulless monotony was, however, by no means the Poor Law Institutions' only vice. It was found true that thousands of Poor Law boys, at sixteen, were turned upon the world with no idea of any trade. So, lacking the initiative and even the physique of the average casual labourer, a disquietingly large percentage drifted into such precarious livelihoods as vending matches in city streets; and this existence failing, many joined the army of crime or drifted back under Poor Law roofs—as adult paupers. Thus the number of their wards thrown back upon the State for support as paupers or prisoners proved, beyond dispute, the paralysing effect of Poor Law barrack schools for *boys*.

The tragedy of Poor Law *girls*, nevertheless, was found even more lamentable, and the problem they presented was certainly more disastrous to Society. Every year hundreds of girls in their middle teens, it was discovered, went forth from Poor Law Institutions without the faintest knowledge of anything wherewith to earn a living. Hence many sank to a life of shame; while among those who retained their purity, appalling numbers, like their Poor Law brothers, returned as adult paupers to Poor Law Institutions, there to become a public charge.

Another discovery was that the spread of contagious diseases in Poor Law Institutions amounted to a plague. Ophthalmia, for instance, was found a continual scourge— hundreds of "State" children being, by its ravages, blinded for life; yet it was but one of many contagious diseases collecting heavy toll.

But, bad as were the general education, the industrial training, the sanitation and even the physical health of Poor Law Institutions, their moral and spiritual status was worse; for within Poor Law walls religious instruction was as stereotyped as other aspects of this treadmill life. "Red tape", formalism and pedantry left their imprint on all sides, and everywhere they stunted the soul. Take one instance the Commissioners brought to light. It was a fast rule that all children whose parents professed "no religion" must be raised according to the rites of the Established Church; and as, in most cases, the parents of Poor Law children were of "no religion", all Poor Law attempts at boarding-out were half paralysed. For frequently it happened that in districts best adapted to boarding-out, few suitable Anglican homes would receive Poor Law children, while, on the other hand, clean, healthy and godly Nonconformist homes were available; but formalism prevented their use. This, however, was but one instance among many, where "red tape" strangled every Poor Law aspiration for a fuller life.

Hardly is it surprising, therefore, that of the thousands of Poor Law children abroad in the land when the Commission was sitting, scarcely any could be cited who had risen to posts requiring initiative or alertness, even in average degree.

But, turning from the Commission's discoveries concerning Poor Law Institutions, what were its findings concerning Barnardo's Homes? The contrast is marked. Of the 4,700 children in the Homes in 1894, less than 10 per cent. lived in barracks : and these were as different from Poor Law Bar-racks as one could conceive. They catered only for the needs of older boys in vocational training, and they were humanized by a hundred attributes breeding fellowship, co-operation and good will. Every Barnardo boy, for example, was in possession of a little spending money; for the monetary value of his labour being estimated every week, he received one penny in the shilling, three-quarters of which he expended as he desired—while the remaining quarter was placed to his credit in the Barnardo Bank, to be added to from time to time as he desired. But providing boys with pocket-money and banking accounts, in proportion to creative service, was one of a score of means whereby Barnardo's developed in their children a sense of initiative and self-control. Twice a week the larger boys conducted organized sports in *public* parks, while again every lad on the "good conduct list" was "allowed out" certain evenings of the week.

Even from the Government's Poor Law officials, came tributes to the genius of Barnardo's Homes. Miss Mason, for example, the "Supervisor of boarded-out children for the Local Government Board in England and Wales", in evidence before the Committee, pointed out the marked superiority of Barnardo's boarding-out system over that which she herself supervised. The State's only machinery for boarding-out, she explained, was based upon a *system of dual control*, engendering friction and inefficiency at every turn. Local Boards of Guardians were solely responsible for "boarding-out" Poor Law wards; but the Local Govern-ment Board was solely responsible for their inspection. Hence, with one body of officials "boarding-out" Poor Law children and another inspecting them, and with each body jealous of its authority, no unified system was devised to advance the welfare of the child. Answering one of the Commission's questions, Miss Mason replied: "But, you see, the difference is, Dr. Barnardo boards out his own boys, and *can have them back when he pleases*. The Local Government

Board do not board out these children, and there is *no central place at which to have them back for training.*"[1]

In Miss Mason's observation lay one of the causes of Barnardo's "boarding-out" success. When twelve or thirteen, practically every Barnardo child boarded-out was recalled from the "foster parent" to a central Home, where generally they received two or even three years' vocational training; for a cardinal point of Barnardo's scheme was that no boy or girl be allowed to face the world unqualified. But co-operation with the central Homes was not the only cause which the Commission found contributory to Barnardo's "boarding-out" success. In the Chairman's words, Barnardo had "the good sense" to place at the head of this system "trained ladies who had become medical practitioners of eminence", and they were assisted by a splendid body of qualified nurses. Hence, under Barnardo's plan, before any child was boarded-out, the house of the "foster parents" was thoroughly inspected by a sanitary expert, while its spiritual fitness was ascertained by a voluntary Local Committee, which, assuming control of Barnardo children in its particular district, co-operated with the inspecting doctor or nurse, who, unannounced, visited every child at least four times a year.

Thus, by means of a highly organized system of inspection, the physical, spiritual and mental well-being of every child was kept in mind, while by withdrawing boarded-out children to Central Homes for vocational training, Barnardo saw to it that all were equipped with some means of honest livelihood. Scarcely is it surprising, therefore, that the Commission discovered Barnardo's boarding-out system to be productive of the most encouraging results, while, on the other hand, the Poor Law's dual system—though better than its Barracks—was but a lame affair. Moreover, although the Poor Law system had ten times more children than Barnardo's Homes, the latter was found by the Commission to be

[1] See *Report of Commissioners*, vol. i, p. 97 f.

boarding-out a larger number both of boys and girls than all Boards of Guardians, the country over.

Or, take another field of comparison. Migration to the Dominions offered, beyond doubt, the finest opportunity for the destitute child, if properly trained. Yet during 1894 all Poor Law Institutions in the kingdom migrated only 299 children, whereas Barnardo migrated 800; and whereas the Guardians followed a policy of "hit or miss", he had a system guaranteeing success. All Barnardo boys and girls sent to Canada under fourteen were *boarded-out* in districts where they were initiated into the life which later they would live: and during school years their board was paid for by the Homes, thus leaving them free on Saturdays, and after school, to roam the fields, explore the woods, pick wild flowers, climb trees, ford streams; chase rabbits, chipmunks and squirrels; and engage in all the pranks which, during summer months, fill the rural Canadian child's heart with glee; while, by winter, they were free to skate, snow-shoe, sled, toboggan and snowball to their hearts' content. Yet, when attending Canadian rural schools and boarding on Canadian farmsteads, they were learning, in play, to ride and drive horses, milk cows, feed pigs and sheep, and to care for chickens, turkeys, ducks and geese; while also they were familiarizing themselves with every variety of farm crop.

Thus, during school years, no Barnardo child had to earn his keep; he was simply being initiated into his environment. Yet Barnardo's was the only Institution sending children abroad which paid for their board while at school. All others, including Poor Law concerns, left them to *earn* their support when at school; and this policy, demanding fruit in season of blossom, curtailed the liberty of the child to enjoy sports. But paying for all their school children, save those adopted, was by no means the only policy which proved the far-sightedness of Barnardo's Emigration Scheme. The Commission specially commended

THE MAKING OF JACK TARS

1. The Watts Naval Training School
2. "We're bound for the Mercantile Marine!"
3. He makes the bell talk   4. Physical jerks

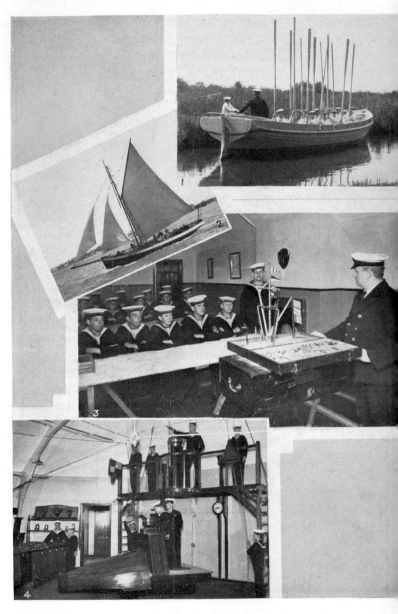

SHIP AHOY! SHIP AHOY!

1. Oar-drill   2. Learning the mystery of wind and sail
3. A naval classroom   4. A "ship on land"

their excellent care of children aboard ship; for always they sent a matron with every forty girls and a master with every fifty boys. Hence the youngsters were well looked after, and not a moment of the sea-journey was allowed to drag; every hour having its programme, including school, play, entertainment, religious services, band music and choral singing. Then, too, for receiving their children in Canada, Barnardo's had excellently arranged "Reception Homes", from which their wards were "placed out"; and by 1894, so completely had Barnardo children proved their worth that Canadian applications for them were eight times greater than could be supplied. But Barnardo's emigration scheme did not stop with finding "suitable places"; far from it. Their supervision machinery in Canada was even more perfect than their boarding-out machinery in Britain; every boy was regularly visited till he was twenty-one, while a parental guardianship was exercised over every girl till marriage.

Again, from an early date, Barnardo emigrated to Canada almost as many girls as boys, whereas Poor Law Institutions sent practically no girls. This fact was seized upon by Mr. Mundella; for, struck by the large number of girls emigrated by Barnardo's, he inquired: "What are the results of this enormous migration?" And Barnardo's reply is worthy of note: "The results, so far, have been *much more favourable than have followed any system of placing out in service in England.*"

This reply leads to Barnardo's examination by the Commission; and, though space permits but a fleeting reference to his evidence, one or two points must be noted. In 1894, at the request of Canada's Minister of the Interior, a careful examination was made into the civic record of every Barnardo ward in the Dominion, when it was dis-covered that, during the ten years preceding the investiga-tion, the annual average of convictions for all causes among Barnardo protégés was only 1·36 per thousand; whereas during the same period the convictions among Canada's

M

whole population averaged 7·55 per thousand. These figures are too eloquent for comment. They represent a standard of citizenship less marred by legal convictions than that of British Members of Parliament during the same years.

Other points in Barnardo's evidence were equally illuminating. His Homes, he explained, kept "a ledger account" of every child who left his roof; while also a monthly "Change List" was sent to Headquarters from each district showing changes in employment, address, contract, etc., which, particularly in the case of wards abroad, proved invaluable. Poor Law children, however, were left to drift. Again, whereas ophthalmia in Poor Law Barracks was a continual scourge, Barnardo's insistence on cleanliness, sanitation and medical inspection had so subdued this dread disease that with over nine hundred girls continually in residence at the Village Home, only ten cases of opthalmia had appeared in the four years preceding Barnardo's examination. Moreover, in order to teach his girls economy and thrift, Barnardo, for two years before they left his Homes, paid each a small weekly wage out of which she bought her own clothes, opened up a savings account and, in a score of ways, conducted her own economic life.

But to appraise the significance of Barnardo's examination, the verbatim account of his evidence should be read; for no summary can reveal its force. The last question put to him, however, suggested the appreciation which these Government-appointed experts came to feel for his Homes: "Having regard to this *marvellous and excellent work you are doing,*" interrogated Mr. Mundella, "*I want to ask you how far it can be carried on without your personal supervision.*" [1]

The concern of this historic Commission for the continuity of Barnardo's work is further expressed in public utterances by both the Commission's Chairman and his chief colleague, Sir John Gorst: the verdicts of both being enhanced

[1] See vol. ii, pp. 346–360.

by the fact that they began their investigations with a bias in favour of the Official System.

" 'I presided,' said Mundella, 'for two years over that Departmental Inquiry which was established by the Local Government Board for investigating the condition of the Poor Law Schools of the Metropolis. In the course of that Inquiry, my Committee felt it was their duty to investigate Dr. Barnardo's methods and to inquire into his success.

" 'I can only say, without in the least flattering Dr. Barnardo, that, at the conclusion of our inquiry, I came to the opinion, *which was shared, I think, by all my colleagues,* that we could wish that in the Local Government Board there was a department for . . . the "Children of the State", and that we had a Dr. Barnardo to place at the head of them.' "

This tribute seems superlative, but hard upon it we read :

"Nothing astonished me more than the magnitude of Dr. Barnardo's undertaking and the faith on which that undertaking seems to be resting. He has raised these institutions till they may be regarded almost as a National Institution. We found, as our Committee went on, that Dr. Barnardo was often boarding out in his Boarding-Out Department more children than the whole of the Local Authorities of this kingdom, and frequently he was emigrating more to the Colonies than all our Poor Law Boards taken together. It is a marvellous work that he has done in the Homes during the last thirty years, and its growth is entirely due to his wonderful energy, determination and character."

Then, striving to penetrate the secret of Barnardo's achievement, he continues :

"With respect to the magnitude of the undertaking, the secret of success is not easy to discover. I think I may say without the least reserve that Dr. Barnardo is not only a born administrator; he is a born master of method. When our Committee came to report, we made what has been deemed by the Local Authorities a very strong report. . . . I may say to you that *most of the reforms that the Committee has recommended, Dr. Barnardo had anticipated and put into practice in the administration of his Institution. We owe him much for what he has done. I think we owe him more for the example he has set us of how to do it."*

Later, attaching a confession to his tribute, the Chairman of the Commission concluded :

"Now it is only fair to make this acknowledgment, and I do it all the more heartily because *I confess that when I started upon the inquiry I had grave doubts about Dr. Barnardo's methods.* I am here to say publicly that *I would to God the same methods were introduced into the administration of the whole of the Poor Law children of the country!"*

Sir John Gorst's review of the Commission's conclusions, published in 1906, is equally strong. Pointing out that by England's Common Law every child possesses "legal rights" to maintenance "until of age to earn its own living", Sir John makes clear the fact that first of all this duty of maintenance falls upon parents. But if, "through any cause whatsoever, whether through inability, negligence or even crime", the parent "fails to perform his duty . . . the child has a second right to maintenance by the community at large". And "the only reason why children do not enjoy the rights which they by law possess, is the imperfection of the administration"—an imperfection "admitted by the President of the Local Government Board". Having thus defined the legal status of the destitute child, Sir John continues: "While the public authorities in the past studiously neglected these children and robbed them of their legal rights . . . Dr. Barnardo stepped in and endeavoured to fulfil them. *In doing this public work, for the public and on behalf of the public, Dr. Barnardo did it in a manner which is an object-lesson, not only to the authorities in England, but to the whole world.* I do not know that you can find anywhere a finer series of Institutions or arrangements, for turning a destitute wastrel of the streets into an honest, healthy man or woman, capable of being of use in the world . . . than Dr. Barnardo's Homes."

Such is Gorst's verdict concerning Barnardo's general labours. But what of particular aspects of his work?

Concerning technical instruction, no man was better qualified to pass judgment than Gorst. For many years it had been his public duty "to visit an immense number of technical schools, both in Great Britain and abroad"; yet in the light of this vast experience he avowed: "*For good solid teaching, which will qualify a boy to earn his own living, there is nothing superior to these Institutions.*"

But contrast this efficiency with the facts of a Poor Law case which came under Gorst's own eyes. When examining

Poor Law Institutions he discovered in an industrial school, mixing among large rough boys, one of the prettiest six-year-old lads he had ever seen. This babe awakened in Sir John a special interest; so he inquired into the facts of the case, which, briefly, were these: the child, found "sleeping under Covent Garden arches", was "brought up before a magistrate on a charge of being destitute" and committed to an industrial school "until sixteen years of age".[1]

On learning these data, Gorst made "desperate efforts to release the child and place it in Dr. Barnardo's care". But to no effect. Although the Home Secretary sympathized with him and "did everything he could to help", the Law would not permit the child's removal, save "by the consent of the Board of Guardians to whom he was chargeable". And this consent being jealously withheld, the infant could only be left to his fate.

Ten years passed by, and the boy, now sixteen, was about to face the world; so Sir John bestirred himself to find what he had learned in this Industrial School. Here are Gorst's own words: "What do you think he has learned in that school? *He has learned to darn stockings! and the darning of stockings is the only technical attribute which this boy has there attained.* . . . If we had succeeded in handing the child over to Dr. Barnardo's care . . . he would have been taught a trade or emigrated to Canada, and put in the way of becoming a prosperous man."

Nor was it only in industrial training that Barnardo's were superior to Poor Law Institutions. At every point, Gorst maintains, Barnardo was in advance of the Guardians. He "sought out" the destitute child; the Guardians took no action till an application reached them. Many Poor Law Institutions treated their children "as criminals"; Barnardo's

---

[1] Commenting on this custom, Gorst said: "It was the practice, if a child were found hungry and miserable, to bring it before a public magistrate and charge it with 'being destitute'. You will be surprised to learn that this is an offence against the criminal law of this country, and the child so offending can be committed to an Industrial School until it is sixteen years old."

youngsters were members of a Co-operative Family. Poor Law concerns exposed many of their children to the pauper taint.[1]

In Barnardo's such contamination was unknown. Poor Law Barracks, herding their wards together, "brought them up by machinery"; Barnardo's made the personal touch supreme. Again, both in Emigration and Boarding-out, Gorst affirmed that any wisdom which State Institutions exhibited they had learned from Barnardo; while comparing health conditions, he pronounced Barnardo's "beyond all praise".

Yet Gorst, like Mundella, began his labours on the Commission "with a considerable amount of prejudice based upon information . . . from periodicals, magazines and the like, against Dr. Barnardo and his system". At the termination of his two years' inquiry, he, like "many other members of that Committee", concluded that Barnardo was *"the man in the whole country, who had inaugurated and was carrying on a system of real and excellent administration for poor children"*.[2]

But not only in *A Review and an Estimate* does Sir John Gorst pay tribute to Barnardo. In his large, scholarly book, *Children of the Nation* (1906), he bestows upon him further praise; pointing out that Barnardo's Homes base their appeal upon "the love and affection dormant in the heart of every child, however its soul may have been suppressed and starved", he declares: "The relation which Dr. Barnardo's system seeks, and that not in vain, to establish is the relation of parent and child, not that of master and servant. Any social student who investigates Dr. Barnardo's establishments cannot fail to be struck with the singular spirit of love which pervades the whole atmosphere." Further on, he says: "The social significance of Dr. Barnardo's Homes is not appreciated by the Public. It is a work not of charity

[1] As late as 1905, one-third of Britain's Poor Law children were living *in Poor Houses or Poor House Infirmaries*, where continually they moved among *adult* paupers.
[2] See Sir John Gorst, P.C.: *A Review and an Estimate*, 1906.

but of ransom. Few of the eight or nine thousand children in the Homes are without a legal right to maintenance and education by some public authority which shovels off its responsibility upon Dr. Barnardo."[1]

The verdicts of these famous Commissioners, however, stand not alone. One of the keenest social studies ever made is that of the Right Hon. Charles Booth and his colleagues in their seventeen-volume series, *Life and Labour of the People in London* (1902). In this monumental work we read: "Dr. Barnardo's institution for the housing and care of destitute children is an enterprise of a similar kind to those for housing the homeless, *but the conception is far higher. Of it no one can say that its aim has been too low. It is, beyond question, the greatest charitable institution in London, or, I suppose, in the world; and its success has been deserved.* The management has been stamped with the impress of a most remarkable personality, and may not have been free from faults; but they have been the defects of its qualities. *It is easy to cavil, but there are few Charities in favour of which so much, and against which so little, can be said.*"[2]

In another volume, approaching Barnardo's work from a different angle, Booth says: "The work of Dr. Barnardo is most remarkable. There is, I believe, nothing in the world like it. . . . With his motto, 'Save the Child', a large and symmetrical structure has been built up, stone by stone, each stone an individual case of child destitution."[3]

Again, turning to Gretton's exhaustive work, *The Modern History of the English People*, a reference to Barnardo's death reads: "His work for destitute children had become such a recognized and admirable part of the life of the Nation that people realized, almost with a shock, its greatness as an individual achievement. He had set on foot forty years earlier, by his own unaided effort, an organization which now possessed Homes in London and the country capable of

---

[1] See especially chap. xiv, *State Children*.
[2] Vol. ii, series 3, pp. 46–47. [3] Vol. i, series 1, p. 127.

housing, educating and training for useful life thousands of waifs and strays of city streets. . . . At his grave, his own great personal devotion was recognized." [1]

But why multiply evidence? Of the fact that Barnardo at every step guided the country towards an enlightened treatment of the destitute child, there can be no doubt. Nor can there be any doubt that to-day the Homes into which he breathed his genius are still far in advance of State Institutions. Lord Brentford (then Sir William Joynson-Hicks), addressing a great meeting in 1927, explained that, as Home Secretary, all reformatories and industrial schools were under his jurisdiction. And, after praying for the decrease of State Institutions and the increase of Barnardo's Homes, he proceeded: "I am here to-day to say to you, and to the people of England at large, that there is no better way of . . . keeping the boy and the girl out of the Reformatory and the Industrial School than by supporting . . . Dr. Barnardo's Homes."

Hard upon the foregoing, his lordship, with marked deliberation, declared: "We both take much the same type of child—sometimes children without parents, sometimes children with unfit parents. . . . But, in my case, most of those poor children must have committed some form of crime to be brought into my homes. Yet I wonder how many of the children who pass through your Homes would have committed crime, if it had not been for your Homes? *If they had not been caught early, if they had not been taken charge of by you, if your Ever-Open Doors had not been open to admit them day and night, how many of these poor children might have fallen into a life of sin and crime, because there was nobody to help them? As* HOME SECRETARY, I THANK GOD FOR DR. BARNARDO'S HOMES, *and for all the work which you have done during the last sixty years.*"

Finally, pronouncing Barnardo "One of the great men of Great Britain for all time", and declaring that through the

[1] R. H. Gretton, vol. ii. (1899–1910).

sacrificial labours of the Chairman, the Committee and other officials of his Homes, "his spirit is going on working to-day", Lord Brentford, after reviewing the "social advantages" Barnardo's confer upon the Empire, proceeds: "But I commend to you this work because I know full well that, side by side—nay, in front of the social work—comes the Divine inspiration which you seek to put into the hearts of these boys and girls, bringing them up to realize that there is something in life higher and better and nobler than merely getting what you can out of life—merely 'doing well' in the world." [1]

Such authoritative verdicts might be quoted at any length—but enough! From 1896, when the Poor Law Committee reported, right up till the present, it has been increasingly clear that Barnardo's at every turn have proved themselves the Government's Guide. And that guidance they are likely to maintain. For never can any Government create Poor Law Institutions which will generate the Christian inspiration that, from the beginning, in Barnardo's Homes has consecrated medical knowledge, science, secular learning and craftsmanship to a purely altruistic end.

[1] For a report of this address, see *Night and Day*, July, 1927.

CHAPTER XII

LITIGATION AND THE "BARNARDO ACT"

"Before the British public will believe anything," declared a keen publicist, "it needs to have everyone concerned either in the dock or in the witness-box. . . . Nothing destined seriously to affect the life of the Nation ever escapes the ordeal of the dock. . . . We would all be without it if we could, yet there are none of us but are grateful for the ordeal after it is over." [1]

This is the judgment of the late W. T. Stead—a man with sufficient experience in the dock to know whereof he spoke. But if Stead had reason to render thanks for forced litigation, so also had Barnardo. And now that old passions have died down, and the perspective of distance has clarified issues, one thing is certain. To a man of Barnardo's temperament and conviction, conflict with the law of the land, as then it stood, was inevitable; for never could this man have been true to Conscience, had he refused to face the Courts. To him the spiritual law was all-supreme; and if the Statutes of the Realm did violence to what he felt certain was the Law of God, then for him no choice remained; his duty—at whatever sacrifice—was to exert his every influence toward bringing the Statute Law into closer conformity with the Law of Christ.

Scarcely is it surprising, therefore, that more than once for Conscience' sake—and his children's sake—Barnardo was compelled to do battle with giants. Yet, knowing his quarrel to be just, he felt himself "thrice armed". Like Luther at Worms, resolutely he held his ground: "Here I stand; I can do no other. So help me, God!"

Barnardo's initiation into the mysteries of legal procedure dates back, of course, to the "Arbitration". But to begin with that harassing episode, and to follow all the vicissitudes

[1] *Review of Reviews*, July, 1896.

of Barnardo's legal struggles, would fill a book; for his vision, initiative and courage landed him in all manner of Courts, defending his Homes. One year, however—1890— stands out as "The Year of Litigation"; the results of which are written into our Statute Books.

In 1890, for days on end, Barnardo appeared as his own Counsel in two important cases before the Court of Appeal: there to be opposed by three veteran barristers. And though on points of Law the verdict in both instances went against him, nevertheless by the consent of all the Lord Justices concerned, the *moral* victory was his. For so completely did he prove the "rottenness" of certain laws that the Legislature was forced into action, and the famous "Custody of Children Act" (1891) was passed—an Act removing from parents who abandon their children all parental control, and known the country over as "The Barnardo Act".

But before approaching the battles of 1890, one or two points must be made plain. That Barnardo was an ardent Protestant is a truth which, if we would understand the history of his Homes, must ever be remembered. His work started as a Protestant Missionary endeavour, and in a Protestant, evangelical atmosphere it took root and grew. Moreover, the fact that his religious life had its birth within Protestant circles in Dublin, predisposed him to no sympathetic attitude toward Roman Catholicism; while also it should be noted that Catholics, as a body, loved Barnardo no more than he loved them. Again, it must be recalled that immediately after Carrots' death, Barnardo made the pledge, "No destitute child ever refused admission." This, therefore, meant that no distinction could be observed as to colour, race or creed. If a child were destitute, he was eligible for entrance; and whether his skin were white, yellow, brown or black; whether he were Protestant, Catholic, Mohammedan or Jew—no barrier was permitted to stand in his way.

In the case of Non-Protestant destitutes, however, Barnardo was always slow to admit *permanently*, if any of their co-religionists could be found willing to relieve him of his task; for any attempt to proselytize was foreign to his scheme. But, from the first, it was made clear that his Homes were definitely Protestant; every child permanently admitted being reared in the Protestant Faith.

For years, moreover, this principle worked smoothly enough. And *never* did Barnardo come into conflict with the Jews, though, from the first, a sprinkling of Hebrew children found shelter under his roof. But of Roman Catholics the same could not be said. Among the destitute children of East London were not a few Irish and Italians, descended from parents at least nominally Catholic. Yet, for many years, the Catholic Church created no machinery to deal with the problem involved. But when, finally, it dawned upon the imperious mind of Cardinal Manning that Barnardo was rescuing from the streets certain children of Catholic parentage, and raising them in the Protestant Faith, a "battle royal" ensued. For when Manning's blood was stirred, he snatched at any pretext to remove children from Barnardo's. The Doctor, however, fighting for a principle, was no less stubborn, and scarcely less imperious, than Manning. Hence, when children had been left in his care for months, or even years, without any suggestion of removal, and then came orders for their return, from degraded parents whom he believed were being used merely as cats'-paws by the Cardinal, it was soon discovered that "the little Doctor" was prepared to fight vigorously for "his children".

In the early eighties the Roman Catholic Church in England awakened to the problem of caring for destitute children of her own Faith. But, at first, her efforts were halting: not till 1887—when Cardinal Manning appointed Canon St. John "to look after the waifs and strays of South London"—was an aggressive policy launched; and from that moment, Manning declared war upon Barnardo's Homes. Agreements entered into between Roman Catholic priests and Dr. Barnardo were peremptorily overridden; and, finally, so exasperated did Barnardo become that, in December, 1889, he published *The Cardinal's Conscience*, or "Proof given of the systematic neglect by the Roman Catholic Priesthood to care for their own Waif and Stray Children, until the latter had been rescued by Christian Agencies from the perils of the streets—when the zeal of Rome begins to wax hot against the rescuers; being a history of certain correspondence between Dr. Barnardo and Cardinal Manning's Secretary." [1]

In this illuminating treatise Barnardo's spirit was thoroughly roused; and, needless to say, he did not mince words. Answering the arguments of many who maintained that in no circumstances should he resist the application of Roman Catholics for the return of any child, however long it had been "a member of his family", he boldly stated his case. Frequently had he been pronounced "bigoted, intolerant and narrow-minded"; in Roman Catholic journals his "motives, methods and personal character" were all made a target for abuse; while certain organs of the daily Press banned him as "contemptible and infamous". Moreover, he had received letters "threatening personal violence". One gentleman, writing from Ireland, informed him that shortly he would be visiting London; and "if you are not then protected by prison walls", he declared, "you may expect your quietus at my hands: for I will knock you on the head"!

Then Barnardo explained the reason of his refusal to comply with certain Catholic demands. Habitually, when Catholic parents or relatives applied for the admission of children, he advised them first to make application to their own priests. But, "in nearly every case", came the reply: "I have done so; he says he cannot help me: the priest has advised me to go to the workhouse myself, or to send my boy or girl to the workhouse, and I won't do that." In

[1] See Supplement to *Night and Day*, December, 1889.

some instances, priests had been angry, and ordered applicants off "as beggars". *Never*, too, had Barnardo received a Catholic child without first making plain to the nearest of kin that it would be reared a Protestant. Yet repeatedly they implored him: "Do take the child, for God's sake!"

Again, Barnardo pointed out that, aside from his Labour House, never had he *admitted* a larger proportion than 5 per cent. of Catholic children, though *applications* for them were —some years—more than 20 per cent. of the total. Of this 20 per cent., however, a large proportion were "Irish Romanists" who told "specious tales", which broke down before "the touchstone of inquiry". Hence, in the case of Catholic applicants, special care was taken to examine into all the facts of the case; and only the *hopelessly destitute* were permanently admitted. Yet Barnardo's trouble grew. Sometimes, after a child had been years in the Homes, the parent was ordered by priests to demand its return; and until this was done Church rites were denied. Meanwhile, too, though Barnardo was being bombarded with applications for the removal of Catholic children, the Catholics were permitting large numbers of their children to sink deep into the sloughs of destitution and crime. "I never once", says Barnardo, "met in the lodging-houses or in the slums, by day or by night, a single priest or other agent of the Roman Catholic Church at work endeavouring to save their own poor children from the nameless infamies which encompass young lives in such environments."

But as Barnardo elaborated the need of a Catholic Rescue work—particularly in London, Liverpool, Manchester and Glasgow—his temperature rose: "Let but our Homes come upon the scene . . . and then no sooner are the children admitted through our portals than the Roman Catholics, who had hitherto been apparently indifferent to the vile surroundings, and worse than heathen-darkness of their lot, grow jealous almost to slaying about the salvation of their children, who, they declare, are being 'robbed of their Faith'."

Farther down appears this illuminating statement:

"I thought, in May, 1887, it was high time to bestir myself and to endeavour to bring the condition of those Roman Catholic young people before Cardinal Manning, in the hope of *urging him* to begin in a satisfactory way the rescue of all children of Roman Catholic parentage, so that they should not be dependent upon Protestant Homes like ours for the rescue they were perishing for lack of. I felt that the destitution in the streets was enormously beyond my power to cope with, and that if the Roman Catholics would only begin by taking those whom they claimed for their own Church, from the places of evil resort where I encountered them, immense suffering, vice and crime would be averted. Moreover, in that case, I would be spared the intense pain of being called upon afterwards to surrender those towards whom—once they had entered the Homes and come under my care—I felt I was, in the Providence of God if not in the sight of the Law, placed in the position of guardian and protector."

This correspondence, opened between Barnardo and Manning in May, 1887, continued more than a year. But it proved futile. Nay, worse! Far from begetting conciliation, it whetted Manning's ire.[1] Hence, when Barnardo published *The Cardinal's Conscience*, legal combat was the order of the day. And if we would understand the issues at stake, certain legal battles must be reviewed.

Most famous among these legal struggles was the "Gossage Case", the facts of which are strangely dramatic.

On September 15th, 1888, the Rev. E. Husband wrote to Barnardo requesting that his Homes receive a boy, Henry Gossage, aged ten. Ten days later, after the usual inquiry, the lad was admitted. Briefly, the facts were these. The boy's mother—an habitual drunkard—had, in a Leamington public-house, given him to two Italian organ-grinders to tramp the country and solicit alms. The boy, moreover, asserted that money was given his mother by the organ-grinders, which,

---

[1] Lytton Strachey's character study of Cardinal Manning, in *Eminent Victorians*, is, in this connection, peculiarly suggestive. The more liberal wing of the Catholic Church, represented by Cardinal Newman, had apparently little sympathy with these attacks.

there and then, was spent on drink. He also declared that twice he had been deserted by his mother, who half-starved him. And now, after tramping for months with these drunken organ-grinders, who sorely maltreated him, he was abandoned in Folkestone.

Discovered by a policeman, he was sent to "The Union". The Rev. E. Husband then had the matter brought before the Mayor and Guardians of Folkestone; and all agreed that the boy be placed in Barnardo's Homes. Accordingly, on September 25th, he was admitted: and Barnardo's, having ascertained the mother's address, wrote, on September 28th, asking if she desired the boy to remain in the Homes, and, if so, requesting her to answer certain questions. The following day she got a local Anglican minister to pen her reply, for she could not write; and this letter, to which she attached her mark, reads:

"DEAR SIR,
        "I shall be pleased if you will keep my son, Henry Gossage, at Dr. Barnardo's Homes as I can't afford to keep him myself.
        "His two brothers are in Canada. I obtain my living by washing, and am so badly off that I cannot keep him. My husband died six years ago. My son's grandfather and grandmother are alive, but they live some distance from here and have many other calls upon them. His relations, aunts and uncles on his father's side, are unable to help.
                "I remain,
                        "Yours obediently,
                        "The mark (X) of Mary Gossage."

This letter received, the boy Gossage was *permanently* admitted, it being taken for granted that the mother professed no religion. In the Homes the boy was happy; but frequently he spoke of two elder brothers being in Canada, and expressed a desire to go there too. Consequently, on November 9th, Barnardo—never dreaming of difficulty—sent to Mrs. Gossage his printed form, requesting her to fill it in and return it; thus granting the Homes permission to send the lad abroad, if such action were considered conducive to his good.

Next day, something quite unforeseen took place. A Canadian gentleman (William Norton) called at Headquarters and, producing instructions from influential Canadians, requested an interview with Dr. Barnardo. This was arranged; and Norton exhibiting a lively interest, Barnardo showed him all round the Stepney Home. Then, returning to the Director's office, they were discussing opportunities for children in Canada, when Norton made it known that the chief reason of his visit was to ascertain whether Barnardo could let him have a bright lad, of nine or ten, to adopt as his son. Further letters were now produced, among them one from the pastor of a Presbyterian Church, who pronounced the Norton home an ideal opportunity for any adopted child.

With Norton's deportment and credentials, Barnardo was eminently pleased. But on one condition only would the Canadian gentleman adopt any child. Repeatedly had he heard of instances where, after adoption, debauched relatives had resorted to vicious practices to obtain money from foster-parents : therefore he would adopt a boy only on condition that his address in Canada be withheld. To this stipulation, after long discussion, Barnardo agreed ; and forthwith several boys were brought up to confer with Mr. Norton—among them Harry Gossage.

Immediately Norton took to Harry : and the lad, being equally attracted, jumped at the prospect before him ; so Barnardo believing the boy's opportunity a rare one, arrangements were quickly made. On November 16th Norton was to receive the child from Barnardo's hand, and a day later they were to sail for Canada. Thus concluded a three hours' interview, and, on the date arranged, Barnardo—bidding Harry farewell—gave him over to Norton's care.

Meanwhile, though unknown to Barnardo, complications arose. When Mrs. Gossage received Barnardo's form, the Anglican clergyman, who had written for her, asking Barnardo to keep her boy, had left for India; consequently she took the form to a person who persuaded her not to fill it in, but to permit him to write Barnardo requesting the boy's transference to a Catholic Home. This letter, which contained no authorization from Mrs. Gossage save the unknown writer's word, was dated November 11th (Sunday), and was received at the Homes, with over one thousand other letters, next day. But, owing to distant appointments, illness and a Continental rest, it was not heard of by Barnardo until after the boy had sailed. Moreover, it was not till January, 1889, that any authorization to transfer the boy was sent by Mrs. Gossage herself; and it proceeded from the "Southam Union", where she was now an inmate. Meanwhile, too, it was ascertained that the boy's father was a Wesleyan Methodist, who before death had expressly desired that the lad be raised a Protestant: though, two years after his death, when the boy was six, the mother, under persuasion, had him baptized a Catholic.

These, in skeleton, were the facts known when Mrs. Gossage applied for a Writ of *habeas corpus* against Barnardo. And after hearing the case in Chambers, Mr. Justice Mathew, on March 13th, 1889, refused the Writ.

But Manning and his lieutenants bided their time. And a few months later, a decision favourable to them in the "Tye Case", caused them to reopen the Gossage Case in the Divisional Court: the salient fact in the Tye Case being that Barnardo, despite a letter received from the child's mother revoking permission, had sent it to Canada.[1]

In the Divisional Court a sensational plea was put forward that Barnardo, in violation of the law, was robbing poor mothers of their holiest rights. And so subtle was the onslaught that not only was a writ of *habeas corpus* issued against Barnardo (November 30th, 1889), but actually the

[1] The Poor Law Commission, which sat from 1894 till 1896, recommended that power be given to Boards of Guardians, etc., to do just what Barnardo did in the Tye Case, viz. send children to Canada without parents' consent, when such action was for the children's good.

Lord Chief Justice "animadverted somewhat severely" upon his conduct.

Barnardo immediately appealed; so on Friday, January 24th, and Monday, January 27th, 1890, the Appeal came before Lord Esher, Master of the Rolls, and Lord Justice Fry. And the facts revealed, as the Doctor pleaded his own case against three prominent barristers, are highly poignant.

After hearing all the witnesses and examining all the affidavits, the Master of the Rolls pronounced Mrs. Gossage "an unnatural brute", who disposed of her child "as if he were a monkey", and who "neither knew nor cared what became of him". He suggested, moreover, that for five shillings she could be persuaded to do almost anything with the boy. "She was a bad woman," he declared, "and is no better now than she was before." Again, her solemnly sworn affidavit, he pronounced, "an impertinent falsehood"; while, as for her statement that her husband had on his death-bed granted her permission to bring up this boy as a Catholic, it was sworn by the Master of the Warwick Workhouse (a disinterested witness) that "just before the death of the said Edward Gossage" he had called Mary Gossage to her husband's bedside, and that "she was, at the time of such visit, in a state of intoxication".

Yet this was the "poor woman" whom the "wicked Dr. Barnardo" had robbed of her "sacred" right to decide the destiny of her child. And the Law, as it then stood, upheld her claim. For the Master of the Rolls, declaring that he could "quite understand" why Norton would be "very anxious indeed" that the mother should know nothing of his whereabouts, nevertheless held that for Barnardo the "real point" was: "If you have broken the Law from the best of motives, you have broken the Law—and must take the consequences."

Toward the close of the Appeal, when already it was evident that the Judges would hold that Barnardo had *broken the Law*, Lord Esher, to illustrate the *legal* position, raised a hypothetical case: "I think if you, after keeping one of these children in your Home for a year, were simply to open your doors and turn it out, it would be cruel of you—and what you would not do; but I do not think, if you did, they could have a Writ of *habeas corpus* against you." This statement implies that Barnardo, not having thrust the boy upon the streets, but having placed him in the way of excellent opportunities in Canada, *was* liable to have a Writ of *habeas corpus* issued against him. And that implication Barnardo followed up; for, elaborating its significance, he rejoined: "My Lords, if that is the Law; if that is to be understood as the expression of your Lordships upon this point, I venture to say that the decision will go to the root, not only of my work, but of that of every Institution engaged in rescuing children from surroundings of the worst class, and from vicious influences."

Then, admitting that, if such were the Law, he might already "in hundreds of cases" unwittingly have broken it, Barnardo pushed on. During the past twenty years he had, without the consent of parents (who frequently were "impossible to trace"), sent many children abroad: always incited by one motive alone—the welfare of the child. What, therefore, was his legal status towards such children? "Am I liable to have these relatives coming to the Courts for aid to bring them back to the misery of their former lot? I would appeal to your Lordships in giving your decision, if it is adverse to me upon this point, to lay down clearly for my guidance—and that of others—what our position is, and will be, under the new and extended application of *habeas corpus*."

During the Appeal it was proved that Mrs. Gossage, now so anxious to have Harry removed to a Catholic Home, had told inmates of the Poor House where she was living that she wanted her newly born child placed under Barnardo's care. Hence, while she was permitting her name and "legal rights" to be exploited for Harry's removal from

Barnardo's, she, at the same time, was bragging that she was going to have her recent baby put into Dr. Barnardo's, where he would be "better looked after" than in the Poor House. This fact, when pressed upon the prosecution by Lord Justice Fry, met with the bland retort that the mother "might not fear the religious influences of Dr. Barnardo's Homes, *while the child was so young*". In reply, one of the Lord Justices pointed the logical sequence: "And when it is old enough to receive religious impressions, there will be another application for a *habeas corpus*, I suppose?" To which suggestion, Counsel for the mother replied: "I do not think Dr. Barnardo would be able to resist it. The statement is not inconsistent with her wish to have her boy brought up as a Roman Catholic. She is, no doubt, a woman who has not behaved with consideration to her child; but she has come under better influences."

At this point a skirmish between the Counsel and the Master of the Rolls, as reported in *The Times*, continued thus:

"THE MASTER OF THE ROLLS: 'Do you mean to excuse her conduct—handing over her child to an organ-grinder, as if he were a monkey? She was *an unnatural brute* '

"COUNSEL: 'We know less about the man to whom Dr. Barnardo has given the boy, than we do of the organ-grinder.'

"MASTER OF THE ROLLS: 'You do not engage my sympathies by such a line of argument.'

"COUNSEL: 'If the mother was a bad woman and handed over her child to a brute, that is no reason for allowing Dr. Barnardo to hand the child to Mr. Norton.'

"MASTER OF THE ROLLS: 'I can see no evidence of her repentance.'

"COUNSEL: 'She now comes to the Court and asks it to help her recover her child, that she may bring it up in her own Faith.'

But before this Appeal concluded, another remarkable admission was made. In reply to a suggestion from Lord Esher that Mrs. Gossage's application was not *bona fide*, in so far as it was being made, and paid for, by a Roman Catholic Institution, Counsel confessed: "I have no doubt the mother was induced to remove her child to a Roman

Catholic Institution, and she might not have taken that step without this influence, but that ought not to affect the Court."

Such facts, however, altered not one iota the legal position. That the parent was the child's natural guardian, and had a right to direct its education, was the ground to which the case always returned. And no proofs of unnatural conduct could affect "the Law".

The "Summing-up" by the Master of the Rolls contains significant remarks. "The history of this case forms", he declared, "a good exposition both of the *undoubted great good which Dr. Barnardo and his Institutions do,* and also of things which are done by him, as I think, beyond the Law." The contention that the mother had now come "under better influences" he spurned: "It is useless to tell me that the mother has come to a better view of her duty to the child. She was a bad woman, and is no better now. . . ." But, though the Summing-up declared that the child had been "betrayed by its mother", the Judgment went against the Doctor: "I say to Dr. Barnardo—that even if the mother had signed the agreement, she might at any time revoke it, and refuse her permission for the child to be sent away. He must hold his agreement subject to that risk." Moreover, the Court held that though Barnardo had not himself received the letter until days after the boy had sailed, his subordinates had received it; and he was responsible. Consequently, it was ordered that: "Dr. Barnardo is bound to use every possible effort to obey the Writ; he must write letters, advertise, and, if need be, go to America to look for the boy."

One passage in the Summing-up is specially pungent:

"I do not say that, in sending the boy away, he (Dr. Barnardo) was not acting for his best interests. *I do not say that I have any suspicion but that Norton was an honest, capable man*; but *legally* Dr. Barnardo has no right to give the child up to him. It was deliberately arranged between them that there should be no means of tracing the child. *I do not wonder at it.* If Norton heard what sort of mother the boy had . . . he would naturally wish to protect himself against relatives coming from the purlieus of London and claiming his adopted child. Dr. Barnardo, however, in giving up the child, did an illegal act. . . ."

So ended the Gossage Case in the Court of Appeal: but one higher tribunal remained; and Barnardo—determined to plumb the Law to its depths—appealed to the House of Lords.[1] Meanwhile, however, the other side—in their zeal to "expose" Barnardo—had filed a new case.

*　　　*　　　*　　　*　　　*

On June 19th, 1888, John James Roddy, on the application of a social worker, and *by his mother's express desire*, was admitted to Barnardo's Homes; careful inquiry having established these facts: This illegitimate boy, nine and a half years old, was frequently running the streets till 11 or 12 p.m.; his mother—a dissolute character who spent her evenings in public-houses—wholly neglected him; their home was a single back room for which the rent (three shillings and sixpence a week) was generally in arrears: and often the neighbours, out of compassion for the lad, gave him food upon the streets. Thus the ground for admission was "gross neglect", endangering the child's life: and the mother signed Barnardo's Agreement passing over to his Homes the care of the boy.

In the Agreement the mother declared herself a Protestant. The boy, moreover, had attended the day-school and Sunday-school of a Protestant Church, and had been baptized a Protestant, while the putative father declared himself the same.

On admission this lad weighed barely forty pounds, though the *average* weight for a boy his age was fifty-six pounds. Good food, however, and regular habits worked wonders, and when, a year and a half after his admission,

---

[1] For a verbatim report of Barnardo's speech on the Gossage Case before the Court of Appeal, see *Before My Judges* (a 56-page Supplement to *Night and Day*, February, 1890).

there came an order for his removal, he was in sturdy health.

But what anticipated this demand, in the mother's name, for the boy's return?

Several times the mother, who, up to this time, had lived with four different men, had visited her son at Leopold House and, more than once, she arrived the worse for drink. But on one occasion she appeared at the Lodge Gate so badly intoxicated that the porter refused her admission; and, being an Irishwoman of violent temper, she stormed and raged. On another occasion, when the boy was allowed to visit her, she got drunk; and Barnardo complained. Again, in September, 1889, the lad had measles; so the mother, calling when he was in the Isolation Ward, was not permitted to see him; though she was told he was getting on nicely, and that in a few days he would be boarded-out in the country—a proposal to which she agreed.

Such were the relations between Barnardo and the mother when, without warning, on December 22nd, 1889, there came a letter, from the firm of solicitors engaged in all the previous actions, demanding, on the mother's behalf, that this Protestant boy—then eleven years of age—be given up to them. What, then, had happened? The facts are simple. On several occasions, when intoxicated, the mother had sworn vengeance on Barnardo for ever refusing her permission to see her son; and once, in quarrelsome mood, she called on her niece—a Roman Catholic—to whom she poured out her spleen. Immediately, the niece insisted on taking her to a priest, and together they persuaded her to transfer the boy to a Catholic Home: it apparently having been told her that some money would be placed in the bank to the boy's credit every week, which she could draw when he left the Catholic Home.

On receipt of the Solicitors' letter, Barnardo was thoroughly annoyed. Already his relations with these lawyers were strained: "For two or three years persistent attempts to remove a special class of children from the Institutions under my care had been made. With one exception, in every instance the relations, whether mothers, fathers or aunts, as the case might be, making these applications, had been persons of either notoriously evil or at least very doubtful character. In all these cases the children had been rescued by me from positions of neglect, physical suffering or destitution, and sometimes from the society of immoral people, or people who had been criminally convicted. But another remarkable similarity ran through every individual case. Although the people were manifestly impecunious, they were, on each occasion, represented by Solicitors and Counsel; and the Solicitors were always the same Firm!"

Naturally, therefore, when these Solicitors demanded the return of this lad to his mother, that he might be placed in "a good School", Barnardo asked questions—which the Solicitors answered, they said, "as a matter of courtesy", maintaining that Barnardo had "no legal right" to put them, and warning him that *in future cases* such "courtesy" was not to be expected. But their answer to the vital question was highly elusive; so Barnardo insisted upon being told the name of this "good School" or, at least, whether it was Protestant or Catholic. That interrogation, in turn, the Solicitors side-stepped: "Our client may perhaps keep the boy under her own care, she being quite able to maintain him." Barnardo knew this statement was misleading so, at once, he directed the Secretary to write to the mother informing her that he should "consider it his duty, as the present guardian of the child, and in its best interests, to seek the advice and authority of the Courts before taking any step in the matter"; and warning her that, if she forced the case into Court, she might have "to satisfy the Judges of the perfect respectability, sobriety and morality" of her own life: for a "searching inquiry" would be made into her "habits and mode of life extending over many years".

But he added, that if she would withdraw her demand, he would have the lad brought to a London Home, to which she could have "the fullest access" compatible with "the Rules of the Institutions".

This letter was not answered by the mother. Apparently she had received instructions to pass all communications to the Solicitors; for forthwith, in her name, they appealed to the Courts: and after an impassioned harangue—during which Counsel read into Barnardo's letter the most sinister of motives—they obtained a *"rule nisi"*.

Thus the Doctor's case, in this Court, was seriously prejudiced, his Counsel from the first being thrust into an atmosphere of suspicion, and even rebuke: so when, on May 19th, 1890, the hearing was concluded, the prospect was dark; and doubly so when the Judges, instead of delivering Judgment on May 20th, as promised, postponed it till "after Whitsuntide" that it might be written.

Among the bundle of Barnardo's unpublished letters passed over to me by his widow is one dated Tuesday, May 20th, 1890. It needs no comment:

"MY DARLING,

"I wired you this morning as soon as I knew that the Judges intend to postpone Judgment till after Whitsuntide.

"I may tell you that my Solicitors and Counsel consider that a *very* bad sign. We have made out a strong case but they are against us, and, to prevent our being successful on appeal, intend to deliver a *written* Judgment. . . . You know I don't 'worry' over *anything*; but this case has *aged* me. Your suggestion is of course intolerable. I may die at my post, but I have never learned to run away. No, my darling, you must prepare for worse if it be God's Will. I can give up my work, if I know He wills it: peacefully lay down the great charge and responsibility I have received from His Hands alone. But, to give up my children to such people to their ruin, *never*—not while life lasts. So now, dear, never suggest that again, as it *hurts* me in my very vitals, and I don't feel right for some time afterwards. [1]

"Meanwhile, to hear the odium under which I at present lie; to submit to imputations of meanness which I loathe—is a heavy Cross

---

[1] Mrs. Barnardo, realizing the tremendous strain to which her husband was subjected, had asked if it might not be wiser to give over the boy Roddy and thus avoid the harassing ordeal of protracted litigation.

indeed. But I have not lost my faith in the overruling Providence of
God. If *He* sits *not* at the helm of this world's affairs, then all is chaos
indeed; but if He be there, calmly but surely guiding and directing, it
is but a little thing for us to trust Him when, amid mist and fog, we lose
our way. *He* has not lost the bearings; He will not abandon His own.
This is my one comfort. Now I must be content to *be* right, rather than
to seem right; and this will I do, God helping me. . . ."

Barnardo's interpretation of the Judges' intention seems
justified by events. The Judgment promised on May 20th
was rendered in two parts—the first, an Order of *habeas
corpus*, on August 5th; the second, an Order for a new
Guardian, on November 4th. "Severe strictures", moreover,
were placed upon Barnardo's conduct, chiefly because of
his letter to the mother; but also because he had sent a
lady to her home district to observe her conduct. Indeed,
the Judges even suggested that Barnardo was "not a fit
person" to have custody of the boy, though, strangely, they
themselves had left him in Barnardo's custody during the
months preceding their order for a new Guardian: and,
again, he was left in Barnardo's care until after the Appeal
Case was heard.

On November 10th, 11th and 12th, 1890, the whole
case came up for rehearing before three Judges in the
Court of Appeal; and there Barnardo acted as his own
Counsel.

To trace the Appeal proceedings would lead us far afield.
Yet certain facts cannot be ignored. As the case proceeded,
Lord Esher (Master of the Rolls) declared: "All I can say
is, after all I have heard in this Case, I think the mind of
the mother depends on 5s. or even 2s. 6d." On one occasion
the mother boasted to neighbours: "I know the Catholics
are going to give me some money soon. If they do not,
after putting me to all this trouble, I will let them know
who I am. . . ." As to her religion, she declared in the
Lower Court she had been a Catholic all her life: yet her
own daughter, twenty-one years old, swore that never had
she known her mother have anything to do with the Roman

Catholic religion, while often she had heard her abuse it. Lord Esher, referring to the mother's veracity, declared: "We (the three Judges) are not children to believe everything she says." Again, it was beyond dispute that she had, of her own choice, signed a contract promising to leave the boy to be reared by Barnardo's Homes; that no reasonable objection could be raised either against the Homes' treatment of the mother or the boy; that the lad was happy in Barnardo's custody, and that he expressed the desire "to remain there". Yet, at this time, the Law robbed these facts of all weight. "When the mother really asked for the child", declared Lord Esher, "you had no right to ask any questions at all. All you had to do was to give it up"; while also he said that, "supposing the mother was the most unfit person in the world to have the custody, nevertheless, if she asks to have the child put into proper custody, then *her unfitness has nothing to do with the matter*".

Now, such a state of the Law meant that the most vicious of parents, if "got at", could be used as puppets by Barnardo's foes. On the maternal rights, therefore, of this drunken, immoral woman, who so cruelly had neglected her child, the whole case hung. "The parent", it was argued, "cannot lose his right by abandonment any more than by agreement."

Barnardo, by *insisting* upon his right to review the Judgment delivered in the Lower Court, including the strictures upon himself, convinced all three Judges not only that, in writing the much-criticized letter to the mother, and in sending a woman to observe her conduct, he was acting in the "best interests of the child", but also that, all considered, it was his "moral duty" so to act.[1] Hence, as the Appeal Case continued, it became obvious that Barnardo was thrown between the horns of a dilemma—the conflict

---

[1] Several persons who, before the admission of the boy Roddy to the Homes, gave evidence regarding the vicious character of the mother, refused to come to Court, some "fearing violence", others timorous of "their trade", etc.

between the Moral Law and the Statute Law: a conflict concerning which all three Judges threw out hints.

The hearing over, the Judges conferred, and requested "time to consider this case". Thirteen days later, on November 25th, their separate Judgments were read.

Lord Esher, commencing his Judgment, declared: "It is said that this is the case of a sensitive mother anxious to have her child under her own care, and wounded at Dr. Barnardo's refusal to let her see it as often as she wished. *I do not believe a word of this.*" Later, he asserted, that when Barnardo received the boy "he was practically upon the streets", and "as poor as he could be"; while, as for the mother's religious motives, he said: "It is absurd to say that she had any religious earnestness; she had nothing of the kind." Then comes a trenchant remark: "It is part of Dr. Barnardo's benevolent business to collect such children as this. I do not know whether the Roman Catholic Institutions do the same. *I can only say that I have not come across any case of a Roman Catholic Institution having rescued a child and Protestant people trying to get it away. If one may say so with all respect, I think Dr. Barnardo is the better scavenger of the two, and picks up most of those gutter children.* The mother deliberately gave the child to Dr. Barnardo, and left it there for eighteen months."

But, despite this high *moral* praise, Lord Esher gave *legal* judgment against Barnardo: "The mother has bound herself by agreement not to take the child away. The Law is perfectly plain. A parent cannot bind himself by any such agreement. . . . The agreement, therefore, is absolutely null." But the ground on which Barnardo was censured in the Court below, he wholly removed: "It was not unnatural that Dr. Barnardo should look closely into the application"; while, again, he asserted that the Doctor, *"not unnaturally,* has this woman closely watched", adding, *"I do not blame him for so doing".* Always, however, the case returned to the iron letter of the Law: "The Law, as Dr. Barnardo has been told before, puts him into this position—that, although he takes a child in at its parent's request and by agreement with him, and expends care and money upon it, nevertheless, whenever the parent chooses to ask for the child, he has no course but to acquiesce, unless he can show some good reason to the contrary." But, ordering Barnardo to "hand over the child", the Master of the Rolls concluded his Judgment thus: "*I do not agree* with the strictures passed on Dr. Barnardo's conduct in the Court below."

Lord Justice Lindley, in passing Judgment, held that, the boy being under fourteen, his illegitimacy in no way interfered with the mother's rights. "I am of opinion that *the Law* requires that the mother's wishes must prevail." Then he added: "*I am not surprised that Dr. Barnardo should feel annoyed at finding his efforts thwarted . . . by persons who do not awake to their own duties to their children until he has rescued them from degradation and ruin.* But the duty of the Court is . . . to administer the Law with absolute indifference to every other consideration; and whilst I *regret that such a contest as this should ever have arisen*, yet, having arisen, it is my duty to say that *the Law* is on the side of the mother. . . ."

Lord Justice Lopes, in his Judgment, suggested that personally he was with Barnardo on all points, legal as well as moral. Emphasizing that the mother "entered voluntarily into an agreement" whereby the child was to be left in Barnardo's Homes "for several years", and that "the desire to remove the child emanates from others, not from herself", he proceeded: "The child, it is to be observed, was happy and desirous to be left with Dr. Barnardo. The child's reputed father had the same desire. *I doubt if the contemplated change into a different atmosphere, with new and different surroundings, will be for the welfare of the child.*" Then, pointing out that the Court below had exercised a legal discretion, he concluded: "In such circumstances, the exercise of the discretion is not lightly to be set aside; and it is for this reason, and this reason only, *I do not dissent* from the Judgments delivered."

But though the decision, on points of Law, went against Barnardo, his moral victory was even more pronounced than in the Gossage Case. For the Judgments were an unanswerable rejoinder to the outcry of many organs of the Press, that "in this case a poor Roman Catholic woman was being refused her very natural desire, to bring up her child in her own faith".[1]

The Roddy Case, as well as the Gossage Case, was taken to the House of Lords. But before either could be decided, certain Bills were before Parliament promising to make for ever impossible such exploitation of parental rights. And the Act wherein this purpose was embodied has, since the day of its passage, been popularly styled "The Barnardo Act".

*   *   *   *   *

The wave of litigation forced upon Barnardo, reaching high-water in 1889-90, left behind it a fertilizing silt. *More than one Judge, after giving a verdict against Barnardo on points of Law, exhibited sympathy for his work by sending a "first donation" to The Homes.* Other effects were more far-reaching. During the long interval between initial steps in the Gossage Case, and its hearing in the Court of Appeal, two important Acts, influenced by facts revealed in this litigation, were passed. One was the *Act for the Prevention of Cruelty to, and better protection of, Children,* which, in certain circumstances, transferred from vicious parents to worthy guardians *all* parental rights.[2] The other was the *Poor Law Act of 1889,* which, in the case of deserted children, transferred to "the guardians of the parish who have supported such children" the parent's normal authority and rights.[3]

[1] For a verbatim report of Barnardo's speeches before the Court of Appeal on this case, see *Am I Unfit*—a 68-page Supplement to *Night and Day*, December, 1890.
[2] See 52 and 53 Vict. cap. 44, section 5, sub-section 1/2.
[3] 52 Vict. cap. 66.

Both these Measures, we repeat, were definitely influenced by facts Barnardo exposed. But the famous *Custody of Children Act*, receiving the Royal Assent on March 26th, 1891, was the immediate outcome of this litigation: and its value to all rescuers of destitute children proved ample reward for Barnardo's pains.

Three Bills were introduced into the House of Lords, and several important debates took place before this Act was moulded into shape. First, a Bill was brought forward by the Earl of Meath, which Debate proved too strong. Later, one was introduced by the Lord Chancellor, which proved too weak. Then a Standing Committee of the House of Lords was appointed, which, after three days' deliberation, forged an acceptable measure.[1] Certain of the Debates, moreover, were spirited and informative. On February 2nd, 1891, the Lord Chancellor exposed the flagrant abuses of the Law as it stood; while Lord Thring followed to show the necessity for reform, and in his speech he plumbed the problem to its depths. The proposed legislation, he declared, was designed to protect "deserted children and waifs and strays" from exploitation by degraded parents, who, after leaving them to be reared by charity, might, years later, when they were an economic asset, appeal to the Courts for the assertion of parental rights. This state of the Law he pronounced "wicked and cruel". Often "the *only* way of saving children is by *keeping them away* from such parents", he avowed. "Is it the object or intention of the Law that these poor children should be handed over to their degradation and ruin? Surely not!"

Countering stock objections, Lord Thring said it was argued: "This measure is an attack upon the home and parental control." But of those raising this argument, he inquired: "*Are the streets a home?*" While to those who quoted the Fifth Commandment as a warrant for inaction, he sug-

---

[1] See "*Bills, Public*", 53 and 54 *Vict.*, House of Lords, July 18th, 1890, December 8th, 1890, and February 6th, 1891

gested that parents who deserted their children had violated the fundamental Law of God, and so had *denied themselves* the filial honour which is a normal parent's due.[1]

But, turning from the Debates, what of the Act? Passed under the title, "An Act to amend the Law relating to the Custody of Children"; its clauses, six in number, prove conclusively with what justice it is styled "The Barnardo Act". (1) The powers of the Court to decline a writ of *habeas corpus* were made emphatic and complete. (2) The Court was empowered, at its discretion, to order repayment of the cost, either whole or in part, for the upbringing of a child. (3) In the case of parents abandoning, deserting or flagrantly neglecting a child, it was specifically stated that an order of *habeas corpus* may be refused, "the Court, in *making this order, to have regard to the conduct of the parent*". (4) In considering a case, the Court was "*to consult the wishes of the child*". (5) In the Act the term "parent" was to apply to anyone at law liable to maintain such a child; while the term "person" was to apply to any school, Institution, etc., which might take over the care of a child. (6) The measure might be cited as "The Custody of Children Act, 1891".[2]

The passing of this Act closed a peculiarly troublesome chapter in the history of Barnardo's Homes; for since March, 1891, they have enjoyed satisfactory legal protection against those who, in the name of unscrupulous parents, could disturb the peaceful tenor of their work. In January, 1892, Cardinal Manning died; and among the first gestures of his successor at Westminster, Cardinal Vaughan, were overtures to Barnardo for an amicable agreement of all matters under dispute. Those overtures were received in the same peaceable spirit in which they were made, Barnardo only requiring that before he would enter into any

[1] See Hansard, House of Lords, February 2nd, February 6th and February 12th, 1891.
[2] The Act passed in the House of Commons exactly as sent from the House of Lords.

Agreement, it must be officially sanctioned by the "Head" of the Roman Catholic Church in England, namely, Cardinal Vaughan. Accordingly, when at last the Agreement was signed, it was of a thoroughly responsible nature; and thenceforth neither litigation nor serious misunderstanding has arisen to mar the cordial, co-operative arrangements which exist between Dr. Barnardo's Homes and the Roman Catholic Church.

The provisions of the Agreement were such as Barnardo had offered from the first. They were thoroughly reciprocal. The usual Catholic demand that every child of a "mixed marriage" be handed over to the Catholic fold, went by the board: only the legal status was admitted. Consequently, Barnardo agreed to pass over to Catholic Homes the children of Roman Catholic fathers, or, if illegitimate, of Roman Catholic mothers, while Roman Catholic Homes, in the case of Protestants, guaranteed reciprocal action. But, in either case, if no steps were taken to receive a child within a fortnight of notification, no later claim could be made.

Years of litigation, therefore, ended in conciliation. But was Barnardo right in permitting himself to be drawn into the Courts? Many warm friends, at the time, answered, "No! Better give up every child for whom a demand is made than be dragged into litigation!" The perspective of distance, however, shows that he was more than justified in his course. Creative imagination made him see plainly that if he surrendered before the challenge of litigation, he was but prolonging the existence of an unjust Law; while faith in the righteousness of his Cause made him fearless of personal attack in pursuit of reform. The result, therefore, was, that out of the travail of this litigation was born legislation which made the legal position of his own, and many other, children secure. Nor was that litigation paid for from moneys sent to The Homes: every penny was raised by a circle of friends.

In spite, too, of all the misrepresentation of Barnardo's

attitude, the Homes' income, during these years of legal contest, had steadily increased. The figures are more eloquent than words. In 1886, the year preceding the outbreak of these disputes, contributions were scarcely £77,000; by 1891, the year "The Barnardo Act" was passed, they had mounted to over £131,000; and increase in every Department had kept pace with increased support. The Children's Champion, therefore, had entered the lists against legal giants not in vain.

CHAPTER XIII

MIGRATION AND EMPIRE BUILDING

IN June, 1921, on hearing of the death of the Hon. James Page, the Federal Parliament of Australia adjourned. For more than fifteen years Mr. Page had been returned, without a break, by the same constituency, to the Australian House of Representatives, where he had held responsible Government posts, including that of Chief Whip: and so sterling had been his honesty, so equitable his conduct, so distinguished his services, that he had won the esteem of the whole House. He was a man of whom the Commonwealth was proud; and, if one might judge from Press reports at his death, he was the most beloved Australian legislator of his day.

But whence came the man to whose career such tributes were paid? Page himself was never too proud to reveal the facts of his early life. As a lad he was a waif on London streets. Nay, worse! He already was learning the trade of a thief when Dr. Barnardo intervened and trained him for a useful career. More than once from public platforms Page told the story of his rescue.

In Cable Street, East London, he, with the help of another urchin, was one day striving to rob a drunken Frenchman carrying a money-box, when Barnardo intercepted him, and finding him homeless and destitute, admitted him to the Stepney Home.

Following a careful training, young Page went abroad, and, after serving with distinction in the Boer War, became a settler in Australia, where, having amassed a fortune of some £50,000, he entered Parliament as a tribune of the Common People. And how nobly he served them all Australia knows. The Prime Minister, under whom he was Chief Whip, described him as "one of the most faithful and trustworthy colleagues the head of any Government could possibly desire"; while the official Secretary of the Commonwealth of Australia in London declared that his "meritorious career" had honoured his adopted country no less than "the Home in which he was raised".

Not only, however, did Page serve faithfully the Australian people: he helped materially to forge a chain of contact between them and The Homes to which he owed all. In 1908, when the Rev. W. J. Mayers was in Australia representing Barnardo's, Page took the chair at his great meeting in the capital, and after telling the crowded audience that he was an "Old Barnardo Boy", related the story of his rescue. But more. He passed a subscription list, headed by a generous personal gift, among Members of the Federal Parliament, and rendered valiant help toward erecting the magnificent "Australasian Hospital' at the Girls' Village Home. In another way, too, did this Old Boy remember the Homes' work: "Many and many a time have I said a prayer for the dear, kind and good benefactor of the poor waif of London"; while, referring to Barnardo's death, he said: "I felt I had lost a relative."

The Hon. James Page is but an outstanding example of the scores of thousands of human lives transformed and beautified by Barnardo's Homes. And although Barnardo miracles are everywhere apparent in Britain, the Homes' richest fruits, as Page's life suggests, are to be found in the Dominions overseas.

For years now the work started by those remarkable sisters, Annie McPherson and Mrs. Birt—the pioneers of juvenile migration—has been incorporated in Dr. Barnardo's Homes. Very fitting, moreover, was that incorporation: for, from the first, Barnardo co-operated heartily with those gifted women; and when, in 1870, they took to Canada the first party of juveniles ever landed on Colonial soil, there was included in that "first hundred" a sprinkling of Barnardo lads; while the whole hundred, incidentally, had been drilled by Barnardo. Again, between 1870 and 1882, when the Doctor started his independent migration scheme, he sent nearly 1,000 of his children to Canada under Miss McPherson: and even after the two organizations worked separately, the warmest harmony prevailed. It was only natural, therefore, that when, after a life of noble service during which nearly 20,000 needy children were placed in Canadian families, the McPherson-Birt work fell on hard times, it should be rescued by Barnardo's.

Hence, these two institutions, long amalgamated, may now be surveyed as one, and legitimately referred to as "Dr. Barnardo's Homes". What a sight, therefore, would present itself could the careers of that army of children sent to New Lands of Promise be reviewed to-day. It would be fifty thousand strong, this Colonial army: which means that more than half of all the juveniles sent from Britain to the Dominions, by all Child Emigration Societies put together, would be included in its ranks. As early as 1870 it commenced its march, and still it is marching on.

If, therefore, on Imagination's wings we could but conceive the spectacle of a Grand Review, a stirring romance would ensue.

Among the fifty thousand Colonial "Old Boys and Girls" are legislators and Cabinet Ministers in Canada and Australia. Among them, too, is a noble band, scores strong, who are Doctors of Divinity, Ministers of Religion, Foreign Missionaries, Y.M.C.A. Secretaries and Superintendents of philanthropic institutions, such as Knowles Home, Kildonan, Winnipeg.[1] In the van of this procession, moreover, are University lecturers, a group of physicians and surgeons, a bevy of barristers and solicitors, together with a company of dentists, civil and electrical engineers, chemists, surveyors, mineralogists, school principals, etc. Indeed, as the Fifty

---

[1] "Knowles Home" for orphan and homeless boys owed its origin to an address made by Barnardo on one of his visits to Canada; its *present* Superintendent, Mr. Maurice Ford, is an old Barnardo boy.

Thousand file by, it will be observed that every branch of the learned professions is honourably represented; while beside them is a goodly number of Church organists, professional musicians and singers, choir leaders, journalists, editors, newspaper proprietors and advertising artists, as well as a large body of nurses who, in thousands of homes, from Atlantic to Pacific, have proved themselves ministering angels.

Then, behind this professional band, comes a keen-eyed battalion of business men and women, numbering well over a thousand: among whom are many proprietors of shops, stores and other commercial enterprises—wholesale and retail. Among them, too, are not a few manufacturers, contractors, builders, bankers, brokers, commercial travellers, insurance agents, grain-buyers, station-agents, postmasters, etc., together with a group of fair cashiers, bookkeepers, stenographers and typists.

Next in this review appear two or three battalions of sturdy, independent mechanics and artisans, whistling merrily as on they march; for like the "Village Blacksmith" they "owe not any man". Among these sinewy fellows are all manner of railway mechanics, including "transcontinental" engineers; for deep is the debt of Canada's railways to Barnardo Boys. Here, too, are captains, pilots, engineers, firemen, pursers, etc., who ply the St. Lawrence, the Great Lakes and other water routes. Within the same ranks is a large company of masons, carpenters, cabinet-makers, plumbers, gas-fitters and electricians who have helped to build scores of thousands of Colonial homes; while marching briskly by their side comes a jolly party of wireless operators, telegraphists, watch-makers, blacksmiths, shoe-makers and other skilled workmen. Then, as the above-mentioned are passing out of sight, accompanied by a fine contingent of Old Girls, who have married into every vocation already reviewed, emerges a corps of policemen, who, with eyes fixed sharply on all in front, are shouting brisk orders that none block the traffic and all keep in step.

It is not, however, among the ranks of the learned professions, among statesmen, business men or mechanics—splendid as their contribution is—that the significance of Barnardo's work is best gauged. Nor can it truly be appraised by the fact that, among the Fifty Thousand are hundreds of Sunday-school officials, a stalwart body of temperance leaders, Grand Masters of many Fraternal Lodges, a fine company of Church deacons, and not a few civic office holders, including Reeves of townships and Mayors or Mayoresses of towns. In a different direction must the majesty of Barnardo's work be judged.

The author, in his book, *Lord Shaftesbury and Social-Industrial Progress,*[1] wrote :

"Wherever the pioneer work of the British Empire is being done to-day, there, with shoulders to the wheel of progress, stand Barnardo boys, an honour to the Institution that mothered them. The writer has been engaged in social work on Canada's frontiers from ocean to ocean; he has laboured among miners, lumber-men, fishermen, prospectors, homesteaders, factory workers and railway builders; yet everywhere, from East to West, on far-flung outposts, he has been confronted with the endeavours of Barnardo boys . . . these frontiersmen toil in an environment where no flag is flying and no drum is beating, but they are, none the less, to be numbered among the true builders of Britain—among the real heroes of Empire."

The above was an observation from first-hand experience over a number of years; and deeper study of this subject has intensified the admiration I then expressed. For, as our review proceeds apace, we see that, among Barnardo's Overseas Army, are thousands whose daily toil marks them as frontiersmen and adventurers : men whose lives are spent in blazing the trail of progress. Among such are many who, in the bowels of the earth, mine for coal, gold, silver, nickel and other minerals; among them, too, are hundreds of homesteaders, ranchers and cow-boys, of fire-rangers and

[1] Third and Popular English Edition, 1928, Allen & Unwin, London.

MIGRATION

1. Off to the "Golden West"   2. The Captain proves a real pal
3. "So this is Australia !"   4. Barnardo girls—Australia bound

EMPIRE BUILDERS

1. "It's Canada for us!"   2. Deck games in mid-ocean
3. "I'll have a farm of my own some day!"   4. A farewell to Old England

trappers; of North-West Mounted Police and prospectors; of river-drivers and lumber-jacks; of road and railroad builders; of fishermen and ferrymen; of foresters, surveyors and the like.

Here follows a fine array of domestic helpers, girls and women, whose practical knowledge of cooking, baking, sewing and domestic science in general, has gladdened many a Canadian and Australian home. But most important of all, and tens of thousands strong, are the massed battalions of food producers whose stakes are in the open fields. Sons of the soil are they, who have cultivated millions of Overseas acres. Some are wheat farmers in Western Canada, some "mixed" farmers in the Eastern provinces; some sheep-farmers in New South Wales; others are dairymen, thoroughbred-stock breeders, bee-farmers, fruit-growers, market-gardeners, etc.—an amazing array: and no small proportion own their own land.

These vigorous yeomen, together with their sister help-mates and the frontiersmen who just preceded them, comprise some 80 per cent. of the Fifty Thousand. What a counterbalancing influence they have asserted against the modern rush cityward! And in what country is that influence more needed to-day than in Canada, where nine-tenths of Barnardo's migrants have taken up their abode? For, though Canada has tens of millions of fertile acres awaiting the advent of the plough, it is notorious the degree to which Canadian farmers' sons are deserting the country-side, and rushing off to city pursuits; while, more notorious is the unwillingness of our city-bred folk to open their eyes, and behold the challenge of Canada's frontiers. In developing our vast resources, therefore, what a contribution Barnardo's protégés have made!—four-fifths of the Fifty Thousand, to say nothing of their progeny, engaged in farming or frontier pursuits!

More than 98 per cent. of Barnardo's Overseas Company have now marched past; and, of all these—his sons and daughters—the "Father of Nobody's Children" would justly be proud: for they are Empire Builders of sterling worth. We wish, therefore, that the review might now stop; but this, honesty cannot permit. Every society has its failures; and Barnardo's Overseas Contingent has not been exempt. More than 98 per cent. have "made good"; but among the remainder are a batch of ne'er-do-wells, some scores who have fallen before the too-alluring temptation to "get rich quick", a pathetic little band whose health has collapsed, a sprinkling of moral failures, a few drunkards, perchance—though almost the whole army are teetotallers— and even some who have served "time" behind prison bars. The miracle, however, is that of such there are so few.

But concerning this remnant a word anon. First let us inquire into the cause of Barnardo's unparalleled success. As early as 1870, when Barnardo, under Annie McPherson, sent his first protégés abroad, it was arranged that only the strong, the alert, the industrious and the dependable should be permitted to embark on the Great Adventure; for none realized more fully than these pioneers, that they were planting seedlings in virgin soil. Hence, when in 1882 Barnardo launched his own emigration scheme, his plans were thoroughly wrought. Only the "cream of the Homes" was sent abroad; which principle eliminated all with physical, mental or moral taint. All parties were accompanied on board ship by Barnardo officials acquainted with the children. Receiving Homes, too, were opened up in Canada, from which the children were placed out on farms: it being a fixed principle that every home be inspected before any child be placed, and that only exemplary Protestant households be accepted—a principle safeguarded by recommendations from a local clergyman, a Justice of the Peace and a medical man. But even after these precautions had been taken, the children were visited, without notice, at least quarterly; while also Barnardo's constituted themselves their *legal* guardians till eighteen years of age, and exercised *parental* guardianship over boys till twenty-one and over girls till married. Thus no Barnardo wards were allowed to drift.

A summary of Barnardo's rules makes his position clear:

"(*a*) That only the flower of the flock shall be emigrated to Canada; those (1) who are in robust health, physical and mental; (2) who are thoroughly upright, honest and virtuous; and (3) who, being boys, have been industrially trained in our workshops, or who, being girls, have had careful instruction in domestic pursuits.

"(*b*) That continual supervision shall be exercised over all these emigrants after they have been placed out in Canadian homesteads; first by systematic visitation; second, by regular correspondence. . . .

"(*c*) That in the case of the total failure of any emigrants, the Colonies shall be safeguarded by their return at our expense, whenever possible, to England."[1]

In the light of these rules, and the splendid training Barnardo children receive before they leave the Homes, this migration achievement begins to explain itself. But when it is remembered that, besides the above-mentioned safeguards, Barnardo's have their own Canadian magazine, *Ups and Downs*, which links their Overseas family not only one to another, but to the parent body in the Mother Land; that their Receiving Home in Jarvis Street, Toronto, keeps an Ever-Open Door to welcome visits from all members of the fold; and that correspondence with the Homes is encouraged at every turn—the achievement is understandable.

Yet, despite the miracles wrought by Barnardo's migration system for sixty years, there has broken out in Canada, from time to time, an epidemic of abuse. From the first his labours have been bitterly attacked by persons with a neurotic tendency to see every venture of faith in the darkest hues—persons to whom *opportunity* spells only *risk*. Moreover, there are to be found in all countries, young as well as old, the proverbial "Mrs. Grundy" and her troop of cronies, who, with beams in their own eyes, are always zealous to

[1] For a fuller statement of early rules of migration, see *Something Attempted: Something Done*, pp. 183–187.

remove motes from their neighbours' eyes. Such persons, while shouting from the house-tops their faith in Democracy, will yet deny to innocent children every opportunity for a decent start in life; and the fact that a child was once destitute, and is perchance of illegitimate birth, is sufficient in their eyes to anathematize it for ever.

From this class of person both Annie McPherson and Dr. Barnardo had to bear the brunt of violent abuse. In 1870, when the first party of juvenile migrants ever sent to Canada were in mid-ocean, the furore broke out. Mad reports were circulated that an army of half-savage street-arabs, collected from London's vilest alleys, were about to be "dumped" in Canada—"wild oats" to be planted in "virgin soil". Accordingly, when Miss McPherson arrived with her "first hundred", including several Barnardo lads, her reception was prepared. Immigration officers were present with Government orders strictly to inspect every boy in the party, and, if need be, to bundle back the lot. When, however, the boat pulled into Quebec, the officials —not Miss McPherson—stood aghast. The boys were sturdy and well-nourished; they filed off the boat in the most orderly manner; they were all keen, affable and obedient; careful tests proved them intelligent and well-trained; and far from exhibiting the marks of "wild arabs", they were courteous and polite.

The tables, consequently, were turned. Mr. Louis Stafford, the Immigration Officer concerned, was so impressed that forthwith he offered to "place" all the boys, adding: *"Canada could do with any number of such lads!"* Miss McPherson, nevertheless, did not accept the offer. She was determined that her boys be "placed" only in Christian households which she had inspected: and from this principle neither she nor Barnardo ever budged, knowing well that they could place and supervise their children better than any Government staff.[1]

---

[1] See L. M. Birt: *The Children's Homefinder*, pp. 63–64.

So ended the attack of 1870. But, years later, when Barnardo, through his own machinery, had sent 6,128 children to Canada, there broke out another hue and cry against the dumping of "gutter-snipes" in "our Fair Dominion", it being contended that these youngsters were criminals "in embryo". The Government, consequently, was again moved to action. But exhaustive investigation proved that only fifty-two Barnardo protégés had ever been convicted of any legal misdemeanour—a record far better than that of our Canadian-born population. That hysteria, therefore, was soon cured: but, decades afterwards, the mania flared forth once more; so the builders of the Canadian Pacific Railway, Lord Strathcona and Lord Mount Stephen, commissioned Mr. Bruce Walker, then a prominent newspaper proprietor in Canada, and now Chief Commissioner of Canadian Immigration from Europe, to undertake a painstaking inquiry into the record of Barnardo boys and girls in the Dominion: and so flattering to these children were the facts revealed, that Lord Mount Stephen presented to Dr. Barnardo Canadian securities worth $250,000, stipulating that they be held in trust, and their interest devoted exclusively to the migration of Barnardo wards to Canada,[1] while Lord Strathcona's appreciation was marked by a generosity only less princely.

*   *   *   *   *

One day we Canadians will awake from our stupor of prejudice to appraise the stupendous debt we owe Barnardo for piloting to our shores his splendid army of young citizens, and watching over them till they became fully-fledged citizens of their adopted land. When that day dawns, we shall erect to his memory a noble monument; for not only was he the greatest champion of destitute children whom History can acclaim, but also he was the greatest pioneer of successful migration Canada has yet known.

[1] This gift was followed by several others, averaging about $50,000.

CHAPTER XIV

POUNDS, SHILLINGS, PENCE

BARNARDO's first public gift was a packet of twenty-seven farthings. Before his death, scarcely forty years later, he had received scores, if not hundreds, of gifts of £1,000 or more. An examination of his *first* Balance Sheet shows that the year's income and expenditure was then just over £200. Now the Homes' annual income and expenditure is more than half a million pounds. And that sum, expressive of the people's love, is contributed from citizens in every walk of life throughout the Empire, from King and Queen, who are patrons of the Homes, to the humblest seamstress and casual labourer, who reckon it an honour to "do their bit": while *outside* the Empire, from persons of every nation and clime, come auxiliary gifts—some from ambassadors at European Courts, some from the grandchildren of cannibals inhabiting Christianized islands in the Southern Seas.

These facts are symbolic. They suggest, first, the amazing increase of interest, the world over, in child-rescue endeavour since Barnardo started his flaming crusade, and, second, the degree to which his Homes are now revered as a pioneer and guide in the delicate process of remoulding juvenile life. But, despite the world-interest manifested to-day in Barnardo's work, the collecting of more than half a million pounds a year in voluntary gifts is an achievement; and well may we ask: "How is it done?"

From the night of that apocalyptic vision, when Jim Jarvis revealed to the missionary-student the existence of the "Don't-Live-Nowhere" tribe, Barnardo determined that "something must be done". Later, under Shaftesbury's influence, he came to see that East London, not China, must be the seat of his life's missionary task. Obvious difficulties, however, stood in the way. No Missionary Society was at hand to finance such work; and whence would come funds? The task, too, must involve a great venture of faith: a venture augmented by Barnardo's religious outlook at that time; for, as an "Open Brother", two of his guiding principles were never to "beg" for funds, and always to obey the Biblical injunction—"Owe no man anything".

For years, too, he adhered strictly to these principles. More than once, when extension programmes were under way, he called off builders, plumbers and painters till money was in hand to complete the work: for of borrowing he would have none. And though he would state the *opportunities* and *needs* of his Mission in organs like *The Christian*, with strong suggestions that here was a field of service for "the Lord's stewards", he would not "beg"; and, except in professedly Christian circles, he would not even make known the claims of his work.

Gradually, however, with the ripening of his religious life, he became less exclusive and more tolerant. Brethrenism, he discovered, was a creed too narrow and rigid for the full expression of his soul's life. Soon, therefore, he was holding fellowship with friends of more latitudinarian views; and with an expanded horizon came a distinct modification of his financial tenets. Increasingly he realized that God-inspired humanitarian endeavours are deeper and broader than most creeds; while, simultaneously, came a multiplication of charity, adaptability and co-operative grace.

In the process of this evolution certain landmarks are discernible: the most significant, in ultimate effect, being the death of Little Carrots, who, it will be remembered, was temporarily refused admission because the Home was full; and "the appointed time" proved "too late". The Director, accordingly, swore there and then before God that *never again* would any destitute child be refused immediate admission: and from that hour his famous pledge became the watchword of his work. But with an increasing army of young destitutes surging through his now Ever-Open Door, his declaration, NO DESTITUTE CHILD EVER REFUSED

ADMISSION, was in time challenged by his principle "Owe no man anything".

Year after year huge enlargement schemes had to be carried out to house and train what soon became "The Largest Family in the World"; and with the "Jubilee" expansion of 1887 it was no longer possible to raise current income sufficient to foot all the bills. Borrowing became a necessity; but by this time Barnardo's interpretation of the aforementioned injunction had so expanded that he could justify his step. In his 1888 Report he wrote:

"I have, during the past four or five years, been busily occupied in acquiring the freehold of much of the property hitherto held only on lease. I have also explained the necessity of replacing . . . old insanitary and inefficient buildings by new, more capacious and more suitable structures. Special gifts were received from generous donors to meet many of those requirements, but the greater portion of the requisite cost still remained to be defrayed out of the General Fund of the Institutions. The policy of piecemeal alterations was however felt to be both expensive and burdensome, and at length my Committee and I came to the conclusion that the wiser and more prudent course to adopt would be to spread the remainder of this *Capital Expenditure* over several years. . . . This expenditure was really one which will permanently benefit the Institutions in the future; and it appeared to us that, in view of this fact, it would be unfair to cripple the operations of the Homes during the current year by diverting so large a sum from the natural needs and development of the work, to *what was actually and principally an investment for the days to come.* Hence the resolution to borrow on the security of the freehold property of the Institution, a sum which was expended solely on increasing the value of the security. . . . Thus it will be seen that, although I am indebted to the Bankers for a considerable amount, yet, as the freehold property on which the advance was obtained is being steadily increased by the sum borrowed, *I have not really been guilty of any breach of the commandment* referred to. The whole matter is therefore simply . . . one of account, which will adjust itself (D.V.) in a few years. . . ." [1]

Twenty years earlier this explanation would have been unconvincing to Barnardo himself: then under no pretext could he have been persuaded to borrow a penny. But was his changed attitude right or wrong? Among those who

---

[1] *Something Attempted: Something Done*, pp. 263–264.

thought it wrong was a tried friend, Lord Radstock, who, years previously, had quietly given £1,000 toward the purchase of the "Edinburgh Castle". Now, he felt that Barnardo, by mortgaging certain buildings and thus extending his work on borrowed funds, was running counter to the Word of God. But for another reason Radstock grieved. He believed the increasingly latitudinarian character of Barnardo's appeals represented a cleavage with his first avowed principle, never to "beg". And, in the commonly accepted meaning of that word, Radstock was right. Correspondence which, during a period of financial strain, passed between these old friends portrays two noble characters who once held fellowship side by side, now journeying on different roads. Radstock was looking back wistfully to earlier days. The spiritual foundations of the work, however, Barnardo believed were as solid as ever: so wherein, and wherefore, the cleavage? The answer points back to the Homes' watchword; for, if no destitute child were refused admission, and if increasingly such children thronged through their doors, then finances had to keep pace. So gradually Barnardo came to believe a duty was laid upon him to *educate* the Christian public as to the "grace" of liberality in "the Children's Cause". And though never would he admit himself a "beggar", right royally did he achieve this task.

"A few fleas", runs an old proverb, "keep a dog on the move." If a human analogy be permitted, the advent of mortgages and debts increased even Barnardo's activity; while, as for his Committee, it goaded them into endeavour on many fronts. For, as the Doctor once confided to Mr. W. Hind Smith, his solemn pledge and the advance programme it forced upon him, often became "a thorn in the Committee's flesh".

But what exactly was the change in Barnardo's financial outlook; and what steps in that change are patent to-day? Now, in facing this question, it should be remembered that,

P

though Barnardo's work was rooted in a soil continually nourished by prayer, never did he, like George Müller, claim to receive his support *wholly* in response to prayer. His *First Occasional Record* makes his early position plain: "I do not want to be mistaken or to be supposed to take higher ground than that I really do. The funds have hitherto not been supplied *simply* in answer to prayer, for I have from time to time very freely made the need known *to believers*." The thought, nevertheless, of being *wholly* dependent upon prayer was, at this time, his ideal: "I can say that I never read that remarkable book entitled *Narrative of Facts*, etc., by Mr. George Müller, of Bristol, . . . without feeling at once encouraged by the example of what living faith in God *can* do, and humbled by contrast with that unto which *I* have attained."

This was Barnardo's *first* official statement concerning money affairs: his *last* was a clarion call to the Nation, challenging her, in Christ's name, to rise up and provide for her every child a reasonable start in life. Yet between these two positions there was no fixed gulf; for, each succeeding year, Barnardo saw more clearly that an essential part of his ministry was to kindle in the hearts of his countrymen a fuller generosity on the Children's behalf. Hence, almost imperceptibly, the challenge of his work led him by stages from the former position to the latter. The death of Carrots he considered a revelation from God. So his pledge never again to refuse prompt admission to *any* destitute child was to him a holy vow. But the fulfilment of this pledge brought an ever-increasing inrush of destitute children, thus compelling the purchase of more land, the erection of new buildings, the extension of old ones, and the freehold-purchase of properties previously held only on lease. These advances, therefore, demanded a huge increase in funds; and remarkable as was the increase that poured in, such a programme as that undertaken in 1887 could never have been met by a single year's donations. Mortgages had to be placed: and although the income, year by year, mounted higher and higher, so insistent was the demand for multiplied facilities, that even till the Founder's death, debt hung, as a black cloud, over the Homes.

This cloud, however, had its use. It forced Barnardo afresh to "search the Scriptures" on the whole subject of soliciting aid in carrying on "the Lord's work"; and the more he searched them, the more was he led to take up common ground with St. Paul, that *generosity* must be stimulated as a Christian *grace*. Hence often did he preach with singular power on St. Paul's words: "Therefore, as ye abound in everything, in faith, and utterance, and knowledge, and in all diligence, and in your love to us, see that ye abound in *this grace* (liberality) also." [1] But his favourite appeal was from Christ's words when, nearing Jerusalem, He sent two disciples to fetch an ass and her colt, instructing them that, if any man say aught, they reply: "*The Lord hath need of them.*" [2]

The manner whereby Barnardo used this text to remind Christian people that, if true to their trust, they are really "God's hands", whereby He conveys "messages of love to His needy little ones", is clearly set forth in his own words, penned in 1889:

"I have, therefore, spoken by word of mouth where possible, and by printed 'appeals' at other times, always animated by the spirit of the message Our Lord once gave to His disciples, and, pointing to money, talents, time and men, have said, with much plainness of speech, 'THE MASTER HATH NEED OF THESE'.

"In short, I have thought that, just as it is the *duty* of faithful ministers of the Gospel to expostulate with their flocks, for any failure to obey the exhortations of the Word of God, in respect to the general obligations and duties of Christian life and service, so it is necessary that there should be from time to time earnest voices raised aloud in the Church, to assert the peculiar privilege and duty of sustaining Home and Foreign Missions, to show that it is more blessed to give than to receive, and to enforce, by every legitimate means, the great truth that *the work of Christ in the world demands self-sacrifice and generous devotion on the part of all who bear*

[1] 2 Cor. viii. 7.   [2] Matt. xxi. 3.

His name. I have tried to point out to thousands who, so far as active stewardship is concerned, are almost cumberers of the ground, that their responsibility to evangelize the masses, to rescue the perishing, to deliver homeless and suffering children from the power of the destroyer, cannot be set aside by giving *an opiate* to the conscience, and that a *literal obedience* to His command, who said, 'Suffer the children to come unto Me', is *the bounden duty of all Christians.* So, far from feeling that such 'appeals' as mine involve a lack of faith, I never dare issue one without committing it in believing prayer to God, and waiting upon Him in daily expectation for results. As regards any loss of dignity in assuming the rôle of a beggar, that in itself, even if it existed, would be to me a very small matter where God's work is concerned. No such result, however, is really involved, for I consider it to be *the distinct exercise of a Christian ministry* of a most important kind, to urge our Lord's people everywhere to give liberally to His work."

In thus urging Christian people to liberality, Barnardo could speak from the depths of rich experience. Nearly seventeen years of service he bestowed upon the Homes without any pay; and when, finally, owing to financial embarrassments, he had to accept a salary, the amount was not half what he could have earned as a medical practitioner. But another fact enabled him to express himself with boldness: from the day of his conversion, he laid aside a fixed proportion of his income for "The Lord's Cause".

With ripening experience, Barnardo's financial outlook came to square itself with Wesley's famous injunction: "*Make* all you can; *Save* all you can; *Give* all you can." For he, like Wesley, came to believe that money honestly made, honourably saved, and generously given to Christ-like ends, becomes a veritable sacrament conveying to the needy the love of God. But, before death, Barnardo would have gone farther and sanctioned the dictum of William Booth: "Give me your money and I will cleanse it; I will wash it in the tears of the fatherless and lay it on the Altars of Humanity." Thus, with the passing of years, the area of Barnardo's appeal was substantially enlarged; but, in conjunction with this fact, it should be remembered that never—no matter how sore his need—would he issue any appeal which was not based squarely upon the Christian faith. More than once it was pointed out to him that, if only he would issue a limited number of appeals without any reference to his Faith, these could be placed in the hands of certain wealthy people, with surety of substantial support. But this he refused to do.

Repeatedly Barnardo declared he had a "special mission to the stingy", and continually he emphasized the belief that all men, whatever their rank, colour, nationality or creed, are stewards of the treasures of God. The implications of his philosophy, therefore, being universal, the doors of his Homes stood open to *absolutely all*: but this fact altered not the *Christian* character of his appeal; and proofs of its effectiveness are legion. On one occasion, in the early days, when addressing a certain drawing-room meeting, he pointed out that his weekly expenses were then £350, and suggested that there were persons present who, if they would fully respond to Christ's call, could support the Homes for a week, or even more. Next morning, among the cheques received at Headquarters was one for £1,400— "to support your family for four weeks".

But, though Barnardo came to feel that a "paramount duty" was "laid upon him", to urge "in the most forcible manner" the claims of destitute children, and thus "awaken sluggish consciences", he believed profoundly that, his utmost done, he was absolutely dependent upon God; and that more than once, in his extremity, Providence had intervened to save the day. He could have said with one of the greatest statesmen of modern times: "I never worry. I always do the *best* I can; I leave the rest to God." Nor was his trust misplaced. The Spring of 1882 found Barnardo in peculiarly tight straits. Week after week his income was exceptionally small; immediately ahead were liabilities exceptionally large: in a few days, accounts running into four figures had to be met. The Homes' extremity was a matter of special prayer on the part of all the staff; yet for days the income continued appallingly low. Faith was tried as in a furnace; but when the situation appeared desperate, an amazing thing occurred:

"On the afternoon of May 3rd," writes Barnardo, "I was informed that 'a person' wished to see me. . . . She refused to tell her business to anyone. I did not know her, she said, but if I would only see her for a minute she would be content. So she sat down among messengers, porters and several poor boys making application for admission. Summoned from a room at the upper part of the house, where I tried in vain to get a few minutes' quiet for necessary writing, I came through the lower hall, where my pertinacious visitor sat, to reach another caller who was waiting in the Sale Room. As I passed, my visitor said: 'You are hard to approach.' I replied: 'Not exactly so, but I am very, very busy, and unless callers have some definite business to communicate, I leave them to my kind helpers. . . .' 'But I have some money for you,' she said. 'Thank you,' I responded, 'I am always glad to receive such help, and just now especially so. Please sit down a moment and I shall be free. . . .' I advanced to meet my other visitors. Quickly disposing of them, I called my pertinacious friend into an inner office; standing at the door of which she said, while tears rolled down her face: 'I bring you this money because your doors are never closed to any poor child. Go on with your blessed work! Never turn away one destitute child. God will surely help you,' and, to my astonishment, she placed in my hand a Bank of England note for £1,000. . . .

"I gasped for breath, while wonder and gratitude struggled for expression. My visitor gave me, however, fresh cause for such feelings, as she added: 'And I rejoice to know that your children are kept free from the workhouse taint, and that you seek to bring them up in the fear of the Lord.' Then another note for £1,000 was placed in my not unwilling hand. I now resigned myself to the inevitable. I could only feel . . . 'Oh, Lord, how wonderful are Thy ways'; and certainly this feeling was increased to utter bewilderment when my visitor slowly took a *third* note for £1,000 from her bag and placed it where the other two already were—in my hands!

"Declining to give her name, or to accept a receipt, but assuring me that she was familiar with every detail of our work, and had visited it, inspected it, and prayed for it, my visitor . . . turned quickly and was gone ere ever I was aware."

Dr. Barnardo's widow has related to the author the following episode: One year, winter setting in exceptionally early, and numbers at the Homes having rapidly increased, blankets were so scarce that rolls of paper had to be used between the quilts. This, of course, could not continue. Blankets had to be procured in large numbers, and no

money was at hand. Ardent, united prayer was raised to
God; and the following morning a Quaker gentleman
called to see Mrs. Barnardo, saying that the night previous
he was unable to sleep, for a Voice kept saying to him:
"Barnardo's children are shivering in bed! See thou to their
want!" This good man, on ascertaining the proportions of
the need, at once wrote a cheque in three figures: next
night every child in the Homes was snug and warm.

Such deliverances the Homes have experienced again and
again. Here is an intervention Barnardo loved to recall.
On the shortest notice, he was informed that £500 must
be paid almost at once or a mortgage would be foreclosed.
Two days before the vital date, not a penny was in hand
which could be devoted to this cause and, to make matters
worse, along came another emergency claim for £50.
The day before the threatened foreclosure receipts were
below par; on the morning of the critical date they were
smaller still. Hope lay vanquished. All Barnardo could
now do was to throw himself on the mercy of the lawyer
who held the mortgage, and such action seemed futile.
With a sad heart, he was making his way to the lawyer's
office, when, passing down Pall Mall, a "military man"
accosted him: "I beg your pardon, sir! But are you not
Dr. Barnardo?" The unknown gentleman explained that
he had just returned from India, and that Colonel —— had
entrusted to him a packet for the Homes. Soon Barnardo
was seated in a Pall Mall club untying a small box. It
contained £650—the proceeds of an Indian bazaar.

Notwithstanding the remembrance of many such deliverances, Barnardo's Committee more than once was
alarmed by the proportions to which the Homes kept
expanding and by the accompanying expense. For, although
income sped forward, expenditure kept pace; and sometimes
shot ahead. Thus, if this year a mortgage was lifted, next
year a further building programme augmented debt. Moreover, Barnardo was a man who would have kept any

Committee awake; for if he believed a course to be dictated by Duty, he was liable to resort to peremptory methods; and then he was extremely difficult to curb. In 1881, for instance, without informing his Committee, he published an article in "*The Christian*," *announcing his intention* to open a Youths' Labour House for "destitute cases beyond the age of boyhood". And in this article the *President* of the Homes saw "*by chance*" the announcement of the scheme, with an accompanying appeal for funds. Next mail brought to Barnardo a trenchant letter: Lord Cairns expressed no doubt as to the "urgency" of such cases, "or as to its being possible to relieve in this way much distress and suffering"; but already he feared the doors of the Homes had been opened too widely, and he "could not accept a share of responsibility for a further increase". Therefore, he wrote "at once" to say: "If an organization of this kind is added, . . . *I must cease to be President.*"

Despite this protest, a "Youths' Labour House" was, that year, added to the Homes; yet Cairns did *not* resign. He remained till death the Mission's loyal President. Often it left him panting to keep Barnardo's pace, but his heart was too closely linked with "the Children's Cause" to give up the race. And, after all, nine times out of ten when differences arose, he admitted later that Barnardo was right.

But Lord Cairns was dead before the financial problem became most acute. The adventurous extension of 1887–88 had saddled upon the Homes a heavy mortgage; and the equally adventurous policy of establishing, in 1891–92, a chain of Ever-Open Doors in Provincial cities brought an unprecedented inrush of eligibles. Consequently, although contributions mounted from £76,000 in 1886 to £150,000 in 1894, so remarkable had been the extension that every penny of increase was consumed in current expenses; and the debt, instead of diminishing, had grown. Not unnaturally, therefore, Committee and Trustees were frightened: "Will there ever be an end to this expansion?" And the more they essayed an answer, the more they felt a halt must be called. Indeed, they argued that, if no other check could be devised, Barnardo's long-cherished pledge, to refuse *no* destitute child, must be revoked.

In this mood, in March, 1893, a joint conference of Committee and Trustees was held. And although it unanimously recorded "unchanged sympathy and warm appreciation of the self-denying labours of Dr. Barnardo", it pronounced the financial situation one demanding "immediate" relief. Five stipulations accordingly were laid down by which, it was agreed, Barnardo must henceforth be bound.

1. No new case admitted which has not the element of *extreme urgency*.
2. Boarding-out reduced until it falls below 500. It shall not be increased without special authority of the Trustees.
3. An average of £1,000 shall be paid off each month of old debts.
4. Tradesmen and other persons accepting orders are to sign a form indicating that the funds of the Institutions alone are liable, and creditors have no claim against any present individual except Dr. Barnardo.
5. An insurance of £20,000 on Dr. Barnardo's life should be effected as soon as possible.

Needless to say, Barnardo did *not* accept, without grave reservations, these stipulations. At once he agreed that the Trustees might insure his life in the Homes' favour for £20,000; but, as for the rest, he appealed, over the heads of Trustees and Committee, to the readers of *Night and Day*: and that appeal represents perhaps the most pathetic utterance he ever made. It opens:

"I stand face to face with the most serious problem which has ever met me during the whole of my twenty-seven years of labour among destitute children. Shall I partly close my doors, and meet the cry of every second destitute child who appeals for aid, as I have *never* met such before, with a refusal?

"That is the question; and the necessity for putting it is the greatest sorrow which has hitherto darkened my life-work.

"I know not how to describe my feelings, as I contemplate this painful alternative. Must it be? Surely Christian men and women, all the world over, who love the Master, and whose hearts cannot fail to be touched by the possibility of their Lord's little ones being turned away from the door of welcome, unrelieved and unsuccoured, will respond with a prompt and decisive, 'No; it shall *not* be'.

"I do not hesitate to say that if I have to adopt my Committee's suggestions, it will do more to shorten my life than anything which has befallen me during all these years. On the one hand, I simply know not how to follow the advice, while on the other I am compelled to admit . . . that it seems a cruel necessity. . . ."

Then, after an explanation of the debt, a reference to the work achieved in 1892, and a review of the situation confronting him, he concludes:

"Dare I . . . in view of all this, now commence to close my doors in the face of a single homeless child? *I cannot believe that this must really be done.* However prudent in the circumstances the course suggested by my Committee may be, it involves to my mind some degree of forgetfulness of that mission into which I was assuredly called twenty-seven years ago, when, as a youth, not then of age, I first heard the voice of Christ bidding me, in His name, to 'shepherd' the 'lambs' of His flock."

The response to this appeal was sufficient to stave off the threatened strait-jacket. The Homes' pledge was saved: and, as for the limitation to Boarding-out, Barnardo lived to see his boarded-out family *seven times* greater than was now sanctioned by Committee and Trustees.

But, though he escaped the strait-jacket, Barnardo agreed that strict economies must be devised: for the work could not continue on all fronts to grow at such a pace: and greater debt would have imperilled financial stability. So, in spite of enhanced income, the scissors were applied. "Deaconess House", which had long rendered excellent service among the poor, was now closed, and "outside" Mission agencies were curtailed, so that all resources might be concentrated upon the "Homes". Several publications, too, were temporarily suspended, and the *Annual Report* was sent only to those who asked for it. Yet, to the credit of all concerned, no "destitute" child was turned away.

At this time, too, an organization was growing up destined to render heroic support.

On a chill November day in 1891, Barnardo admitted an unusually large number of children, among them two crippled girls and a blind boy. Towards midnight, he was seated before his fire, meditating on the problem of such admissions, when, falling asleep, he had a significant dream.

Walking by a narrow, rapid stream, he was startled by a shrill cry: "Help! Help!" A lad had fallen into the torrent and was being carried headlong. Barnardo rushed to his assistance, shouting "Help! Help! Help!" as he ran. Getting just ahead of the drowning boy, he stretched over the brink of the stream; but his arms were "not nearly long enough", and he thought in his dream he could not swim. The boy, nearly exhausted, was carried past him. Again he rushed along the bank, crying loudly for help: on reaching a point of vantage, the lad was still beyond his grasp. He was about to despair, when some children, having heard his call, rushed up: "We'll hold you, sir! Don't be afraid!" Throwing himself upon the bosom of the water, as the children held his feet, he grabbed the drowning boy; a moment later, both were safe on land. The lad had been saved just in time!—and by the children's help!

Like his dream before the founding of the Village Home, Barnardo considered this a revelation. Why not bind "the children of privilege", safe on shore, into a rescue-band for saving their brothers and sisters perishing in the turbid vortex of ignorance, vice and sin?

A few days later, the Young Helpers' League was born; and although it began in the humblest way, to-day it raises over £50,000 a year. Yet its service to the children of privilege is not less than its service to young destitutes; for, true to its purpose, it is producing "a culture of the heart". Few sights could be more impressive than the annual display in the Albert Hall, under the auspices of this League, when, thousands strong, the children of opulence meet face to face the children of destitution, and learn of the achievements the latter acquire in the Homes. The growth of the League, too, was remarkable from the first. Conceived on November 20th, 1891, its contributions in 1892 were £2,186: in the year of Barnardo's decease (1905) they already were £17,000.

But, despite increased funds and rigid economy, Barnardo never lived to see the mortgages lifted. Among "old boys" were those abroad who every year, as a thank-offering, sent him twenty-five to thirty frozen sheep, or equally generous gifts; ingenious devices, too, like match collecting-boxes, helped to swell the funds, so that the Doctor lived to see his annual income mount to over £200,000: but he also lived to see his average daily family number more than 7,000, and his annual *migration* parties over 1,100. Finances, therefore, remained, till the end, the most acute problem he faced.

There lies before me a large pile of correspondence between Barnardo and Mr. Harry Elmslie, his brother-in-law, the Homes' Chief Steward. Not a few of these letters are dated 1904–5; and if ever correspondence revealed a desperate effort for economy, this does. Yet, however straitened his funds, Barnardo would have nothing shoddy; and many a tradesman learned, to his sorrow, that inferior goods could not be "dumped" on the Homes. Referring, for instance, to certain garden seats delivered as a "bargain" to meet an emergency at the Girls' Village Home, Barnardo writes: "They buckle up if you look at them. No two are pitched in the same way. A little child passes them and touches them with her skirts, and they fall back flat, turning up their heels in the air." Then he asks: "Is there no way to hold these people liable for the delivery of such inferior articles?" In another letter he inquires: "Could you not get the rascal who sold those horrible, ginger-bread, ill-balanced, ill-devised garden seats . . . to apologize and take them back, and pay us for our disappointment in having to use them for a while? Anything more rotten I never saw." This was not the only dishonest tradesman made to quake before Barnardo's wrath.

When the Doctor died, the debt hanging over the Homes totalled almost £250,000. But then, the nation realized with a shock the majesty of the life it had lost, and set itself to make amends for its insufficient support. William Baker, an old helper, dropped a lucrative practice at the Bar to become *voluntary* Director; while the late Howard Williams (the Homes' veteran Honorary Treasurer), supported by a strong Committee of Christian gentlemen, started a Memorial Fund; and contributions being received from the Throne to the slums, every penny of debt was wiped away.

How Barnardo must have rejoiced, as, from the Other World, he beheld this National tribute to his life's work!

Since this appreciative gesture, financial strain has been greatly eased. The Committee has since had monetary troubles, but never again has such a cloud of debt hung over its head: and as, with continued advance, still greater generosity became imperative, the challenge of Barnardo's heroic life has called forth the needed support. So, till this hour, the Homes' pledge has been kept.[1] But another asset has stood the work in good stead. Dr. Barnardo, throughout life, kept abreast of the best thought on biology and co-related sciences. Hence at a time when scientists and theologians were engaged in barren conflict, he was proving to the world the essential unity of science and faith: for to him all truth was of God, and practical Christianity was sufficiently comprehensive to embrace all established scientific fact. He wrought, therefore, a work such as never could have been wrought by either science or faith, labouring alone; and this unity is to-day a fixed principle in the Homes' work.

[1] *Permanent* admission is, however, now denied to epileptic and weak-minded children, for the State has at last evolved excellent institutions for their care.

Moreover, despite the enhanced demands which increased numbers and the opening of such ambitious institutions as the "Boys' Garden City", the "William Baker Technical School", the "Russell-Cotes Nautical School", etc., have brought, the Doctor's *methods* of finance have been carefully preserved. To this day the appeal is wholly Christian: yet, as much as ever, the Homes consider it their duty to stimulate the grace of liberality. Like Barnardo, pointing to money, talents and time, they say to believing men and women: "The Lord hath need of these."

The avenues of support opened since Barnardo's death cannot here be explored. Enough to say that the motive behind every advance has been—as always it was—the resurrection of buried joy, and the rebirth of childhood in the hearts of destitute bairns. That miracle, too, continues to be performed in the name, and through the power, of Barnardo's Christ.

Children's pennies which might have been spent on sweets, the sacrificial shillings of the poor, the £1 and £5 notes of the middle classes, the larger gifts of the "well-to-do", thousands of anonymous donations, large and small; Church and Sunday School collections, the income of concerts and bazaars, flag-day funds, and legacies—these are among the sources from which flow the half-million pounds and more which every year are required to feed, house, clothe, educate, industrially train, place out in life and follow up with "after-care" the Largest Family in the World. One post-Barnardo revenue, however, claims a passing word.

Scarcely had Barnardo's remains been laid to rest, when Miss Effie Bentham, a voluntary worker who for years had declined Barnardo's offers of a paid post, experienced a peculiar "call". On a visit to Middlesbrough, Yorkshire, she dreamed she was passing a great factory yard when cries of children, in great anguish, burst upon her ears. Hurrying through the factory gates, she saw a vast concourse of workmen standing about: but none heard the children's groans. She, accordingly, rushed through the throng, and, in the centre of the yard, found a group of small boys and girls lying on the ground, bound hand and foot, and bleeding from many wounds. She knelt to release them; but the fetters mocked her strength. What could *she* do? At this moment strong hands were placed under her arms, and, as she was lifted up, she observed that all the workmen had gathered around, while from a thousand voices came the chorus: *"We'll loose 'em, miss!"*

Miss Bentham had no doubt as to the purport of her dream. Strong workmen had promised support: hers was the duty of organizing it. To this task she applied herself with zest; and now the "International Farthing League", which she established, collects, through the coppers of industrial workmen, some £45,000 a year.

Again, mention must be made of the boundless generosity of two veterans recently passed to rest. No man stood more staunchly behind Dr. Barnardo than the late Howard Williams, son of Sir George Williams, world-founder of the Y.M.C.A. For a generation, right up till his death in 1929, Howard Williams was Honorary Treasurer of the Homes; and how generously he supported them the world will never know. One suggestive incident, however, happens to be known. In recognition of his war services on behalf of the "boys" at the front, thankful fathers and friends presented him with a gift of £10,000; to which was added £4,000 by retail drapers who did business with his firm. All was passed over to Barnardo's; and most of it was spent in opening up a sunshine Home in Folkestone, for the special treatment of children with tubercular bones. But in no circumstances would he hear of this institution being called the "Howard Williams Home": he insisted that it bear the name of a friend—a great surgeon; so to-day it is flourishing as the "Bruce-Porter Home".

This incident is symbolical of a selflessness the Homes

know well. The late Chairman of the Governing Council, William McCall, whose death followed so closely upon that of Howard Williams, was no less generous than his old colleague and friend, while also he was as unassuming in everything he did. At an age when most men look only for rest, and at a crisis of some gravity in the Homes' affairs, he took upon himself the whole burden of directing their work: and, like Barnardo and William Baker before him, bore it till death.

To these men a destitute child was just a friend in need; and what can a man do more than lay down his life for his friends, as each of them truly did? If the trumpets ever sound, without doubt they sounded when these great souls passed over to the Other Side. The Council of Dr. Barnardo's Homes pray for help to follow in their footsteps without failure, and without fear.[1]

[1] As a Williams-McCall Memorial, special donations are now being received to rebuild some of the old houses in Stepney Causeway and provide more and better accommodation for the reception of destitute children.

CHAPTER XV

THE MAN AND HIS MEMORIAL

THE most astounding phenomenon of history is the degree
to which pioneers and prophets, who were despised and
persecuted by the potentates of their age, have emerged
slowly as spiritual teachers and honoured emancipators:
while simultaneously the said potentates, who bustled about
with so much show of power, have receded into the habita-
tions of pigmies and ghosts.

Jesus Christ was first crucified and afterwards acclaimed
"The Saviour of the World". But the "mighty" men of his
day are now remembered chiefly for their weakness and
arrogance, their lack of vision and faith. Every civilization
yet known has repeatedly been guilty of first stoning
its prophets and *afterwards* erecting monuments to their
memory.

Nor has quite modern history much deviated from this
ancient rule! Many of the one-time celebrities whose three-,
four- or even five-volume "Lives" filled honoured places on
our grandfathers' shelves are not even a name to-day,
oblivion having claimed them. But, even as they fade away,
a tiny band of their contemporaries have emerged as giants;
and, strangely, these latter were generally treated by the
former with contempt. The former were mostly militarists
and party politicians, intoxicated by the flattery of creeping
sycophants, or obsessed by the notion that they were born
to rule: the latter were chiefly crusaders and pioneers who,
looking forward in faith to a Better Age, inspired their
fellows to work for its dawn.

Few names, for instance, kindle such admiration to-day as
those of William Wilberforce, Lord Shaftesbury and
Abraham Lincoln. All were pioneers of great emancipating
crusades. All were inspired by an idealism which led them
to consecrate their every talent, not to a career but a cause.

Q

All endured bravely the most bigoted buffoonery; all became targets of malice and ridicule; all were lampooned and despised by the "great and wise". Yet, while their maligners have either vanished from the stage of History or shrivelled into ghosts with thin, sepulchral voice, they and their kind are standing out, ever more distinctly, as the liberators of their age.

Now among the pioneers and prophets whom the perspective of distance is increasingly marking out as great, is Dr. Thomas John Barnardo. As "Emancipator of the Outcast Child", he is worthy to hold a place abreast all three emancipators cited above. But especially should his name be always associated with Shaftesbury's: for, if the maxim be correct, that "lasting reform must start with the child", then Shaftesbury and Barnardo are two of the most sagacious reformers of all time. Both dedicated their lives to social labours among unfortunate, exploited or destitute children; both worked for To-morrow rather than To-day: both believed profoundly that if a people would cleanse the springs of its National life, it must start by purifying the child's environment and sowing the seeds of integrity and utility in the hearts and minds of the young.

How significant, moreover, were the results of their endeavour is suggested by no less honoured a child-welfare worker than the Rev. Benjamin Waugh, founder of the National Society for the Prevention of Cruelty to Children. "In protecting the young from the evils to which they are exposed", he declared, *"Lord Shaftesbury and Dr. Barnardo were our pioneers."* And Waugh knew well whereof he spoke; for, through the spiritual succession of the Sunday School and the Ragged School, Shaftesbury and Barnardo, by persistent endeavours, awakened first the British public, then the English-speaking peoples, and, finally, Christendom in general, to a new appreciation of child-life: to new and mighty exploits on its behalf.

But the above is somewhat abstract: and the subject of

this chapter is highly concrete. What then, we hasten to ask, made Barnardo the great pioneer he was? What were the dominant attributes of his character? And wherein have those attributes impressed themselves upon the national character of the people he served? In brief, what was the mental and spiritual stature of this man who, year by year, in the perspective of distance, holds an increasingly high place among the pioneers and prophets of the race?

In preceding chapters certain of these questions have received a partial answer: now the time has come for tighter grips.

First and foremost among the forces which moulded Barnardo's character and made him great was, beyond doubt, the religion which inspired his initial endeavours and sustained him through all the vicissitudes of his life-crusade. To him religion was a more intimate part of his being than the air he breathed or the food he ate. It was to him the be-all and the end-all of life.

From conversion till death, Barnardo was an avowed Evangelical. But this does not mean that his religion was static. Quite the contrary! The evolution of his convictions is apparent. In youth, under the influence of Brethrenism, he inclined to the belief that the Lord's Table should be open only to the immersed. In middle-age, a liberal Non-conformist, he was much less concerned about doctrines and dogmas as such: while, during his last twelve years, a lay-reader in the Church of England, he was ready to co-operate with all, whatever their affiliation, if only they "loved the Lord Jesus Christ in sincerity and truth".

The cardinal tenets of Protestantism were to Barnardo the foundations of his religious life. The Open Bible in the vernacular, Salvation by Faith, and the Priesthood of all True Believers, were principles which, to the end, he cherished increasingly. Without the Open Bible in a people's native tongue, he believed religion was liable to degenerate into a system of semi-magical rites. Christian works, he maintained, were as much a property of saving faith as light is a property of the sun; while all true Believers, he avowed, were priests, because they needs must minister in Holy Things.

Admittedly, Barnardo's anti-Catholicism was tinged with prejudice; but this, in view of the treatment he received from Cardinal Manning's underlings, if unfortunate, was natural. For if, as an Irish Protestant, Barnardo had a "bee in his bonnet" concerning the "errors of the Papacy", Manning repaid him by releasing a swarm of bees, which, whenever his name was mentioned, stung reason out of court. But the primary cause of Barnardo's aversion to Catholicism lay in his devotion to a principle the Papal hierarchy opposed: Liberty of Conscience. To him the idea of an infallible Pope or an infallible Church was nauseating; he abhorred the assumptions and dogmatisms of an hierarchical caste; while the record of the Inquisition was to him always a symbol of perverted spiritual power.

But though Barnardo had little sympathy with the Roman Catholic interpretation of Christianity, he, nevertheless, was "Catholic" in the truest sense; his outlook was universal, and he had no patience with exclusive denominationalism. Moreover, anything in the shape of priestly arrogance was to him highly repulsive, no matter from what communion it came. A letter to a young Anglican curate, whose bigotry out-distanced his knowledge, is representative of Barnardo's deepest feelings. The curate had strongly reprimanded him for, as a Churchman, associating with "unchurchly Christianity"; and Barnardo, believing this attitude a denial of all Christian charity, spoke plainly his mind. The most trenchant parts of his reply are typical of the man:

". . . I stand aghast at the ferocity of a certain Churchman who is prepared to empty the pulpits of Dissent at one stroke, and to re-establish the Acts of Uniformity. Preserve us all! And when next I enter a Chapel, not a Church, may you *not* be there to see it!

"Well, I humbly agree with Dr. Johnson in liking a good hater.

But it fairly makes my hair stand on end to listen to you 'a swearing like anythink' at Dissent.

"My dear friend, you are suffering from *Church fever*, and you 'see red' when the bare walls of Little Bethel swim into your ken! But you know you have one or two bits of History, a few chapters of literature, an influential movement or so in matters ethical and social, and several awkward facts to explain away, before you can whisk out of consideration that moiety of our population content to dub itself Dissenter and Nonconformist. Go to!

". . . I sit up and testify that the average Nonconformist has done as much as, or more than, we Churchmen to hold up the pillar of orthodoxy and to keep sweet the life of England. You will find the Dissenting minister at the bed-side of the sick and dying, and in the thick of the fight for purity and goodness, as readily, and as numerously, as you will find the Bishop, the Vicar, the Rector, and *even the Curate*. I speak that which I know. I confess to you that such names as Horton, Archibald Brown, Dr. Whyte, Spurgeon, Fairbairn (to go no further; and I don't profess to know Dissent as widely as I might) are enough for me to kill and bury fathoms deep any such indictment of Dissent as a whole, as your fulmination implies. And I humbly submit that our civil and religious liberties owe somewhat to the Quakers. We have all heard something of Elizabeth Fry, of John Howard, of John Bunyan, and of a few more like significant names! While I do believe that we owe a great deal in our own day, as regards the social problem, to Cadbury and Lever Brothers; to Chivers and the Frys and Colmans.

"No, sir! They have given us a capital lead in many a field, have these same despised Noncons; and both classes and masses in this old England, owe them a bit of a debt, and not a little respect, as well.

"But then you put your knowledge at the back of your ban! With all diffidence, I don't think it can be representative. And with this final dig at your omniscience, and craving permission still to exist as a Dissenter from your sweeping conclusions, I subscribe myself in all humility:

"Yours obediently,

"T. J. BARNARDO."

Among Barnardo's private papers, no answer from the Curate is to be found.

The catholicity, the tolerance, the charity and the broad humanity of Barnardo's religious outlook might be illustrated in many ways. All the Chapels, for instance, at his various Home centres have been *dedicated*; but none consecrated. Were they consecrated, each would be under control of the Bishop of its diocese, thus becoming more or less distinctly Anglican. But, being dedicated instead, their pulpits may be opened to any minister or layman possessed of a real message. Hence, though most of the Homes' Chaplains are to-day Anglican clergymen, they, like Barnardo, are broad Evangelicals, who co-operate freely with Nonconformists.

Barnardo's religion had no relation to long-faced piety or sanctimonious gloom. Once he chaffed an austere parson that he looked "as though his religion did not agree with him"; and his thousands of sermons are shot through with Gospel promises, with faith, hope, love and joy. Continually he emphasized the "sinfulness of sin" and the devastating folly of the ungodly life; but always he presented the Gospel as Glad-Tidings, and Christ as the personal Friend, as well as the personal Saviour, of man. Love, briefly, was the Alpha and the Omega of his religion; and if ever a man's teaching was Christo-centric, Barnardo's was. His *last* address, delivered to a party of his children about to migrate, illustrates well this truth. Speaking from Acts xxvii. 29, "They cast four anchors out of the stern, and wished for the day", he took as his subject, "Anchors of the Soul"; and under four headings urged his boys and girls, when seeking their fortune in the New World, to "stand fast" by: (1) the Bible, (2) Prayer, (3) a Good Conscience, (4) Christ Himself. Under this last heading his points, written in his own hand on paper now lying before me, were: (*a*) Christ the Best Friend, (*b*) He loves *you*, (*c*) Love Him, (*d*) Choose Christ, (*e*) Trust Him, (*f*) Stand up for Him.

This address is suggestive of hundreds. But neither in his sermons nor in his addresses can we best gauge the depth and breadth of Barnardo's Faith. It is life's overwhelming bereavements that most severely test the soul; and of such Barnardo had his share. Three of his five sons preceded him to the grave: yet faith bore him up. In *Night and Day*, replying to hundreds of condolences which reached him after the death of Herbert, a promising lad of nine, who fell a prey to diphtheria, he wrote:

". . . This loss has only intensified my desire to continue . . . that work of child-rescue committed to my care. As my dear boy lay gasping in my arms, and I gazed into the little pinched face, growing cold in death, hundreds of other child-faces appeared to me through his, while other wistful eyes looked out at me by the waning light of his dear eyes. I could but resolve afresh, as I then did, that, by God's grace, I would consecrate myself anew to the blessed task of rescuing helpless little ones from the miseries of a neglected and sinful life. *Now I know the vows of God are on me.* I dare not turn aside from this work. By His help I will not! The little ones are His; yes, assuredly *the children* belong to Jesus Christ. Let it be my task through life to fold and shepherd them for Him."

The qualities of Barnardo's mind and heart were profoundly influenced by the Faith which brought harmony and poise to a singularly many-sided career; yet they deserve separate notice. Dr. Grattan Guinness once referred to Barnardo's "beaming face, cheery voice, broad brow, big brain, glowing heart, indomitable courage, tender sympathy, intense philanthropy, unwearied activity, and marvellous practical ability". This tribute seems fulsome; but it is the pen-picture of one who knew Barnardo as few had the opportunity of knowing him, and, upon examination, we see that if any of these characteristics were omitted, something essential to a life-portrait would be missed; for from many independent sources, comes evidence that every trait here ascribed to him was woven into the warp and woof of his being.

Barnardo had a scientifically trained, a well-stored and a logical mind. His private library contained more than four thousand volumes; and of these he knew "something in all, and everything in some". Nor is this amazing, for between midnight and three a.m. he habitually spent an hour or two among his books—the one life-long recreation he indulged. And how well he could marshal his knowledge is proved by his efforts, as his own Counsel, in Court. Had he been a barrister he would have been second to no K.C. of his day. Yet for all his breadth and depth of reading, he assumed no "airs". No one could apologize more generously; and always he held that "they who alter no opinion, correct no mistake". No man or institution, he knew, can "corner" truth, and he would have agreed wholly with Tagore: "If you shut your door to all error, Truth will be shut out!"

But not to his logical acumen, tenacious memory, or well-stored mind did Barnardo owe his phenomenal power; rather was it to a singleness of purpose, intensified by a red-hot earnestness and a volcanic vehemence of soul. He disowned all kinship to Professor Dry-Dust: his mind worked in closest co-operation with his heart; and the latter, not the former, first urged him forward as the Champion of the Destitute Child. His conversion meant the dedication of his every talent to Christ's Kingdom: therefore, never could he compromise with his conscience, and a thousand incidents show that he was incapable of choosing simply the easy course. To him all problems were essentially moral: "Is a certain course right or wrong?"

By nature Barnardo was endowed with quick perception, with imagination, originality and courage; with a marked individuality, an affectionate disposition, and an unusually systematic mind. By concentrated effort he developed a rare power of vision, the art of terse, vigorous expression, an uncanny command of detail, a mighty organizing ability, a rare faculty for "placing" workers, and an audacity of action which often left his associates gasping with awe. His cab was known throughout East London as "The Flying Scotsman"—a name symbolic of more than his cab.

Nevertheless, it would be folly to suggest that Barnardo was free from the faults of his qualities. He was autocratic, impetuous, peremptory, highly emotional and impatient of restraint even from his own Committee; and being a Titan for work, he expected of his associates more than they could reasonably be asked to perform. Again, by no leap of imagination, could caution or expediency be included among his strong points. But this admitted, he was a great soul! His audacity, naturally, won him bitter enemies; yet hatred or revenge he never harboured. Like Lincoln, whom he resembled in many ways, he exhibited "malice toward none, and charity toward all". Finally, too, this charity bore rich fruit, for, in his later years, hundreds were swearing by him, who once were swearing at him.

Every power of Barnardo's mind and heart was yoked in the service of the child. Asked why he looked so much younger than his years, he answered: "Why, to live with and for children, is the secret of perennial youth!" Often, too, he declared that never had he seen an ugly child. Every child, he held, has a beauty peculiarly its own, especially as a baby; and squarely he endorsed Emerson's dictum: "Infancy is the perpetual Messiah which comes into the arms of men and pleads with them to return to God." In consecrating his every talent to child-service, therefore, he believed he was giving "his utmost for the highest". And who will make bold to say he was wrong? In singular degree "the Emancipator of the Outcast Child" had entered into the mind of Christ; hence, to him, the guileless "little one" was the symbol of the Heavenly state.

Always Barnardo was a true "pal" among boys and girls: and hundreds are the reports of his children's rejoicing when he appeared. No one could play with youngsters more spontaneously: yet, play over, he could lead them in impromptu prayer, with equal zest; for prayer to him was as natural as play. But the most touching of all Barnardo's relationships with "his children" are reflected in letters to his wife, after visits to certain of his Homes for incurables. These tell of how the afflicted children's faces "beamed with joy" on seeing him, of how he kissed them, talked, played and prayed with them, picked them up in his arms, carried them about and stroked their "pale, pinched little faces". More than once, too, he tells of how, "after staying an hour" among these "poor, little, afflicted ones", when finally he "had to go", he could not suppress tears, as the "little dears" tugged at his clothes and begged him to stay "just five minutes more!"

Little wonder, then, that with such love for children Barnardo had a keen admiration for all who worked disinterestedly in "the Children's Cause"; and the fact that he and his methods were sometimes misunderstood by such workers in no sense diminished that admiration. Once, for instance, William Quarrier, founder of the Scottish Homes which bear his name, acting impulsively on erroneous second-hand information, published a damaging criticism of Barnardo's Homes. The Doctor's friends, cut to the quick, advised him immediately to publish a reply. Instead he waited till the storm passed. Then, knowing well the excellent work which Quarrier was doing, he published this good Scotsman's picture in his magazine, along with a generous appreciation of his Homes.

Spurgeon once said: "I like Barnardo for his goodness and his *fun*." Another intimate friend declared that he was "full as an egg of humour, playfulness and jokes". These observations go deep. Once, on meeting some fellow-workers at dinner, he assumed a funereal expression, and, in doleful tones, said he had just lost one of his oldest friends. The party expressed warmest sympathy. Then, coyly smiling, Barnardo told them he had just returned from the dentist, and bade all guess the identity of his "life-long friend". On one of his visits to Canada, he left Headquarters to go "shopping". On his return he walked up to "a relative"— a member of his party—and in a careless manner exclaimed: "I say, old man! I find I've left a little parcel behind me at the corner shop. Run down and get it for me, won't you?" His relative returning in a lather of perspiration, the party was convulsed with laughter. The "little parcel" was a huge water-melon which had to be carried a mile!

Such sportive sallies were characteristic of Barnardo to the last. The year of his death offers a dozen illustrations of his irrepressible jocularity. Early in 1905, recuperating from a severe illness, he answered the letter of a lady he knew well, requesting him to address a meeting on March 24th. Explaining that, on his doctor's advice, his wife had taken him in hand, he wrote: "I am not a free agent. I am under the vilest form of despotic authority—Petticoat Government." Then:

"I am fighting a pretty stiff battle to defeat the Government. I am using dynamite and bombs, and I hope I have overthrown some of the principal buildings and shaken the autocracy; so that it is possible I may be able on Wednesday, the 1st, to write you a note, or send you a wire: 'The enemy has fled. I will be with you.' But, if by that time the Government is reinforced by Boreas, I am afraid I will have to surrender without making terms. I dare say your husband knows, poor man, what such capitulation involves!"

On July 27th, 1905, scarcely eight weeks before his death, Barnardo wrote a "chatty" letter to his eldest son, Stuart, in Trinidad. Addressing him as "my dear old chap", he told about Founder's Day activities at the Homes, and the meeting convened and presided over by the Lord Mayor of London in the Mansion House to celebrate his sixtieth birthday. Messages of congratulation had arrived from every quarter of the world, among them a "very jolly telegram" from the Queen. The speakers, too, included the Duke of Argyll, the Recorder of London, Lords Brassey and Reay, Bishops, and great Nonconformist divines. After a racy account of it all, Barnardo continues in a strain quite his own: "According to them all, I am an angel in pantaloons and spectacles, and I have been looking at the glass since then to see if my wings are sprouting, but cannot discern any sign of plumage on either shoulder: so I expect the angelic business is a little overdone!"

Again, for realistic humour, the last article Barnardo ever wrote rivals the most vivid passages in *Oliver Twist*. It is entitled *Some Queer Children I have Met*, and, written shortly before his death, it never was completed or revised: yet it bubbles over with fun. The little characters, even in print, are uproariously alive. "Jack and Jill" were wholly insuppressible. One burning summer's day the matron discovered "these two imps enjoying their midday bath in the cistern containing the drinking-water of the House". It was much more spacious than the prosaic bath-tub in which they ordinarily had their splash.

Mary Smith was a little gipsy girl, born in a van. At first she was "as difficult to control as a wild-cat"; and her flashing eyes, dishevelled hair and untamed expression gave her a feline air. Besides, "Mary could fight and scratch and bite—and she *did*". For days she was the terror of the Home. Then a miracle was wrought. The Matron was turning out an old cupboard when, among the treasure, appeared a battered, broken doll.

"Mary seized it at once. 'Oh, the dear *live* dolly! May I keep it? May I keep it?' 'It is not a *live* dolly,' said one of the other children. . . .'It is,' said Mary, and she hissed and spat at her. 'It is, *it is*! a real, live dolly!' and she stamped in rage. The Matron intervened. 'No, my dear, dolly is not alive. What do you mean?' With difficulty Mary pointed out that Dolly had two eyes, a nose, a few locks of hair on its prematurely bald head, and a few garments that could be taken off and put on. If that was not a real, live dolly what could be? She had never seen the like before. 'What—have you never had a dolly?' 'Yes, ma'am.' 'Well, what was it like?' And Mary explained that it was a bit of stick picked up in the hedgerow, around which was tied a scrap of rag—and there you were! That was Mary's *only* previous dolly!"

The Matron now had her chance. Mary might keep the *live* dolly if she were good. That was the beginning of this little gipsy's transformation. From then on she submitted, without fighting or biting, to have her hair combed, to be bathed, and even to be put to bed.

"Sammy and Smut" is the best story of the group. Sammy was a character Dickens would have loved. This "snivelling, sniffing, squinting" youngster, whose face and hands were covered with "constellations of warts", was an urchin Barnardo had picked up one night in Covent Garden Market; while Smut, the ally of all his exploits, was a torn-eared and tailless mongrel terrier, which, "in a weak and foolish moment", the Doctor allowed Sammy to bring with him into the Home. The uproarious escapades of this urchin and his canine accomplice cannot here be related. Enough to note that masters, matrons and monitors, as well as Barnardo himself, "were nearly driven out of their seven senses trying to circumvent the numberless and daily dodges of Sammy and Smut".

Barnardo's keen sense of jollity helped not a little to make his relationships with his staff both human and cordial. The author has had the privilege of protracted interviews with many who worked under Barnardo for years; and, if ever a staff was unanimous in praise of its chief, his was. One veteran says: "The spirit the Doctor instilled into all his colleagues might be expressed in one word: 'Come'—not 'Go'. We all felt that however hard we worked, our Chief set us an example that left us far behind!" Another old worker remarks: "I doubt if ever there lived a man possessed of greater genius for inspiring in his associates the desire to do only their best. His example taught us the meaning of the 'Second-Mile' life." Similar observations might be quoted by the score. Few leaders of men have ever expected more of their lieutenants than Barnardo: and few have had their expectations so splendidly fulfilled! No colleagues were of any use to him whose hearts were not in "The Children's Cause"; and, attracting such to him, he possessed an uncanny power of placing them. Once he said: "I would rather have ten minutes' interview with a man than a bushel of testimonials". And results justified his claim. He was endowed with a rare faculty for penetrating a man's soul.

Yet, despite his insistence upon personal interviews, occasionally he was deceived. Among his private letters I find one, in his own hand, to his wife, written from a special-treatment centre, in 1889. After a description of his "little darlings" and their ailments, he concluded: "Sister M——, who is in charge, does not care one atom for them.

She has never kissed a child since she came! She has no heart for the poor dears that need more love than medicine. She *goes* on the 18th!"

Often Barnardo exclaimed: "Love is the power which rules these Homes." Never could the monument of his life-work be described as an institution: it was a series of Homes, wherein a Family Spirit prevailed. No one understood more completely than Barnardo that the ultimate success of his Mission depended upon the character of the men and women he gathered around him; and a noble, devoted band they were. Repeatedly he paid high tribute to their faithfulness, ability and zeal, pointing out that among them were those who, for twenty-five years on end, had never missed a day from work, save when on annual holiday. But perhaps never was his gratitude more tersely expressed than on his fiftieth birthday, when his staff presented him with a handsome grandfather clock. Acknowledging his "great indebtedness" to his "faithful fellow-labourers . . . to whose continuous and unceasing toil any success which God has given us is chiefly due", he proceeds: "Credit is often given to *me* that really belongs to *them*. . . . I am often ashamed at the prominence given to my personal share in an undertaking the real burdens of which have been silently and heroically borne by a great company of splendid workers, male and female, of whose names even our subscribers are ignorant."

This appreciation, however, he expressed in more tangible ways. On his sixtieth birthday, being presented with a purse of £100 as a *personal* gift from a few friends, he kept not a penny. All was put into a special fund he had started for the benefit of his workers.

"I would not exchange my life and work", said Barnardo, "for any man's that I know of. If I had to live over again, I would do exactly the same thing, only . . . with fewer mistakes." This enthusiasm for his Cause helped

largely to breed in his workers their devotion to him. They
all knew his soul was in his work; and his example was their
shining light. But his loving encouragement also strengthened
their resolve and beckoned them on. Here is a characteristic
letter to a tried worker:

"I don't want this season to come and go without sending you a few
earnest and hearty words of thanks for the splendid service you have
rendered our work during another year. I am becoming more and
more sensible of your great ability, and more and more thankful that
I have secured so loyal and indefatigable a colleague. God bless
you, my dear fellow, and may we long work side by side. This little
cheque which I want you to accept as my Christmas-box is a beastly
thing to offer you—but, to tell the truth, I did not know what to buy
and have left it to you; you will get something you really need, and
which will remind you of your old pal.

"All Christmas blessings be yours and Vere's!"

Few men have been happier in their family relationships
than Barnardo; yet few have been so robbed of time for
their enjoyment. The demands of his Homes continually
overshadowed those of his home: for fathering "the Largest
Family in the World" deprived him of much time which
naturally would have been expended upon his own children.
Rarely on weekdays did he eat any meal save breakfast at
home; and frequently on Sundays was he off speaking
"on the Children's behalf". Nevertheless, breakfast-hour
was a time of true fellowship, for always it included Family
Worship: the Doctor presiding as "High Priest".

Holidays, too, were both a happy anticipation and a
sacred memory; for then, Barnardo's family claiming him
for their very own, all romped and played together—truants
from the school of life. But if Barnardo was a "big brother"
among his own children, he none the less was able to counsel
them as only the wisest of fathers could. How many fathers
have ever written a more understanding letter to a growing
son than the following to Barnardo's youngest son, Cyril,[1]
then at school?

[1] Cyril is now a barrister in Winnipeg, Canada.

". . . I hope, my dear boy, you are going to work *really well* this term. It is a good plan to put one's whole heart into whatever you are engaged in, whether play or work. Some fellows are very enthusiastic over football and cricket and bicycling, but have no interest in their lessons, and so never put their heart into them, and never really get on. Now, I hope *you won't be like that*, but will just work hard and fairly, at your lessons, as well as at your sports. Above all, dear boy, 'Never do a *mean* thing'.

"It *is* mean to lie.

"It *is* mean to allow another boy to be blamed for your Fault.

"It *is* mean to take advantage of a fellow who does not know about things as well as you do.

"It *is* awfully mean to take anything that is not yours, even if only a foreign stamp, or a pencil or a button.

"Keep *honest*, dear Cyril, and always quite *straight* in little things.

"Always speak the truth and only the truth, at all times.

"Keep your mind and thoughts *pure* and *clean*. Never listen to a boy saying dirty, rude things. Never look at another fellow doing rude things. Never soil your dear lips that Mother has kissed, by talking about rude, nasty things.

"Remember you are *my* boy, Dr. Barnardo's own boy, and keep from everything wrong and dishonourable, for my sake and Mother's.

"Don't forget to pray *every day*. If we ask GOD to keep us and mean it, *He will*. And then, when we are tempted, we will be strong to resist the devil.

"*Don't tear up this letter;* but keep it carefully till I see you. Read it over *two or three times by yourself*, and ask Mother to explain it all.

"Good-bye, my darling. God bless you and keep you ever!

"Your loving father,

"THOS. J. BARNARDO."

The intimate relationships of Barnardo's family circle, whether those of sorrow or joy, helped greatly to quicken his understanding of the whole child problem. No mother's heart could be more gentle, more sympathetic; and no mother, confronted by bottomless grief, could be more tenderly tactful. His son Kennie, endowed with remarkable gifts, was the idol of his heart. Yet, in the hour of promise, this lad was stricken by Death. Barnardo's cup of sorrow was full. Nevertheless, at the funeral in Bow Cemetery, Kennie's coffin, covered with wreaths, chancing to pass the grave of an East End child about to be buried without a flower, Barnardo, taking two of Kennie's wreaths, approached

DR. BARNARDO'S MEMORIAL IN THE MIDST OF THE WORK
HE LOVED

the heart-broken parents: "These flowers are from my child to yours."

*　　*　　*　　*　　*

Shortly before his fiftieth birthday, Barnardo experienced the first symptoms of the heart-disease which, later, laid him low. As an infant he was puny; but before he was ten, he had developed a robust constitution, and for forty years enjoyed exceptional health. "During this period", said an old friend, "he had a giant's energy, and used it like a giant." In the early days he frequently was "combing London streets" till the small hours; and, having at this time several beds in different slum areas, he slept in the one nearest the scene of his immediate exploits. But even when not so employed, he retired late; for many a book he read after midnight. More than one of his earliest workers have remarked that often he retired at three or four a.m. to rise at eight. And, till the end, he sacrificed sleep to a reckless degree. One night, when the Roddy case was in the Court of Appeal, he did not go to bed at all, but spent the whole night preparing his brief. Then, about an hour before his appearance in Court, on that January morning, he took a brisk swim in the cold-water pool at Stepney Causeway, and proceeded, very wideawake, to plead his own case. Throughout the forty years of his rescue-work it is doubtful if he averaged six hours' rest per night; and often, for months, he worked sixteen to eighteen hours a day.

The cause of the heart-disease, therefore, which, during his last years, attacked him from time to time, is not difficult to trace. Yet, if, after the first attack, he had husbanded his energies, he might have lived another twenty years. But rest and leisure were foreign to his temperament. If ever a man was predestined to wear out, not rust out, he was. Enforced idleness for any considerable time would have eaten out his soul. It is not surprising, therefore, that his doctors found him a difficult patient! Immediately following

R

his first illness, in 1895, he made good resolutions to shorten his working hours. But the demands of "the Cause" were insistent: and as long as he had energy, he must spend it. Besides, medical doctor though he was, he cherished a deeply-rooted idea that work never killed any man; so, if his days were numbered, why not make the most of them?

Six or seven times he had heart attacks so violent that his doctors sent him to *Bad* Nauheim for special treatment, which certainly did him good: but as a patient he was incorrigible to the end. Once he admitted: "I only obey my doctor when it suits me!" And never would he stay at Nauheim long enough to give the treatment a fair chance. Then, too, even when on health trips, his soul was in East London. After three days on the Riviera, he wrote: "I actually began to feel ashamed of myself for lingering among the idlers, who basked in luxurious ease on the Mediterranean coast. . . . Spite, too, of the lovely surroundings, the glowing landscapes, and the almost tropical abundance of foliage and fruit, I felt a thousand times that 'the old was better', and that nothing would induce me to exchange the dear, familiar haunts of the East End, with all its drawbacks, for a prolonged residence in the 'Sunny South'."

Barnardo's final illness came in the summer of 1905. On August 31st, his doctors ordered him off to *Bad* Nauheim. *En route*, at Cologne, he suffered a severe attack of lumbago; and at Nauheim, the disease did not respond to treatment as previously. He felt, as by premonition, that he should be at home under his wife's care. So for home he started. But, on September 9th, Mrs. Barnardo received a wire from Paris: he was stricken with a severe spasm of angina pectoris. Immediately Mrs. Barnardo, Cyril and Dr. Frederick Barnardo rushed to his side, and found him in a condition so critical that French specialists could do nothing. His wife's nursing, however, worked wonders; on September 14th she brought him home. For two days following hope rose and fell. On the third day he rallied sufficiently to look through a ponderous pile of letters; next day, he called in his amanuensis and for hours dictated replies to matters of urgent concern. September 19th found him similarly employed. From 10 a.m. till 4 p.m., correspondence consumed his time. Then, having bid his secretary good-bye for the day, feeling exhausted, he reclined in his chair and slept peacefully. At a quarter to six he awakened, and immediately tea was served, of which he began to partake with apparent enjoyment, when, turning to his wife, he cried: "Oh, Syrie! My head feels so heavy!" And laying it on her breast, he gasped for breath. A moment later, at exactly six o'clock, his spirit passed into the Great Beyond.

Thomas John Barnardo was at death *sixty* years old: he had fathered *sixty thousand* destitute children.

The Great Reaper found Barnardo's house in order. The Doctor had known from the nature of his disease that death, when it came, would come quickly; and such was his wish. He was not afraid of Death. Twice he was on trains when fellow-passengers in his own compartment were killed, and during certain of his heart attacks Death's shadow hovered over him. One of his latest letters was to a friend who had lost her husband: "I have looked into the face of Death. Three times has my life been given back to me. . . . But oh! I can tell you Death, to the Christian, is not so dark as it is painted. I felt as in the embrace of a friend. . . ." His will, too, was made; and though he left little of this world's goods, he bequeathed to his successors a glorious Declaration of Faith. The *first* article of his will reads: "Death and the Grave are but temporary bonds; Christ has triumphed over them! I hope to die, as I have lived, in the humble but assured faith of Jesus Christ, whom I have so imperfectly served, and whom I acknowledge to be my Saviour, my Master and my King."

Messages of sympathy poured in endless stream upon

Mrs. Barnardo from her husband's admirers the world over: including the King, the Queen, the Archbishop of Canterbury, cabinet ministers, statesmen, divines, missionaries, educationists, social workers, "old boys and girls", and the East End poor. Within twenty-four hours, it was obvious that a public funeral must be arranged.

On September 22nd the body was removed from the Doctor's home in Surbiton to the Edinburgh Castle, Limehouse, where so often Barnardo had preached the Gospel to the poor: and there for five days it lay "in state", when from dawn till dusk a throng filed by the flower-embanked coffin, to catch a last glimpse of him who now was universally recognized as "the Poor Child's Emancipator and Friend". On the intervening Sunday, too, a Memorial Service was held in the Castle; and of those seeking admission, only a small percentage could get near the door. But it was on Wednesday, September 27th, that the People's affection was most manifest. The funeral procession, making its way from the Castle to Liverpool Street Station, passed through the heart of East London; and neither before nor since has the East End witnessed such a demonstration of affection. In the procession were 1,500 "Barnardo boys", present and past; in it also were representatives of numerous philanthropic, social, religious and educational bodies, as well as officials of the Homes and a great concourse from every walk of life. The pall-bearers were all chosen from among Barnardo's fellow-workers; and immediately behind the hearse, "Peer", for twenty-five years the Doctor's coachman, led his horse—pulling an empty cab. The "Flying Scotsman" would never again be seen dashing along its accustomed route!

It was not, however, in the procession, but in the crowded thoroughfares, that the supreme demonstration of East London's affection was most memorably expressed. Scores upon scores of thousands crowded all the streets through which the body was borne; business along the route was suspended; Christians and Jews alike did reverence to the greatest friend East London and the outcast children of Britain have known. All heads in this multitude were bared as the cortège passed by; most were bowed: among the throng were groups of newspaper boys, who had pooled pennies to buy wreaths for the Doctor's bier, and thousands of poor mothers, who thanked God their children were living under happier conditions than would have been possible had Barnardo never started his "Save the Child" crusade. All along the three-mile course traffic was held up; and everywhere the multitude expressed the homage and reverence paid only to those most dearly loved. Men, women and children were audibly sobbing. One poor woman, in uncontrollable emotion, expressed the pent-up feeling of thousands: "O God, O God, give him back to us! Give him back!"

At Liverpool Street Station Mrs. Barnardo joined the mourning multitude; and there again traffic for some minutes was suspended, as, to the sound of muffled drum, the coffin was carried through the dense throng to a special train.

Under cover of an enormous marquee, erected within the grounds of the Girls' Village Home, the public service was conducted by the Bishop of Barking, assisted by other divines. And although a torrent of rain was falling, the monstrous tent was crowded to overflow: hundreds standing outside, among them many Village girls, sobbing bitterly. The funeral sermon was preached by Canon Fleming, who, *inter alia*, declared: "To know Dr. Barnardo was to love him; while to work with him was to catch a breath of the spirit of Christ." Henceforth, he predicted, Barnardo would take his place alongside the great friends and emancipators of men—alongside John Howard, Elizabeth Fry, William Wilberforce, Lord Shaftesbury and such other practical saints as have been the salt of the earth.

The service over, the body was placed in the Village

Home Church, where again it lay "in state" several days. Then, in fulfilment of Barnardo's desire, it was cremated; the remains, on October 4th, being laid to rest in perhaps the most beautiful spot the Village can boast.

Over the grave, on Founder's Day, two and a half years later, was unveiled a stately monument, the finest work, by universal consent, of that eminent artist, the late Sir George Frampton, R.A. Topmost is a huge bronze figure of Charity, bearing two babes at her breast; central is a bust medallion of Dr. Barnardo; below, just above the base, is a magnificent piece of sculpture depicting three Village Home girls—one a cripple. Around the sides of the monument, in semicircular fashion, are spacious stone seats, along the top ledge of which is carved, "Suffer little children to come unto Me: and forbid them not, for of such is the Kingdom of Heaven", and, "Inasmuch as ye have done it unto one of the least of these my brethren, ye have done it unto Me"; while at the centre-base is engraved an extract from the first article of Barnardo's will, quoted above.

If all the tributes paid Barnardo within a month of his decease were collected, several tomes would be filled. The head of a Press-Clipping Agency, of long experience, said that never, save at Queen Victoria's death, could he recall such an outburst of popular appreciation. No State Honours had been conferred upon this missionary to the poor; but now the People rose up to honour him as few titled persons have ever been honoured. In all sections of the Press, secular and religious, whether published in Britain, Canada, Australia, the United States, or Continental countries, high tribute was paid to his achievement, it being fully recognized that the Kingdom of Childhood, the world over, owed him a boundless debt.

Excerpts from four or five journals must suffice. *London Opinion* said: "We well may mourn for him, for few of us have looked upon his like, and fewer still will look upon his like again. He passed with silent steps through reeking slums; like some good angel sent by Grace Divine, and stretched a helping hand to helpless infancy, throwing the mantle of his boundless charity around the crouching figures of the homeless poor. The man was great; the milk of human kindness flowed from him as dews from heaven; nor creed nor colour, caste nor kind, had weight with him. His lofty soul reached beyond the bounds of nationhood, girding the world with love."

The editor of *Punch* wrote eight verses, "In Memoriam". The fourth, fifth and sixth, following a vivid description of "that true disciple" of Christ, ran:

> "By birthright pledged to misery, crime and shame,
> Jetsam of London's streets, her 'waifs and strays'
> Whom she, the Mother, bore without a name,
> And left, and went her ways—

> "He stooped to save them, set them by his side,
> Breathed conscious life into the still-born soul,
> Taught truth and honour, love and loyal pride,
> Courage and self-control.

> "Till of her manhood, here and overseas,
> On whose supporting strength her state is throned,
> None better serve the Motherland than these,
> Her sons, the once-disowned."

The *Daily Telegraph*, referring to this "very remarkable man" and his "marvellous work", proceeded: "Dr. Barnardo, whose unexpected death will be heard of with regret wherever philanthropy is honoured and children are loved, had to pass through the fire of sharp and adverse criticism. But it left him unscathed, and for many years past the disinterestedness of his labours, the sincerity of his motives, and the magic of his influence have been accepted without challenge. . . . his mistakes were few, his triumphs innumerable. . . ." The *Daily News* said of this "indomitable man": "His name will be held in lasting remembrance, and worthily coupled with the authors of the Factory Acts and the pioneers of national education. . . . The death of Dr. Barnardo leaves not this or that private individual, but the people of England and their rulers, as the essential legatees to, and executors of, his work. Let us see to it that they perform their trust."

The Times, having elaborated upon the "astonishing magnitude and diversity" of his work, declared: "He may justly be ranked among the greatest public benefactors whom England has in recent times numbered among her citizens. With no adventitious aid from fortune or connections, with no aim but to relieve misery and to prevent sin and suffering, he has raised up a noble monument of philanthropy and of public usefulness. Notwithstanding the inroads of disease, he remained bravely at his post, and his premature death was no doubt largely due to his devotion." The *Daily Mail*, describing him as a man "great in the extent of his work, the novelty of his plans and the success of his campaign", pronounced him "much more" than the supreme philanthropist of his age: "Starting in a slum, he became a real Empire Builder, whose influence and work reach to the shores of the Pacific." Other organs called him "the world's greatest child-helper"; while the *Daily Chronicle*, designating him "a man of whom any nation might be proud", asked: "Who could desire a nobler epitaph than that which might well be written on his tomb: 'He saved sixty thousand unwanted and destitute children from suffering, vice and crime'?"

*   *   *   *   *

From time to time there are raised up great prophets, who, supersensitive to the ills of their less-privileged fellows, stoop down and bear their yoke; who, deploring "man's inhumanity to man", reveal afresh the love and mercy of God; who, themselves inspired by the vision of a New Day, cease not to toil for its dawn.

These prophets are the salt of the earth: and such a one was Barnardo. The Kingdom of Childhood, the world over, has forever been made more joyous by the life he lived. Confronted by an age whose economic gospel was the *laissez-faire* policy of drift, he opposed a mighty, creative Faith; and in the strength of that Faith he led "the Children's Cause" to victory. As long as the merry laughter of boys and girls continues, his influence will live.

INDEX

GEORGE ALLEN & UNWIN LTD
London: 40 Museum Street, W.C.1
Cape Town: 73 St. George's Street
Sydney, N.S.W.: Wynyard Square
Auckland, N.Z.: 41 Albert Street
Toronto: 77 Wellington Street, West